w0rldtr33.net – Internet Trekker

Password: m1st3rw1nt3r

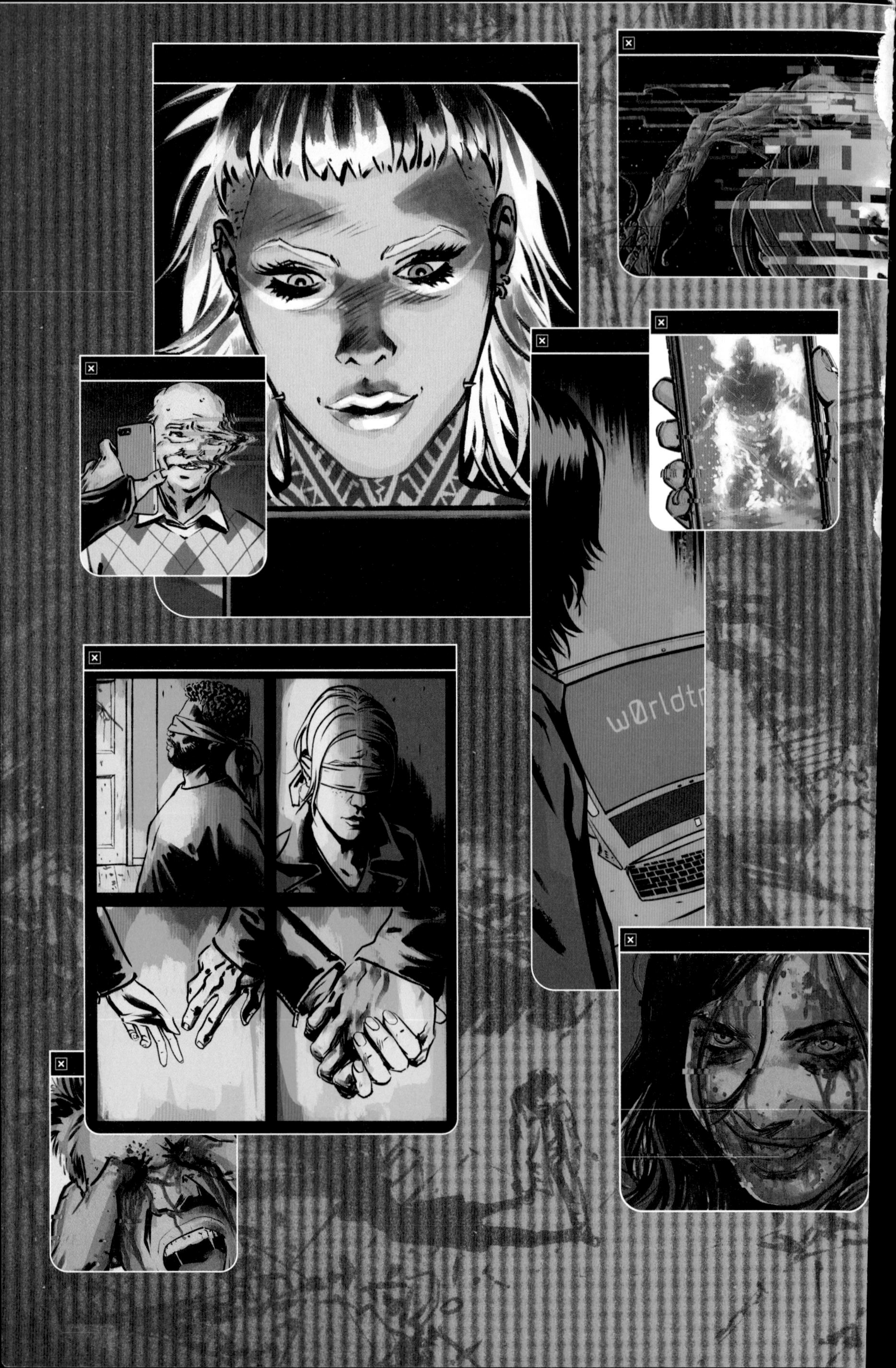

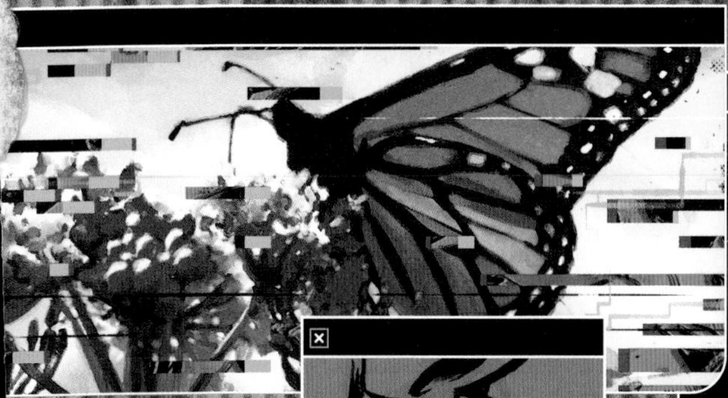
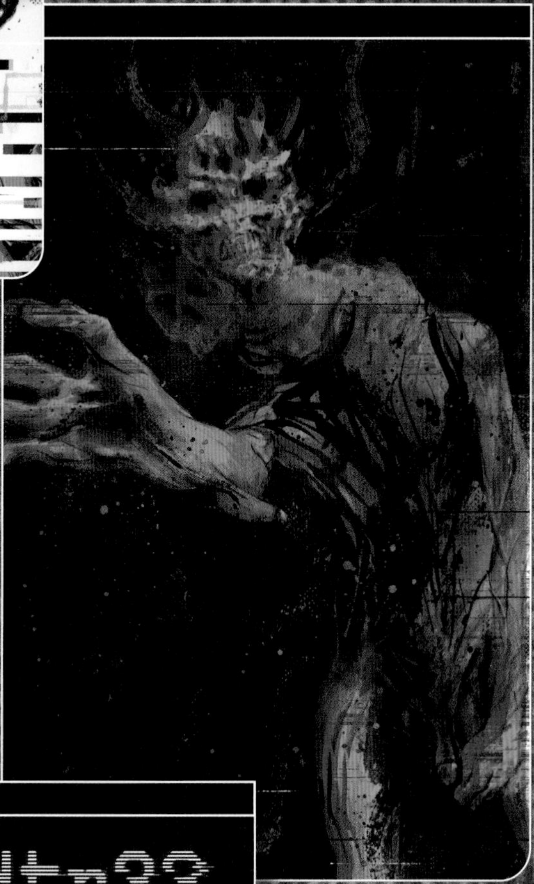
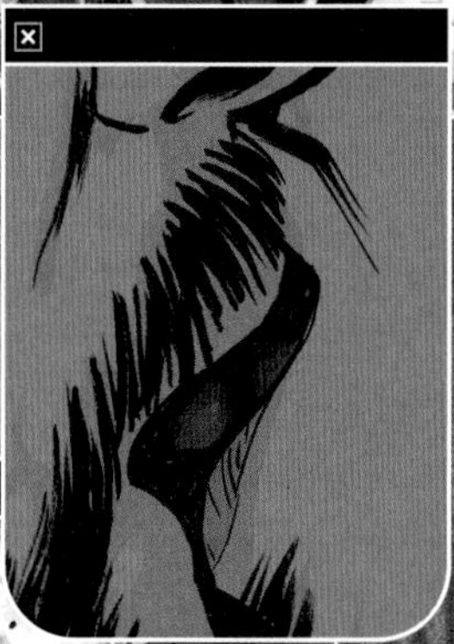
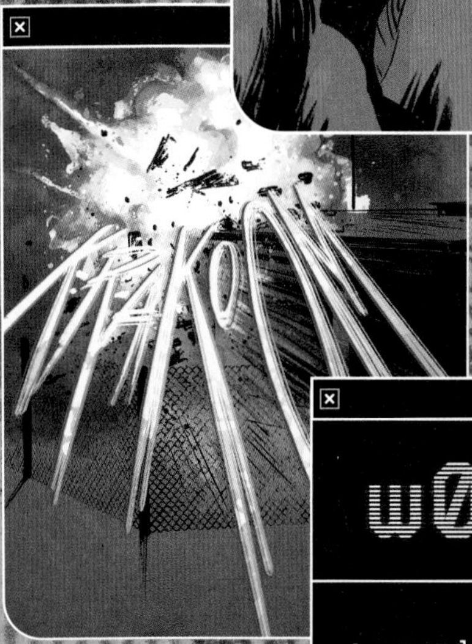

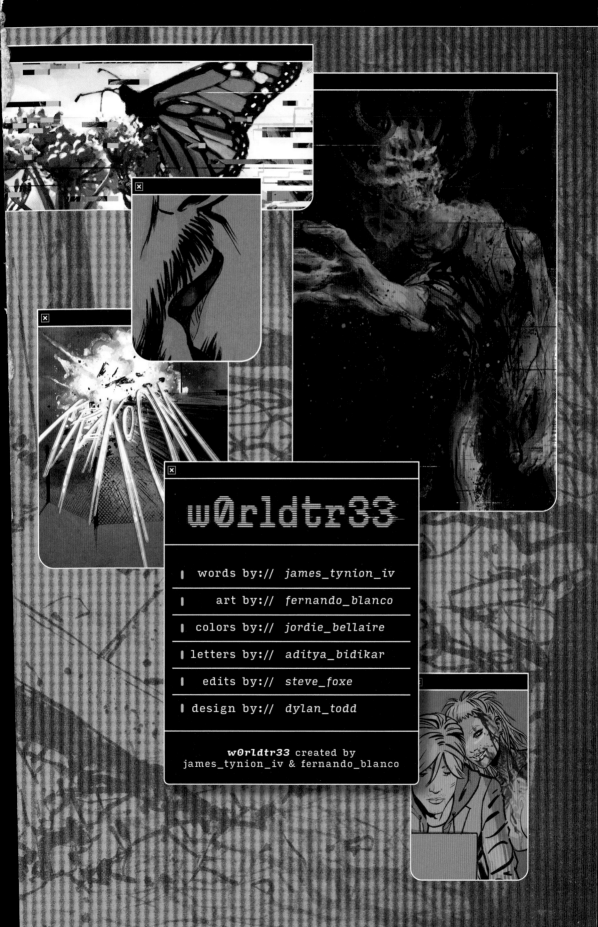

w0rldtr33

- words by:// *james_tynion_iv*
- art by:// *fernando_blanco*
- colors by:// *jordie_bellaire*
- letters by:// *aditya_bidikar*
- edits by:// *steve_foxe*
- design by:// *dylan_todd*

w0rldtr33 created by
james_tynion_iv & fernando_blanco

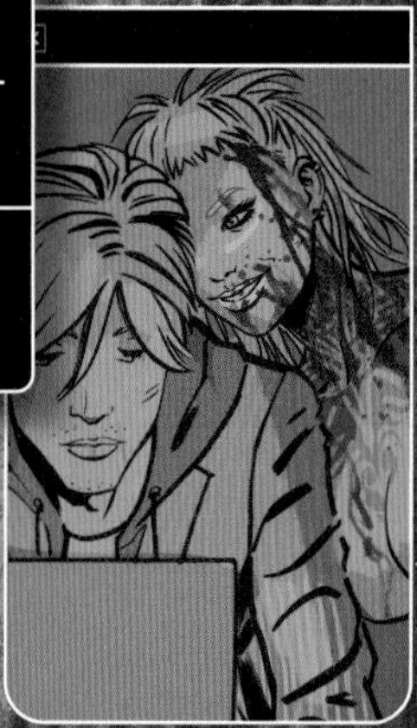

To all the weird little people
on the internet who made me into
who I am today. And to everyone else
who has to put up with it.
>://*James*

For Ismene.
She knows the whys...
25 years of whys.
>://*Fernando*

Kara, you wild bitch,
you would have loved this one.
>://*Jordie*

For Rumi—past,
present and always.
>://*Aditya*

W0RLDTR33, VOLUME 1: TERMINAL

First printing. November 2023. Published by Image Comics, Inc. Office of publication: PO BOX 14457, Portland, OR 97293. Copyright © 2023 James Tynion IV & Fernando Blanco. All rights reserved. Contains material originally published in single magazine form as WORLDTR33 #1-5. "w0rldtr33," its logos, and the likenesses of all characters herein are trademarks of James Tynion IV & Fernando Blanco, unless otherwise noted. "Image" and the Image Comics logos are registered trademarks of Image Comics, Inc. No part of this publication may be reproduced or transmitted, in any form or by any means (except for short excerpts for journalistic or review purposes), without the express written permission of James Tynion IV & Fernando Blanco, or Image Comics, Inc. All names, characters, events, and locales in this publication are entirely fictional. Any resemblance to actual persons (living or dead), events, or places, without satirical intent, is coincidental. Printed in the USA. For international rights, contact: foreignlicensing@imagecomics.com.

>:// Standard edition ISBN: 978-1-5343-9865-8 // Barnes & Noble exclusive ISBN: 978-1-5343-9727-9 // Indigo exclusive ISBN: 978-1-5343-9765-1

SHOPTINYONION.COM

image

Image Comics
Presents...

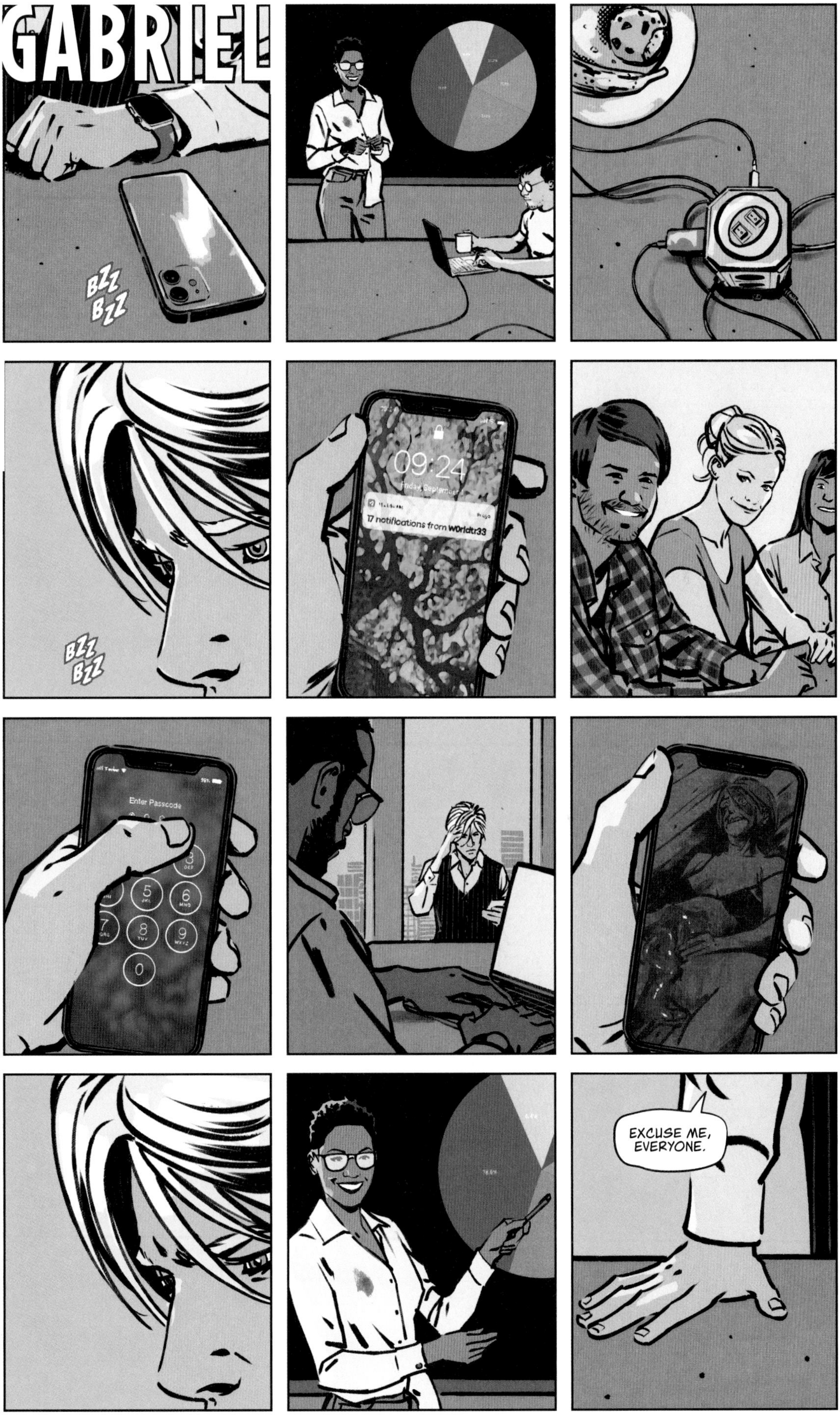
GABRIEL
BZZ BZZ
09:24
17 notifications from w0rldtr33
BZZ BZZ
Enter Passcode
EXCUSE ME, EVERYONE.

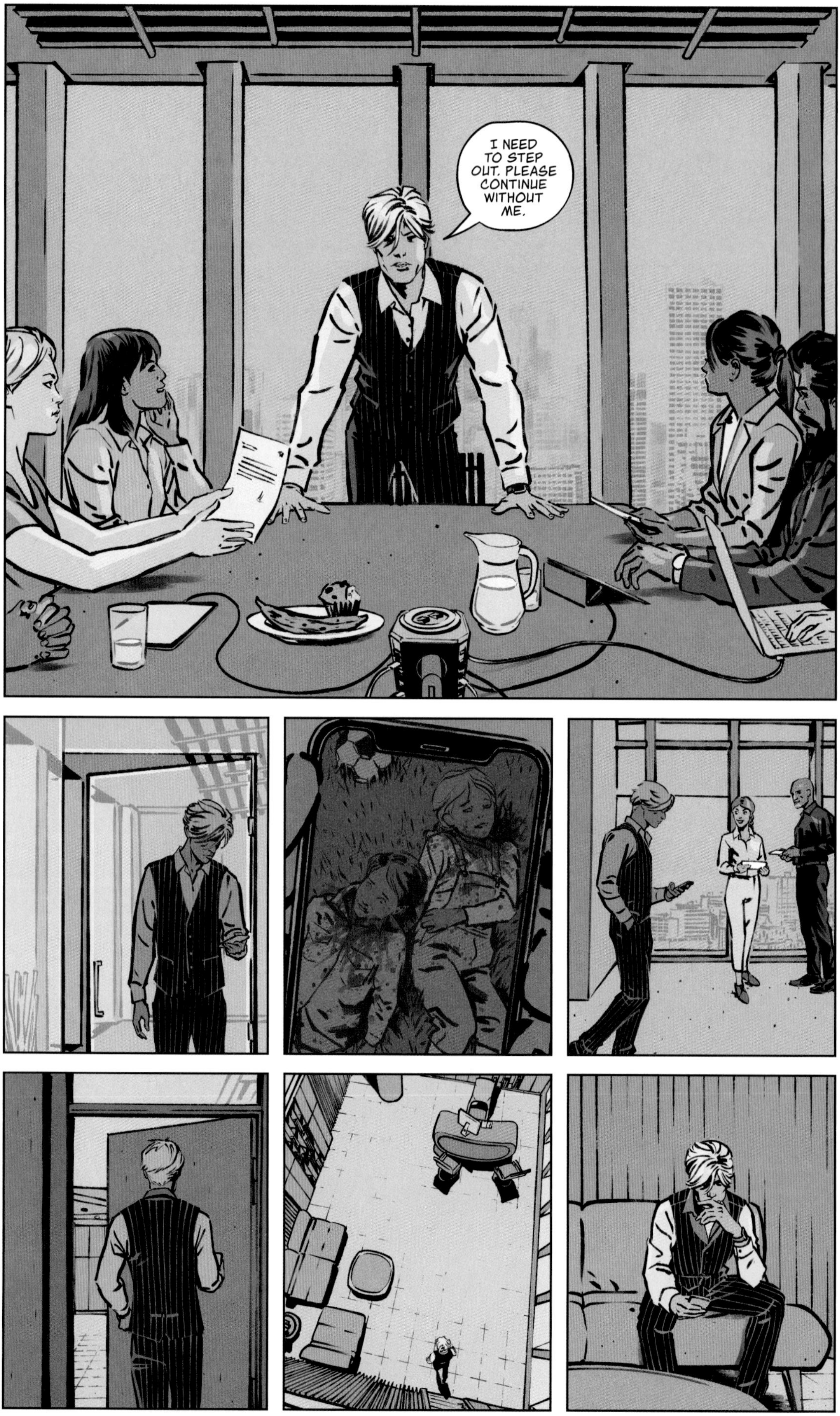
I NEED TO STEP OUT. PLEASE CONTINUE WITHOUT ME.

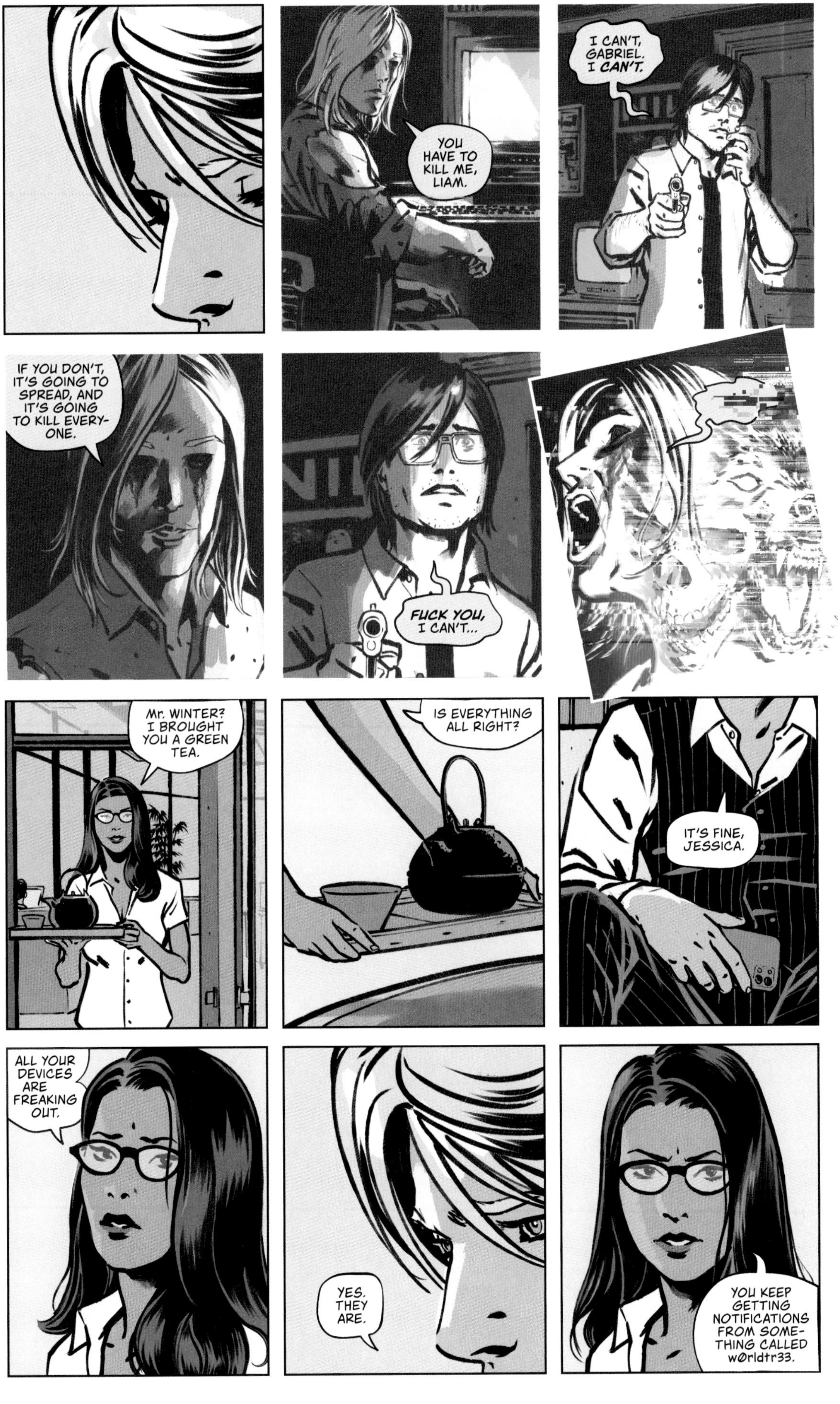
YOU HAVE TO KILL ME, LIAM.
I CAN'T, GABRIEL. I ***CAN'T.***
IF YOU DON'T, IT'S GOING TO SPREAD, AND IT'S GOING TO KILL EVERY-ONE.
FUCK YOU, I CAN'T...
Mr. WINTER? I BROUGHT YOU A GREEN TEA.
IS EVERYTHING ALL RIGHT?
IT'S FINE, JESSICA.
ALL YOUR DEVICES ARE FREAKING OUT.
YES. THEY ARE.
YOU KEEP GETTING NOTIFICATIONS FROM SOME-THING CALLED w0rldtr33.

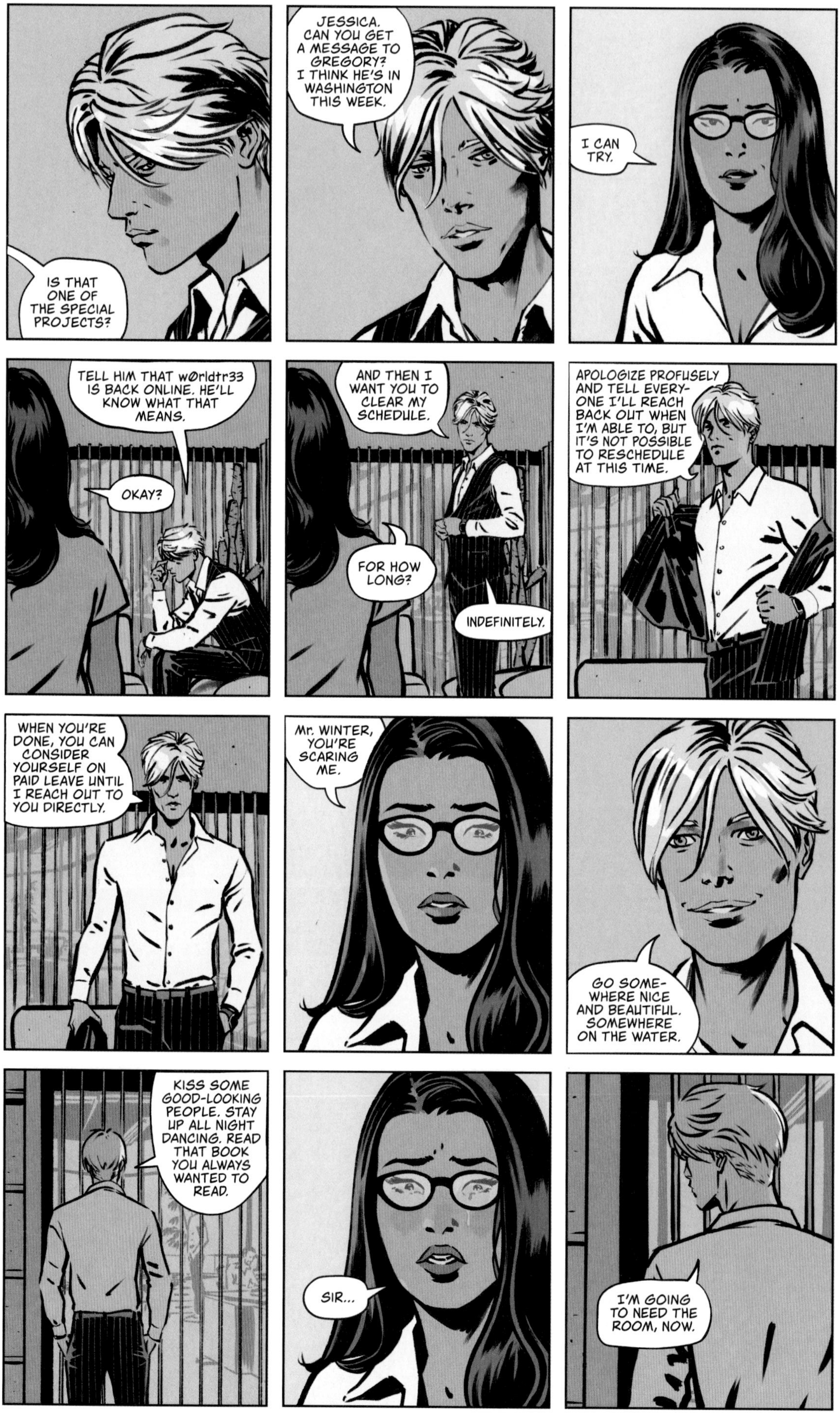

IS THAT ONE OF THE SPECIAL PROJECTS?
JESSICA. CAN YOU GET A MESSAGE TO GREGORY? I THINK HE'S IN WASHINGTON THIS WEEK.
I CAN TRY.
TELL HIM THAT w0rldtr33 IS BACK ONLINE. HE'LL KNOW WHAT THAT MEANS.
OKAY?
AND THEN I WANT YOU TO CLEAR MY SCHEDULE.
FOR HOW LONG?
INDEFINITELY.
APOLOGIZE PROFUSELY AND TELL EVERY-ONE I'LL REACH BACK OUT WHEN I'M ABLE TO, BUT IT'S NOT POSSIBLE TO RESCHEDULE AT THIS TIME.
WHEN YOU'RE DONE, YOU CAN CONSIDER YOURSELF ON PAID LEAVE UNTIL I REACH OUT TO YOU DIRECTLY.
Mr. WINTER, YOU'RE SCARING ME.
GO SOME-WHERE NICE AND BEAUTIFUL. SOMEWHERE ON THE WATER.
KISS SOME GOOD-LOOKING PEOPLE. STAY UP ALL NIGHT DANCING. READ THAT BOOK YOU ALWAYS WANTED TO READ.
SIR...
I'M GOING TO NEED THE ROOM, NOW.

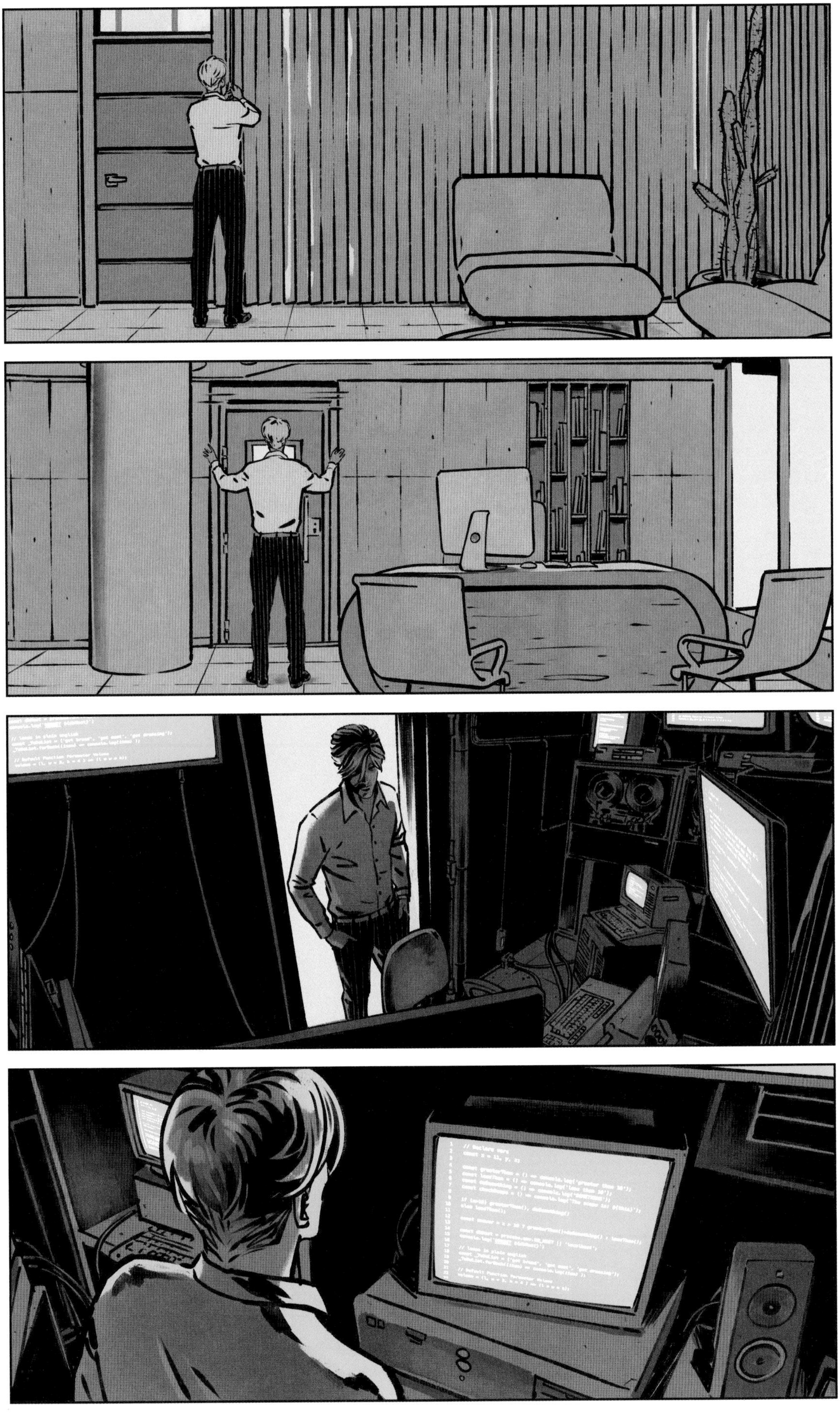

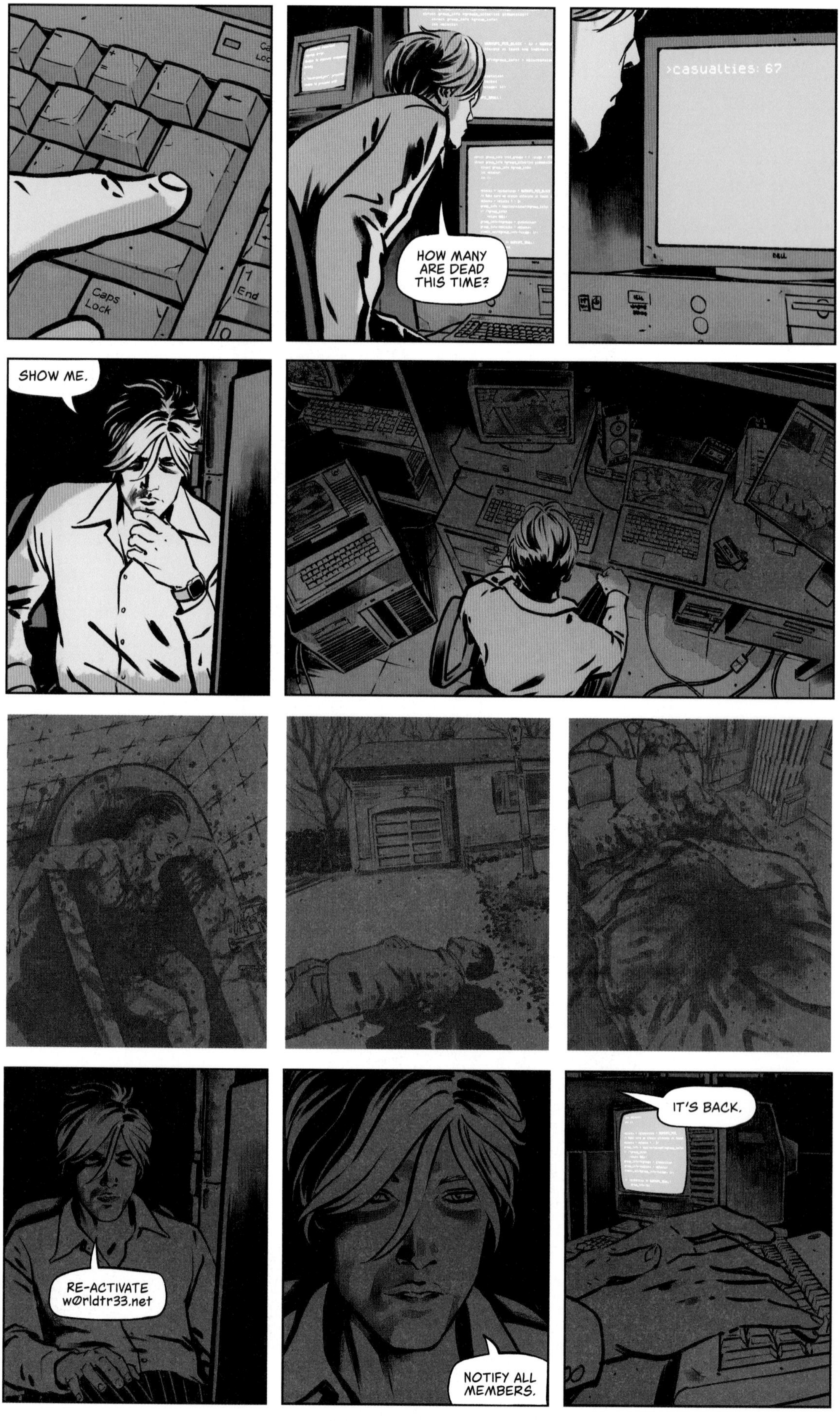
HOW MANY ARE DEAD THIS TIME?
>casualties: 67
SHOW ME.
RE-ACTIVATE w@rldtr33.net
NOTIFY ALL MEMBERS.
IT'S BACK.

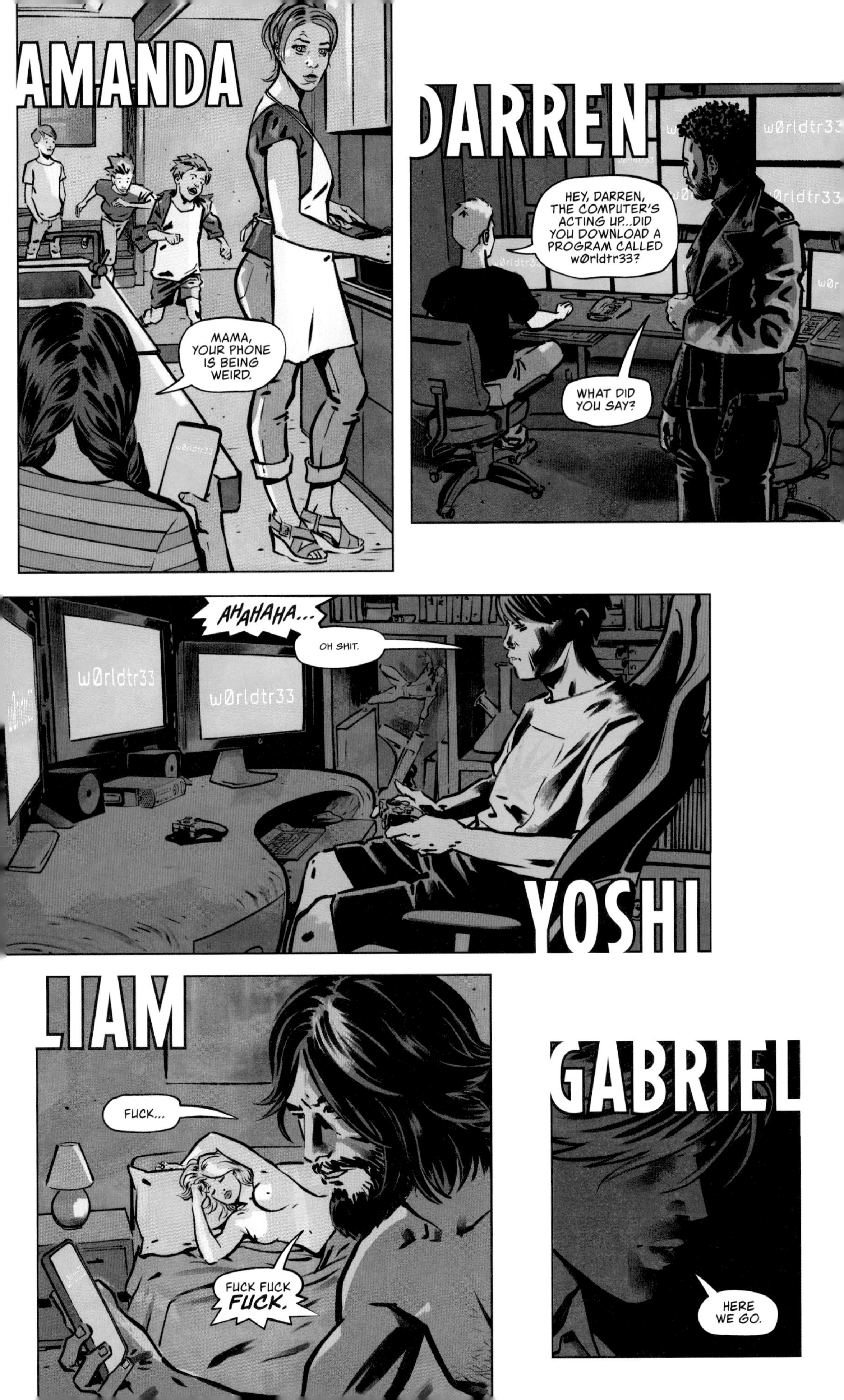
AMANDA
w0rldtr33
MAMA, YOUR PHONE IS BEING WEIRD.
DARREN
w0rldtr33
HEY, DARREN, THE COMPUTER'S ACTING UP...DID YOU DOWNLOAD A PROGRAM CALLED w0rldtr33?
WHAT DID YOU SAY?
AHAHAHA...
OH SHIT.
w0rldtr33
w0rldtr33
YOSHI
LIAM
FUCK...
FUCK FUCK FUCK.
GABRIEL
HERE WE GO.

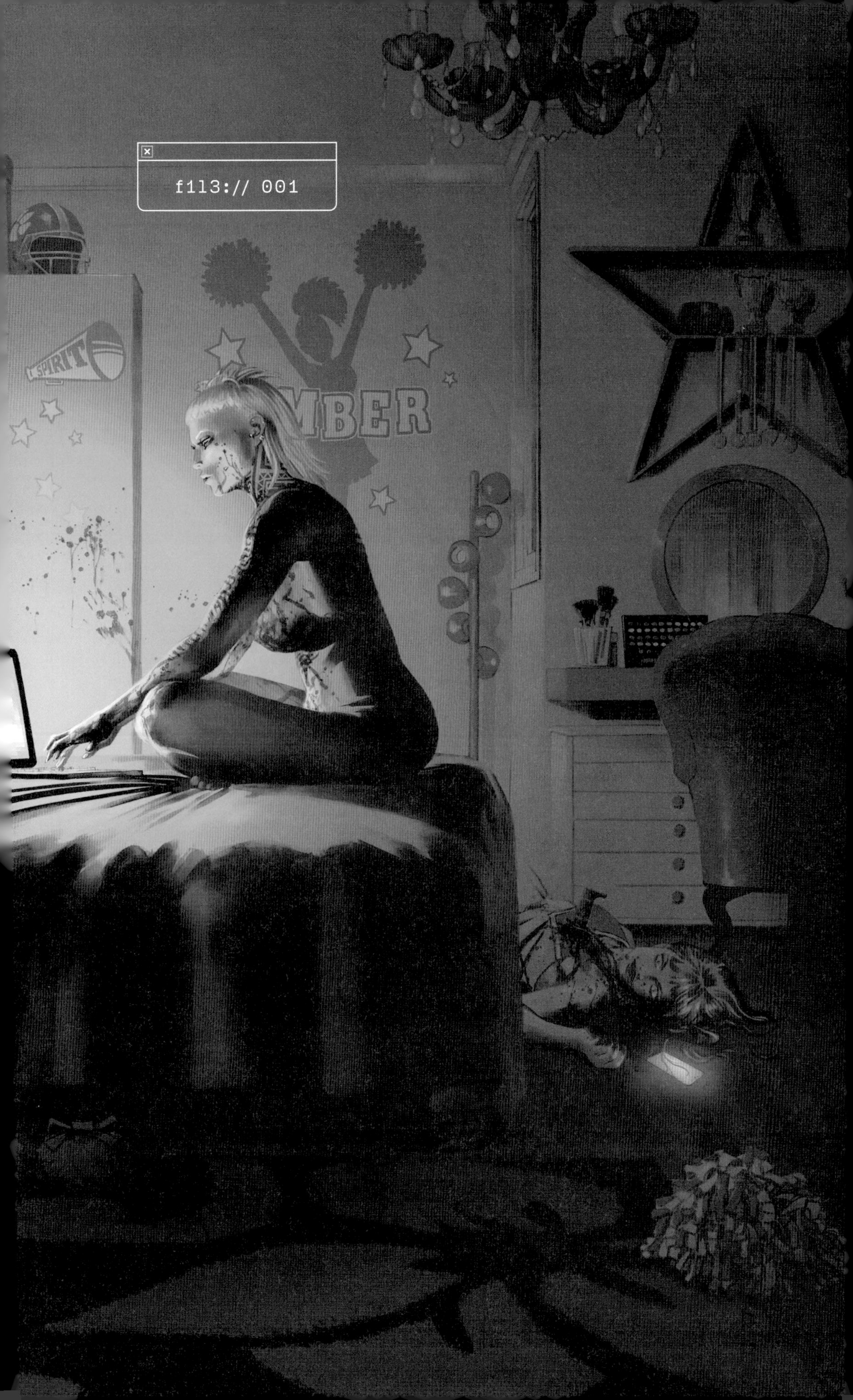
f113:// 001
SPIRIT
MBER

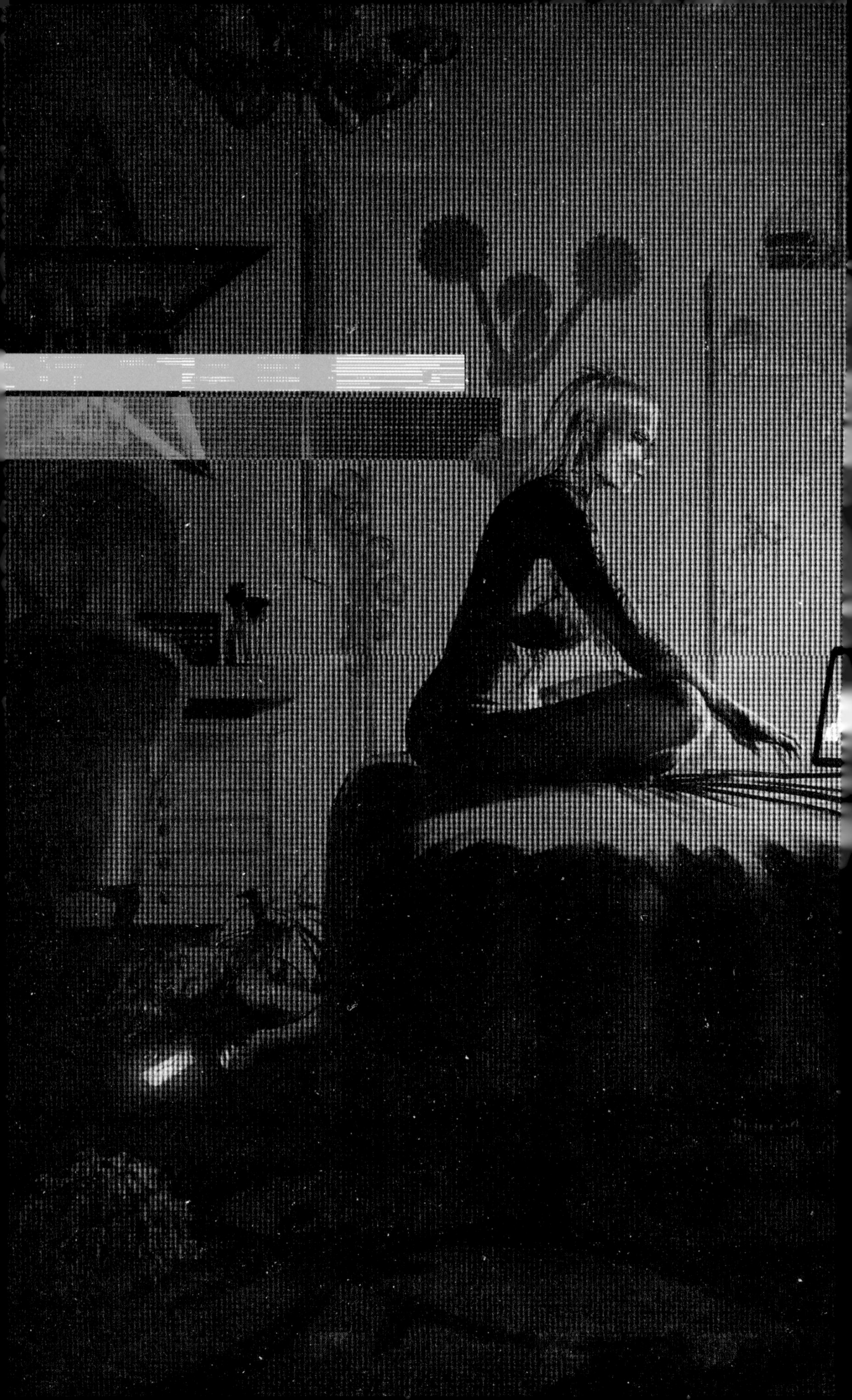

2024

"LET ME TELL YOU HOW MUCH I'VE COME
TO HATE YOU SINCE I BEGAN TO LIVE."

-- Harlan Ellison,
"I Have No Mouth, and I Must Scream"

PH34R

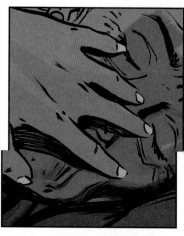

PH34R
****
Connect
KLIK
deeeeet-DOOTDEETDOOTDO
Connecting
ding-daah
SKREEZE
RRRAWWW
Connection Established
Accessing Undernet
29134
KLIK

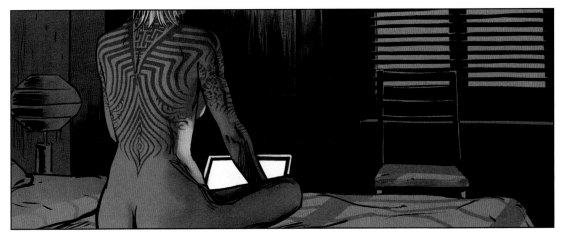

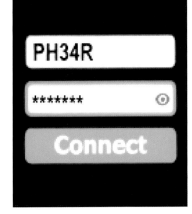

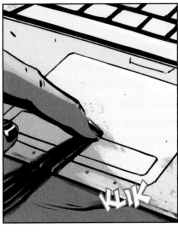

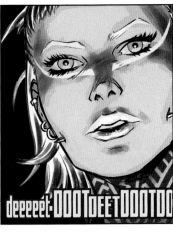

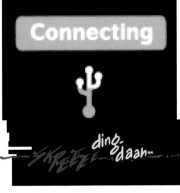

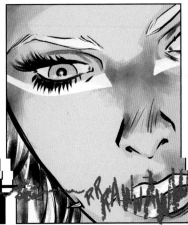

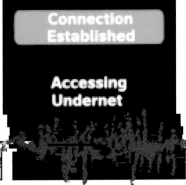

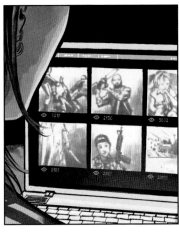

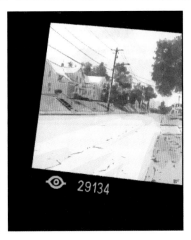

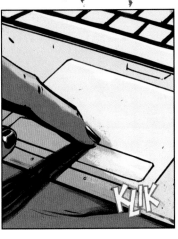

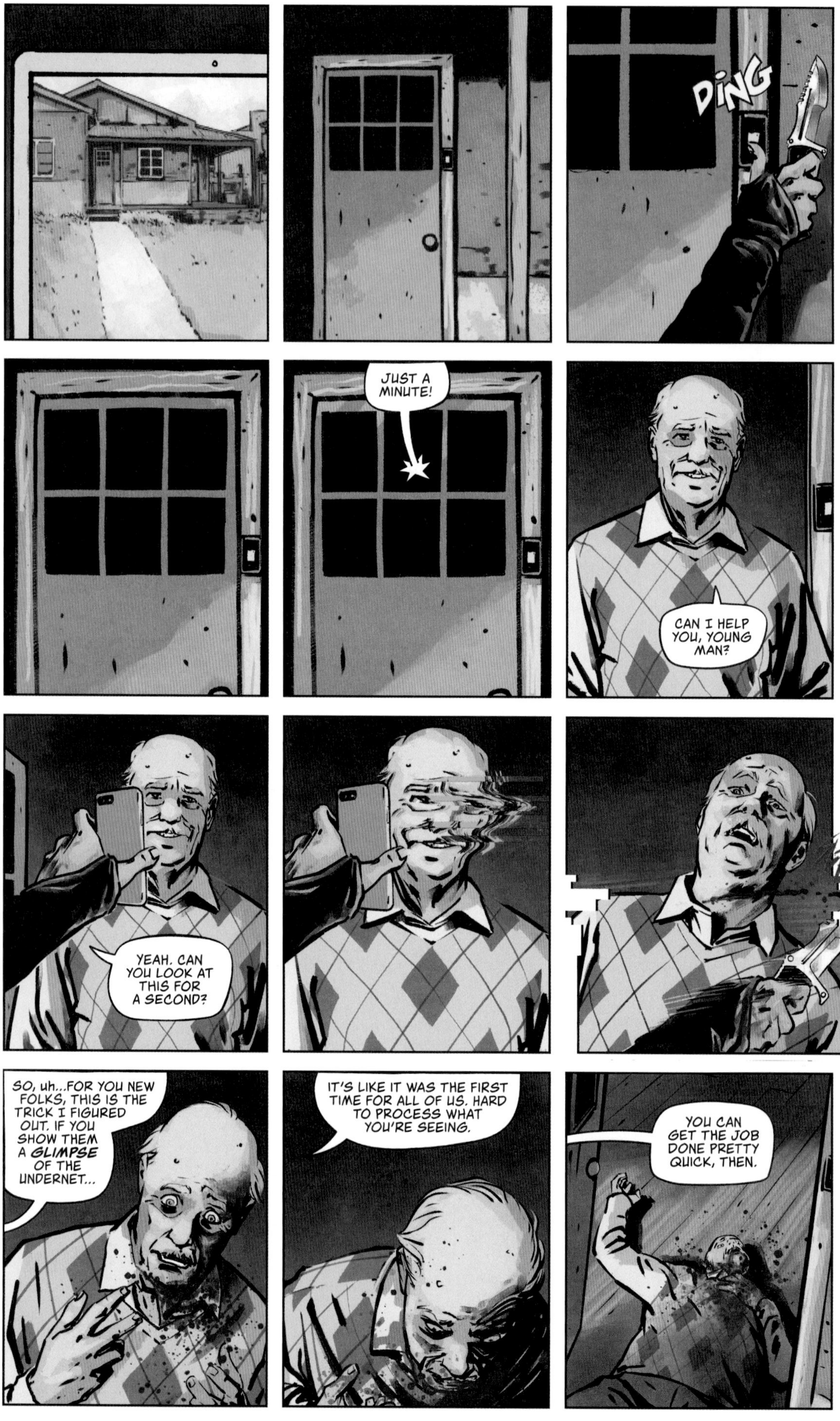
DING
JUST A MINUTE!
CAN I HELP YOU, YOUNG MAN?
YEAH. CAN YOU LOOK AT THIS FOR A SECOND?
SO, uh...FOR YOU NEW FOLKS, THIS IS THE TRICK I FIGURED OUT. IF YOU SHOW THEM A GLIMPSE OF THE UNDERNET...
IT'S LIKE IT WAS THE FIRST TIME FOR ALL OF US. HARD TO PROCESS WHAT YOU'RE SEEING.
YOU CAN GET THE JOB DONE PRETTY QUICK, THEN.

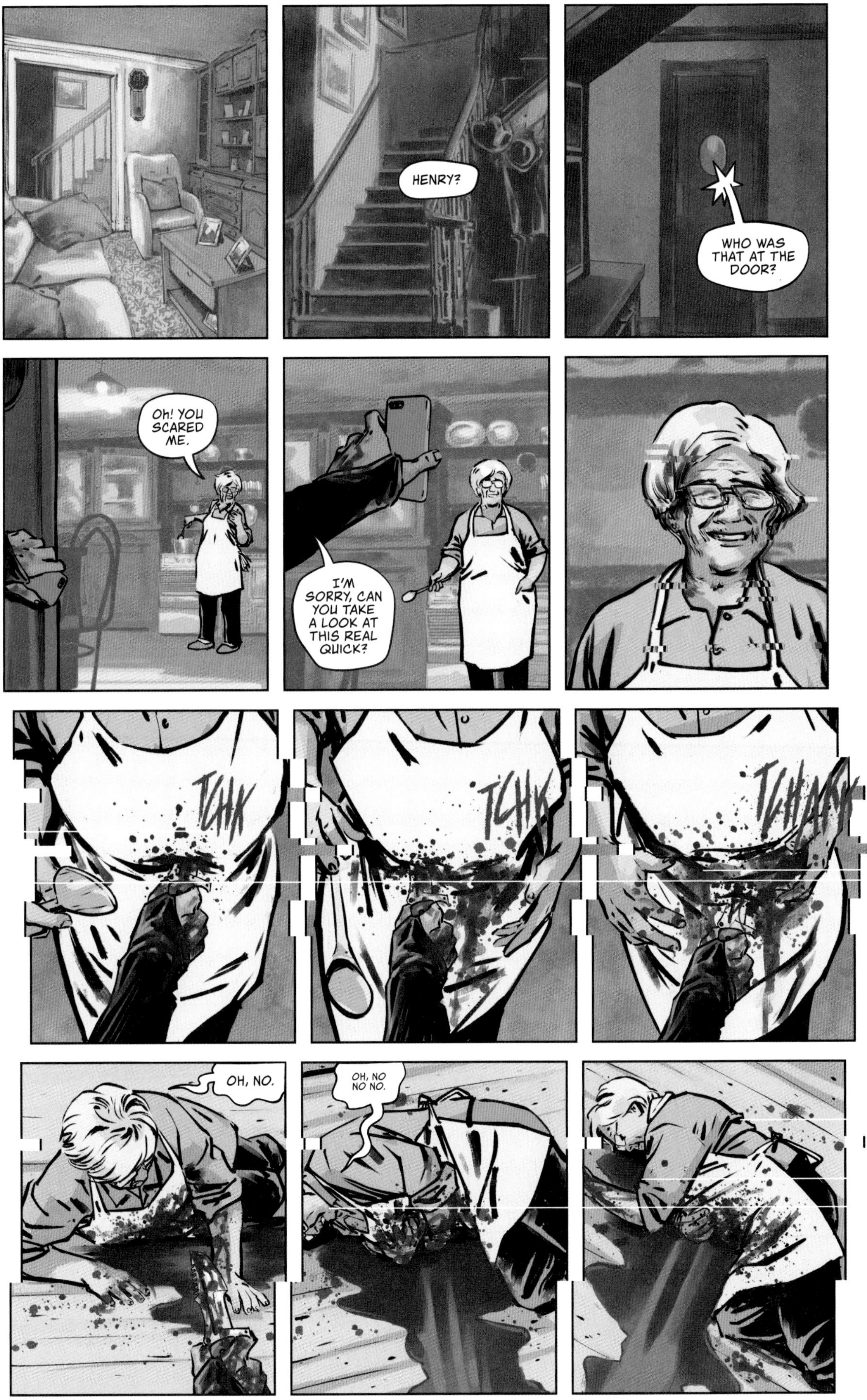
HENRY?
WHO WAS THAT AT THE DOOR?
Oh! YOU SCARED ME.
I'M SORRY, CAN YOU TAKE A LOOK AT THIS REAL QUICK?
TCHK
TCHK
TCHAK
OH, NO.
OH, NO NO NO.

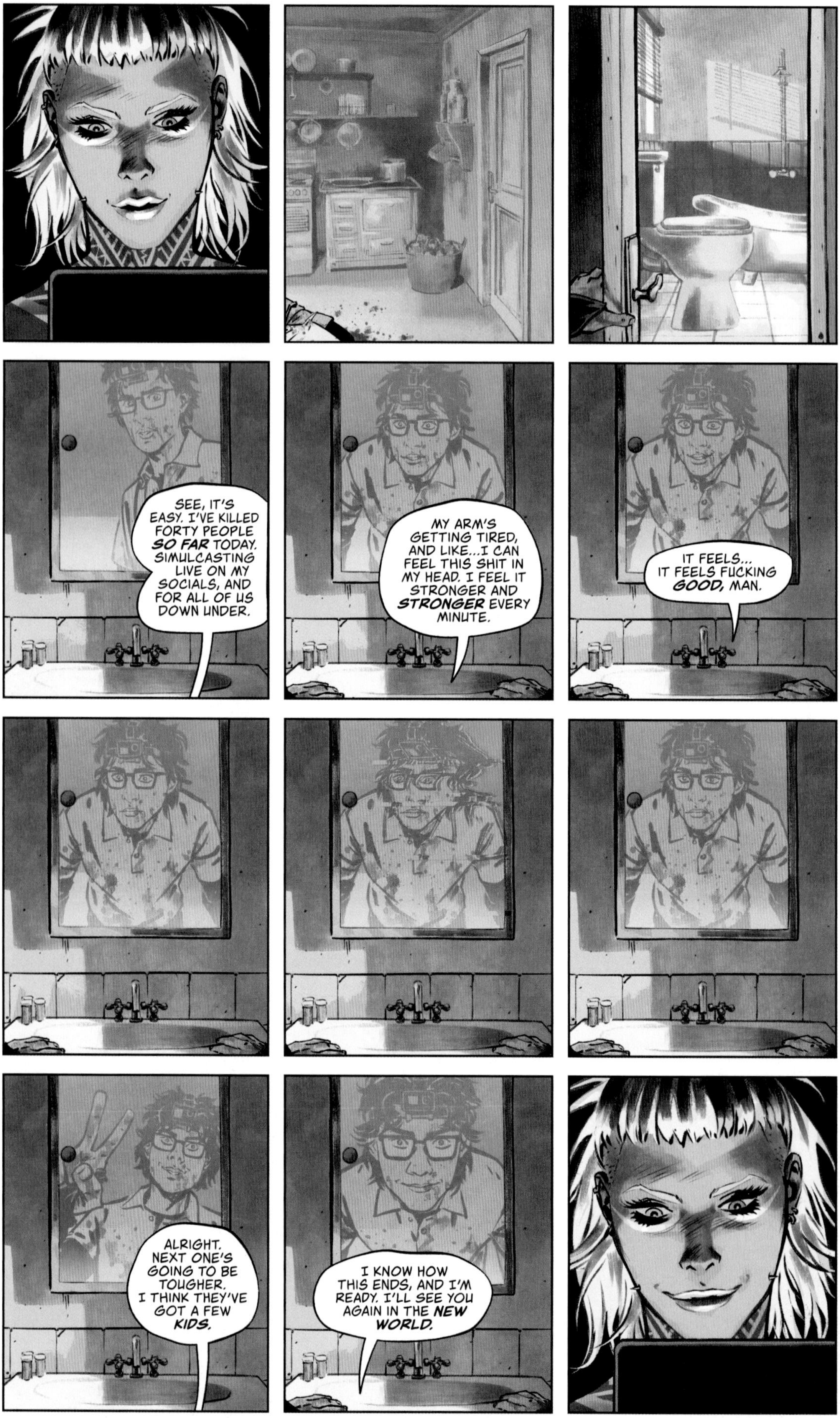
SEE, IT'S EASY. I'VE KILLED FORTY PEOPLE SO FAR TODAY. SIMULCASTING LIVE ON MY SOCIALS, AND FOR ALL OF US DOWN UNDER.
MY ARM'S GETTING TIRED, AND LIKE... I CAN FEEL THIS SHIT IN MY HEAD. I FEEL IT STRONGER AND STRONGER EVERY MINUTE.
IT FEELS... IT FEELS FUCKING GOOD, MAN.
ALRIGHT. NEXT ONE'S GOING TO BE TOUGHER. I THINK THEY'VE GOT A FEW KIDS.
I KNOW HOW THIS ENDS, AND I'M READY. I'LL SEE YOU AGAIN IN THE NEW WORLD.

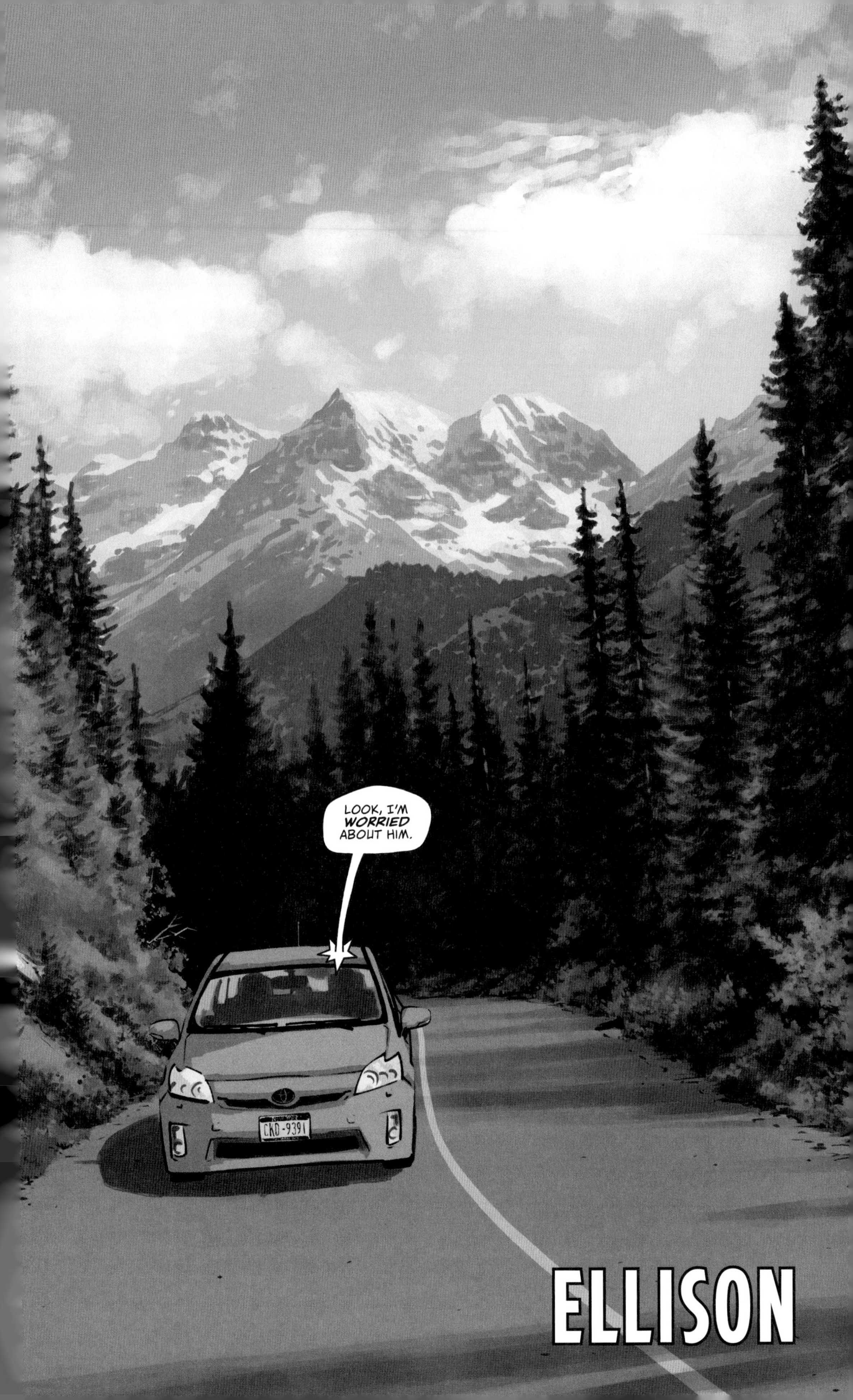
LOOK, I'M WORRIED ABOUT HIM.
ELLISON

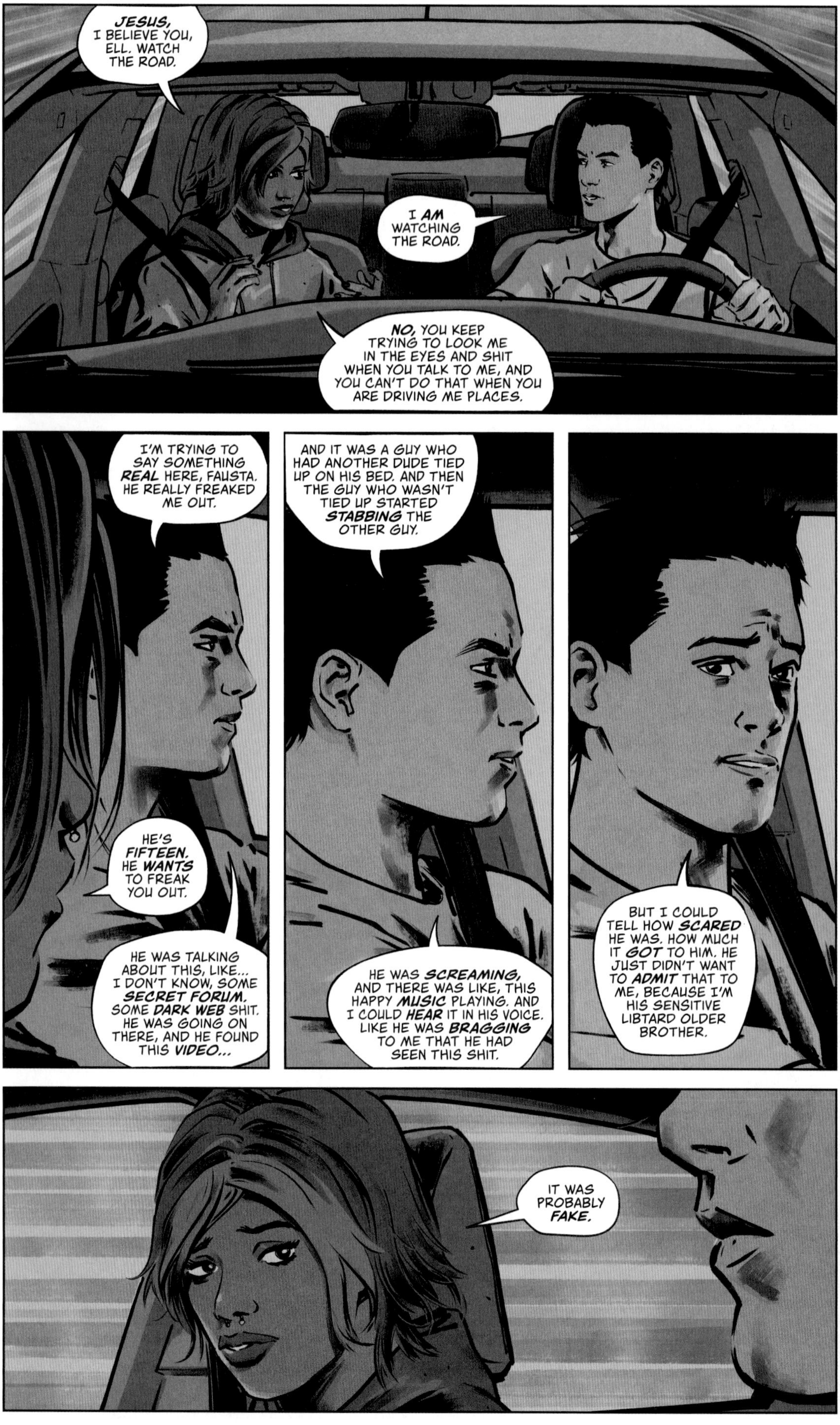
JESUS, I BELIEVE YOU, ELL. WATCH THE ROAD.
I AM WATCHING THE ROAD.
NO, YOU KEEP TRYING TO LOOK ME IN THE EYES AND SHIT WHEN YOU TALK TO ME, AND YOU CAN'T DO THAT WHEN YOU ARE DRIVING ME PLACES.
I'M TRYING TO SAY SOMETHING REAL HERE, FAUSTA. HE REALLY FREAKED ME OUT.
HE'S FIFTEEN. HE WANTS TO FREAK YOU OUT.
HE WAS TALKING ABOUT THIS, LIKE... I DON'T KNOW, SOME SECRET FORUM. SOME DARK WEB SHIT. HE WAS GOING ON THERE, AND HE FOUND THIS VIDEO...
AND IT WAS A GUY WHO HAD ANOTHER DUDE TIED UP ON HIS BED. AND THEN THE GUY WHO WASN'T TIED UP STARTED STABBING THE OTHER GUY.
HE WAS SCREAMING, AND THERE WAS LIKE, THIS HAPPY MUSIC PLAYING. AND I COULD HEAR IT IN HIS VOICE. LIKE HE WAS BRAGGING TO ME THAT HE HAD SEEN THIS SHIT.
BUT I COULD TELL HOW SCARED HE WAS. HOW MUCH IT GOT TO HIM. HE JUST DIDN'T WANT TO ADMIT THAT TO ME, BECAUSE I'M HIS SENSITIVE LIBTARD OLDER BROTHER.
IT WAS PROBABLY FAKE.

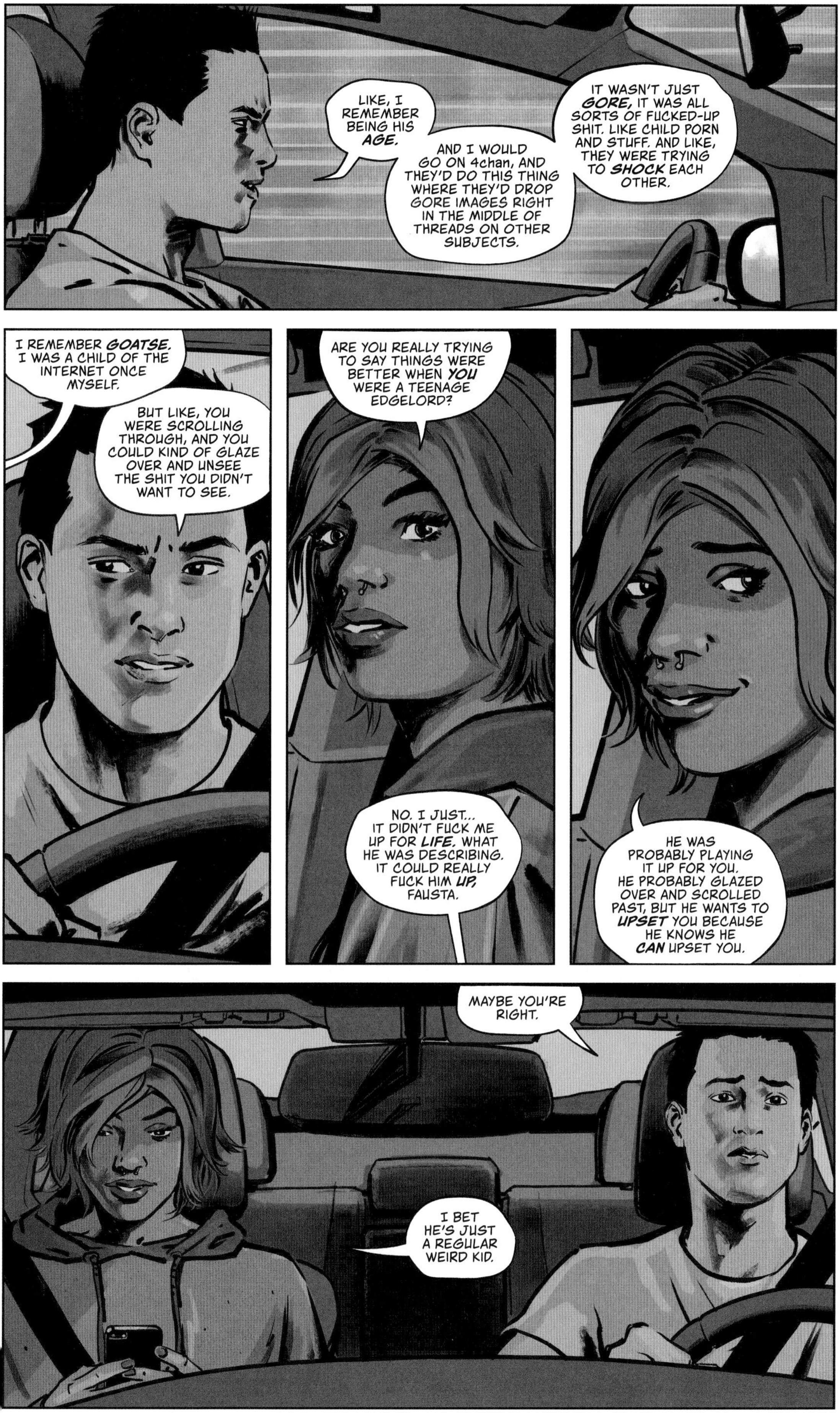
LIKE, I REMEMBER BEING HIS AGE.
AND I WOULD GO ON 4chan, AND THEY'D DO THIS THING WHERE THEY'D DROP GORE IMAGES RIGHT IN THE MIDDLE OF THREADS ON OTHER SUBJECTS.
IT WASN'T JUST GORE, IT WAS ALL SORTS OF FUCKED-UP SHIT. LIKE CHILD PORN AND STUFF. AND LIKE, THEY WERE TRYING TO SHOCK EACH OTHER.
I REMEMBER GOATSE. I WAS A CHILD OF THE INTERNET ONCE MYSELF.
BUT LIKE, YOU WERE SCROLLING THROUGH, AND YOU COULD KIND OF GLAZE OVER AND UNSEE THE SHIT YOU DIDN'T WANT TO SEE.
ARE YOU REALLY TRYING TO SAY THINGS WERE BETTER WHEN YOU WERE A TEENAGE EDGELORD?
NO. I JUST... IT DIDN'T FUCK ME UP FOR LIFE. WHAT HE WAS DESCRIBING. IT COULD REALLY FUCK HIM UP, FAUSTA.
HE WAS PROBABLY PLAYING IT UP FOR YOU. HE PROBABLY GLAZED OVER AND SCROLLED PAST, BUT HE WANTS TO UPSET YOU BECAUSE HE KNOWS HE CAN UPSET YOU.
MAYBE YOU'RE RIGHT.
I BET HE'S JUST A REGULAR WEIRD KID.

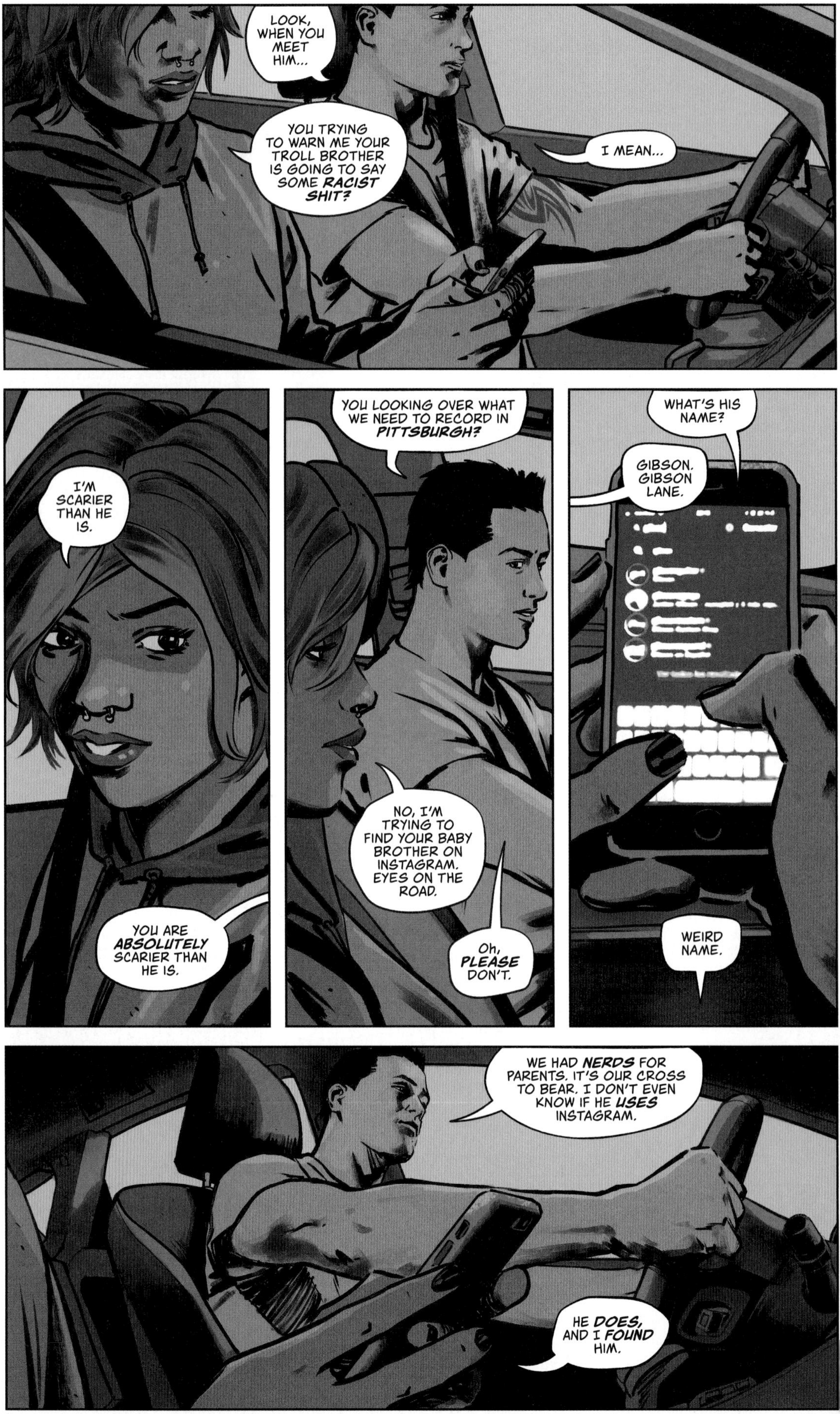
LOOK, WHEN YOU MEET HIM...
YOU TRYING TO WARN ME YOUR TROLL BROTHER IS GOING TO SAY SOME RACIST SHIT?
I MEAN...
I'M SCARIER THAN HE IS.
YOU ARE ABSOLUTELY SCARIER THAN HE IS.
YOU LOOKING OVER WHAT WE NEED TO RECORD IN PITTSBURGH?
NO, I'M TRYING TO FIND YOUR BABY BROTHER ON INSTAGRAM. EYES ON THE ROAD.
Oh, PLEASE DON'T.
WHAT'S HIS NAME?
GIBSON. GIBSON LANE.
WEIRD NAME.
WE HAD NERDS FOR PARENTS. IT'S OUR CROSS TO BEAR. I DON'T EVEN KNOW IF HE USES INSTAGRAM.
HE DOES, AND I FOUND HIM.

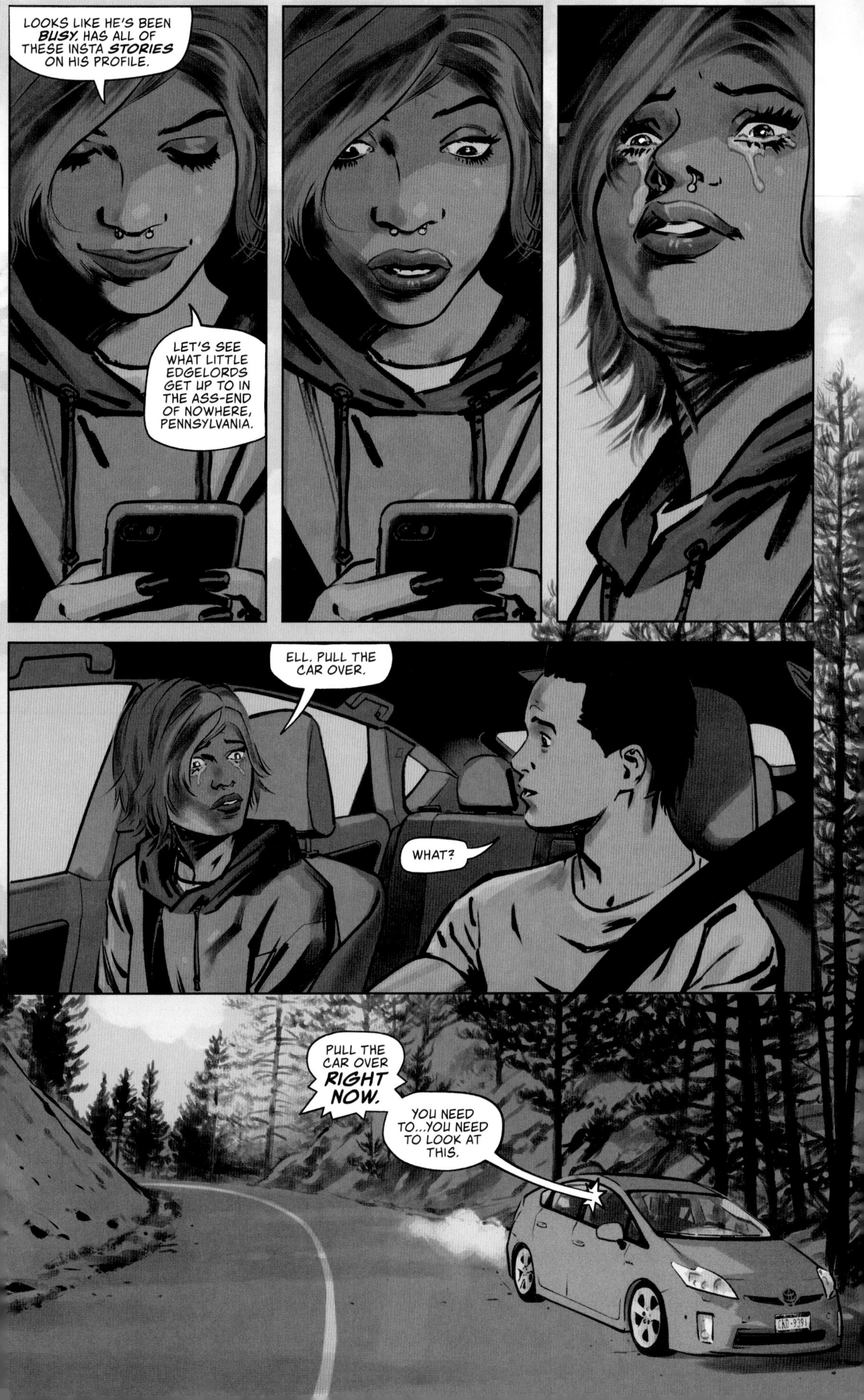
LOOKS LIKE HE'S BEEN BUSY. HAS ALL OF THESE INSTA STORIES ON HIS PROFILE.
LET'S SEE WHAT LITTLE EDGELORDS GET UP TO IN THE ASS-END OF NOWHERE, PENNSYLVANIA.
ELL. PULL THE CAR OVER.
WHAT?
PULL THE CAR OVER RIGHT NOW.
YOU NEED TO...YOU NEED TO LOOK AT THIS.

GABRIEL

"SHOCKING SCENE OUT OF CAMBRIA COUNTY, PENNSYLVANIA..."

DEADLY MASS KILLING

BREAKING NEWS

"...WHERE A TEENAGE BOY MURDERED **DOZENS** OF HIS **NEIGHBORS** OVER THE COURSE OF FIVE HOURS. AND HE POSTED ALL OF THE MURDERS **ONLINE**."

"THE VIDEOS HAVE SINCE BEEN TAKEN DOWN, AND THE TEENAGER, **GIBSON LANE**, HAS BEEN TAKEN INTO POLICE CUSTODY."

DEADLY MASS KILLING

BREAKING NEWS

"SO FAR, WE CAN CONFIRM THAT HE TOOK THE LIVES OF NEARLY **SIXTY** PEOPLE, BUT POLICE ARE STILL SEARCH--"

DEADLY MASS KILLING

BREAKING NEWS

DEADLY MASS KILLING

BREAKING NEWS

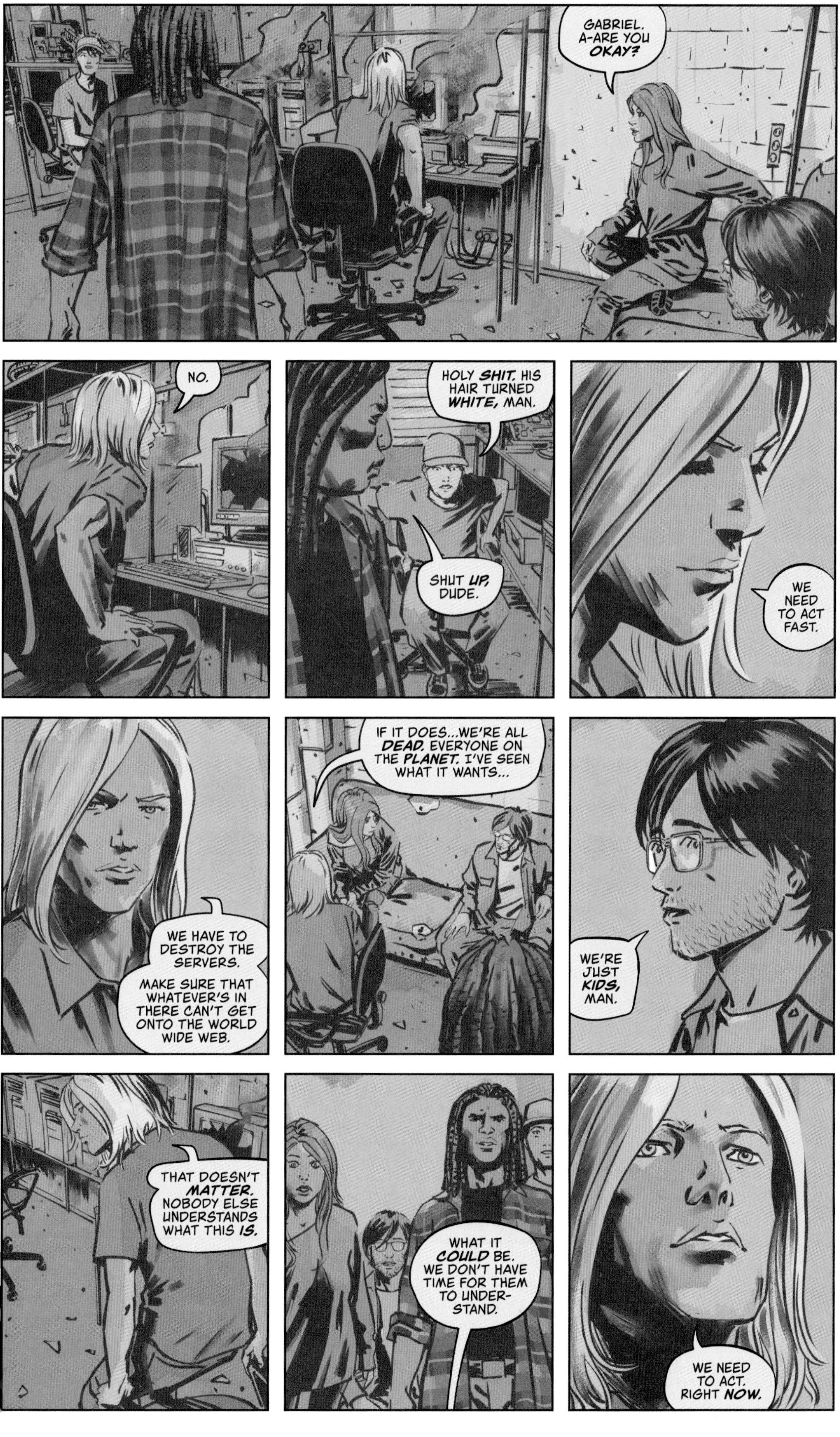
GABRIEL. A-ARE YOU OKAY?
NO.
HOLY SHIT. HIS HAIR TURNED WHITE, MAN.
SHUT UP, DUDE.
WE NEED TO ACT FAST.
WE HAVE TO DESTROY THE SERVERS.
MAKE SURE THAT WHATEVER'S IN THERE CAN'T GET ONTO THE WORLD WIDE WEB.
IF IT DOES...WE'RE ALL DEAD. EVERYONE ON THE PLANET. I'VE SEEN WHAT IT WANTS...
WE'RE JUST KIDS, MAN.
THAT DOESN'T MATTER. NOBODY ELSE UNDERSTANDS WHAT THIS IS.
WHAT IT COULD BE. WE DON'T HAVE TIME FOR THEM TO UNDER-STAND.
WE NEED TO ACT. RIGHT NOW.

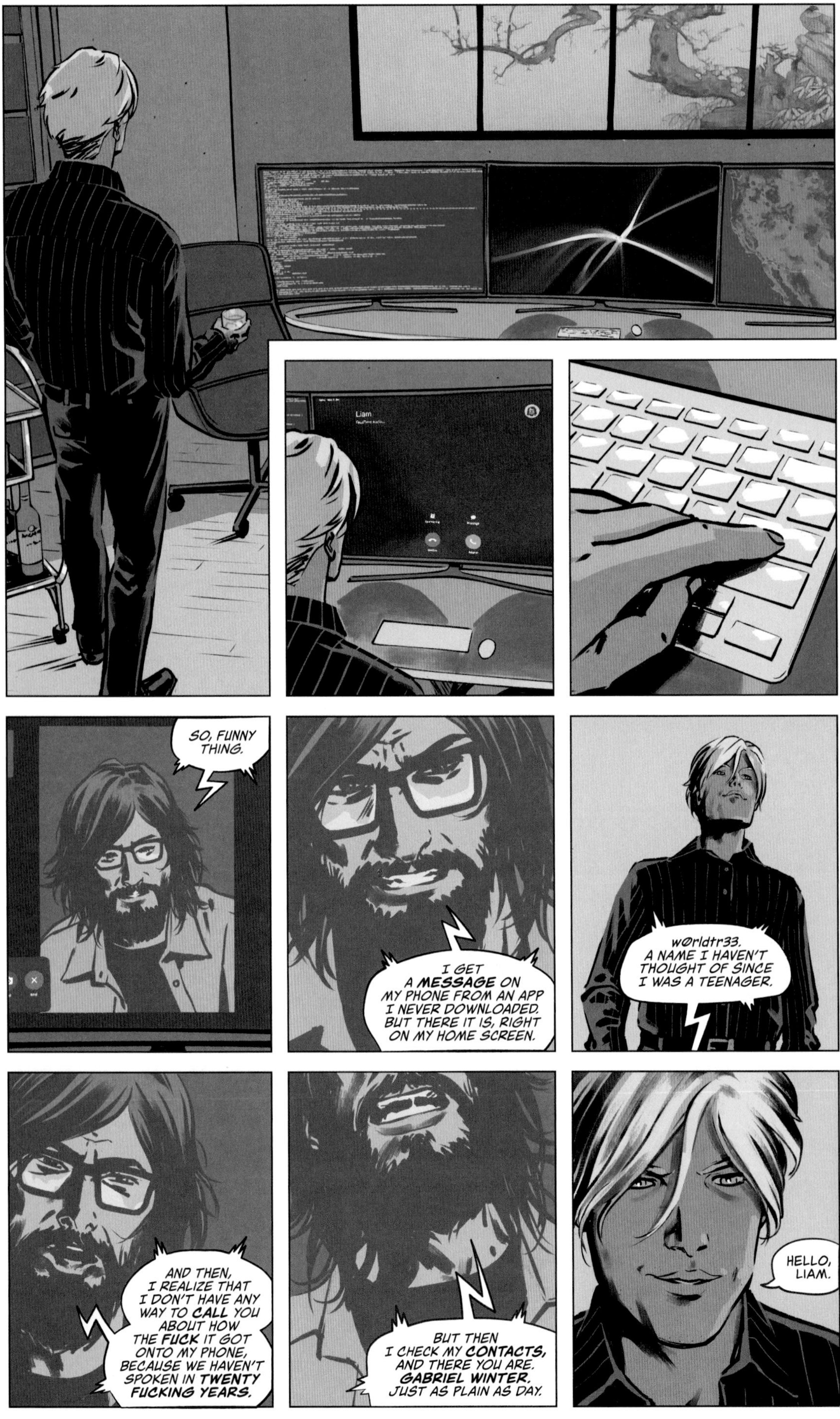
Liam
SO, FUNNY THING.
I GET A MESSAGE ON MY PHONE FROM AN APP I NEVER DOWNLOADED. BUT THERE IT IS, RIGHT ON MY HOME SCREEN.
w0rldtr33. A NAME I HAVEN'T THOUGHT OF SINCE I WAS A TEENAGER.
AND THEN, I REALIZE THAT I DON'T HAVE ANY WAY TO CALL YOU ABOUT HOW THE FUCK IT GOT ONTO MY PHONE, BECAUSE WE HAVEN'T SPOKEN IN TWENTY FUCKING YEARS.
BUT THEN I CHECK MY CONTACTS, AND THERE YOU ARE. GABRIEL WINTER. JUST AS PLAIN AS DAY.
HELLO, LIAM.

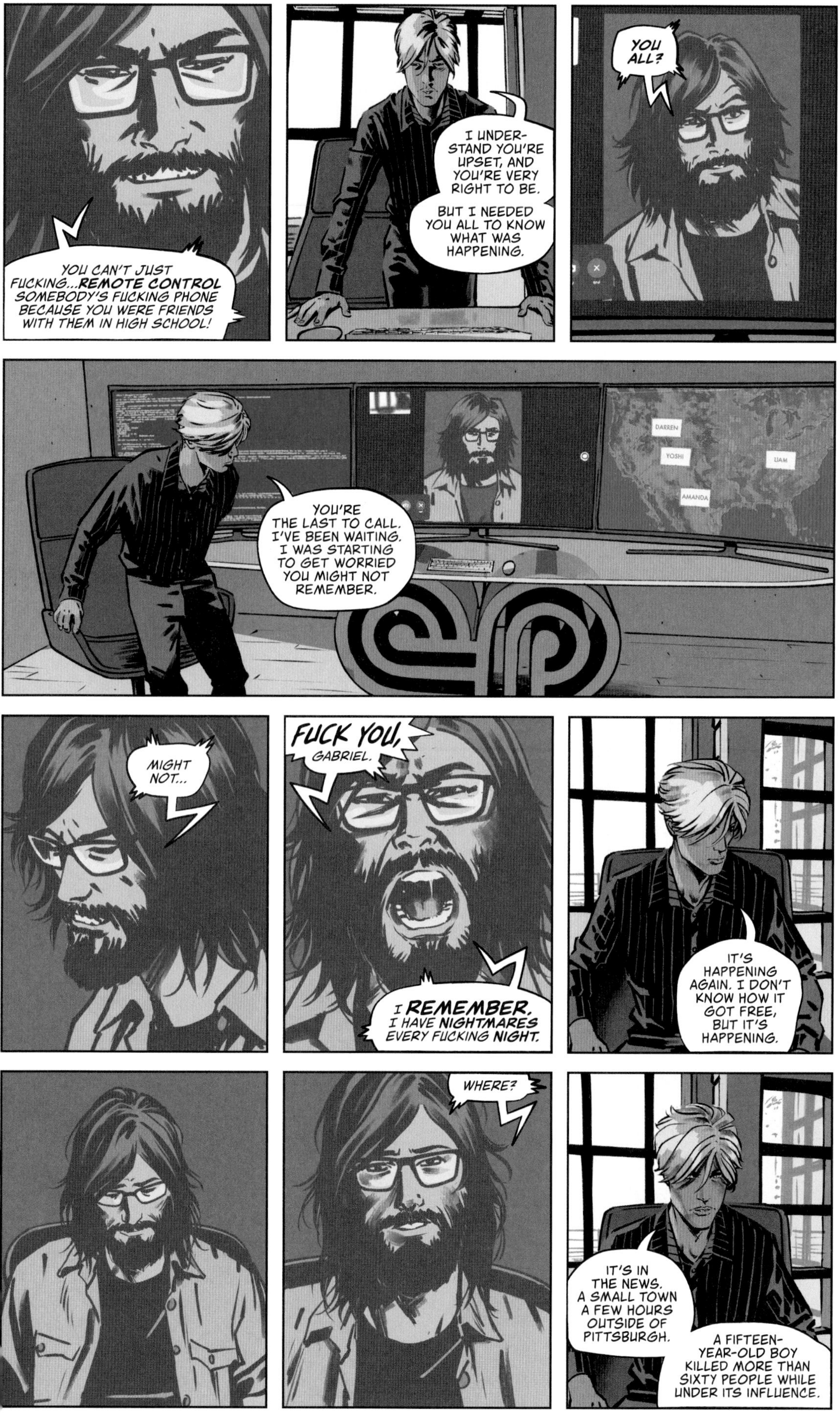
YOU CAN'T JUST FUCKING...REMOTE CONTROL SOMEBODY'S FUCKING PHONE BECAUSE YOU WERE FRIENDS WITH THEM IN HIGH SCHOOL!
I UNDERSTAND YOU'RE UPSET, AND YOU'RE VERY RIGHT TO BE.
BUT I NEEDED YOU ALL TO KNOW WHAT WAS HAPPENING.
YOU ALL?
DARREN
YOSHI
LIAM
AMANDA
YOU'RE THE LAST TO CALL. I'VE BEEN WAITING. I WAS STARTING TO GET WORRIED YOU MIGHT NOT REMEMBER.
MIGHT NOT...
FUCK YOU, GABRIEL.
I REMEMBER. I HAVE NIGHTMARES EVERY FUCKING NIGHT.
IT'S HAPPENING AGAIN. I DON'T KNOW HOW IT GOT FREE, BUT IT'S HAPPENING.
WHERE?
IT'S IN THE NEWS. A SMALL TOWN A FEW HOURS OUTSIDE OF PITTSBURGH.
A FIFTEEN-YEAR-OLD BOY KILLED MORE THAN SIXTY PEOPLE WHILE UNDER ITS INFLUENCE.

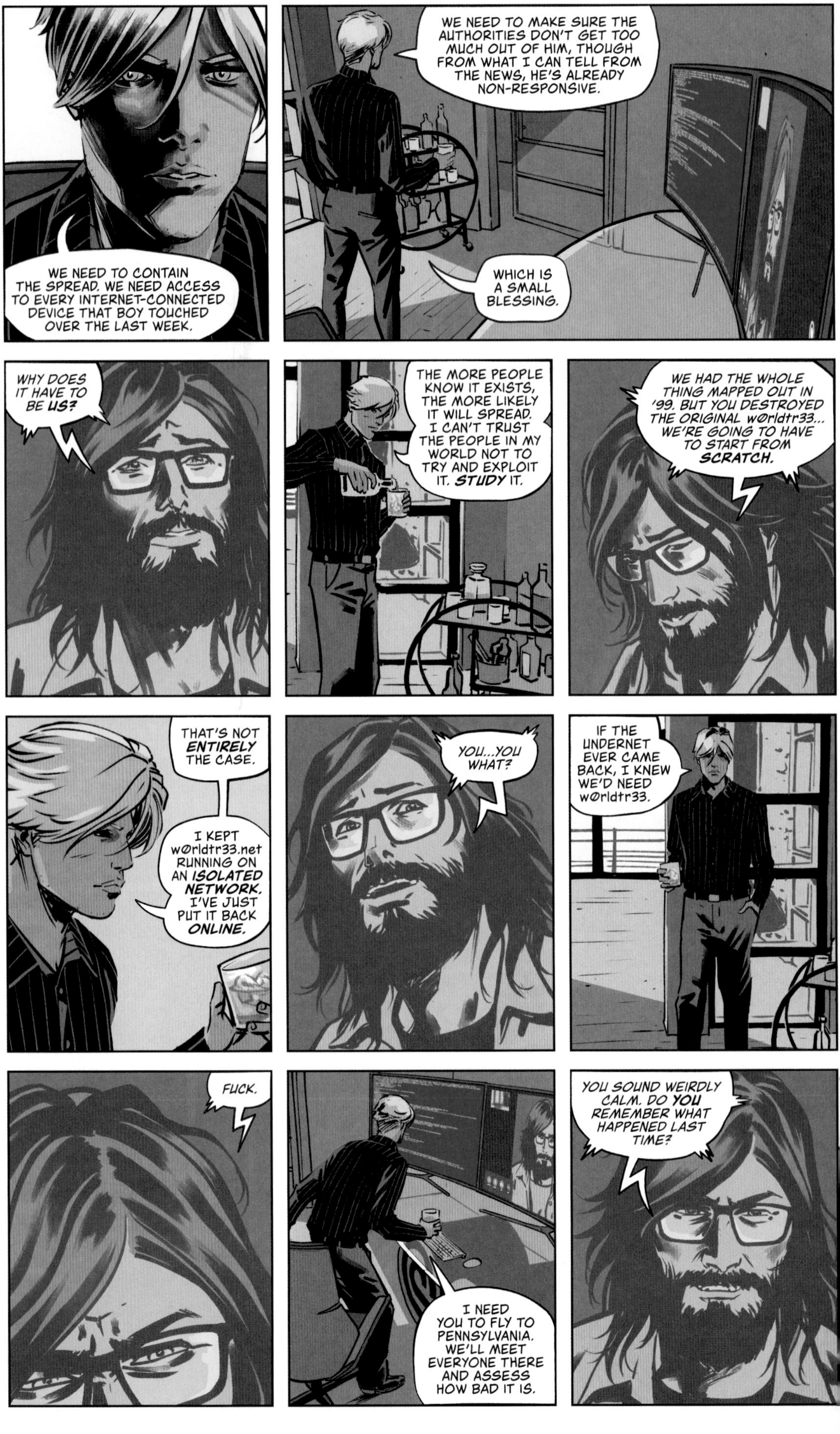
WE NEED TO CONTAIN THE SPREAD. WE NEED ACCESS TO EVERY INTERNET-CONNECTED DEVICE THAT BOY TOUCHED OVER THE LAST WEEK.
WE NEED TO MAKE SURE THE AUTHORITIES DON'T GET TOO MUCH OUT OF HIM, THOUGH FROM WHAT I CAN TELL FROM THE NEWS, HE'S ALREADY NON-RESPONSIVE.
WHICH IS A SMALL BLESSING.
WHY DOES IT HAVE TO BE US?
THE MORE PEOPLE KNOW IT EXISTS, THE MORE LIKELY IT WILL SPREAD. I CAN'T TRUST THE PEOPLE IN MY WORLD NOT TO TRY AND EXPLOIT IT. STUDY IT.
WE HAD THE WHOLE THING MAPPED OUT IN '99. BUT YOU DESTROYED THE ORIGINAL w@rldtr33... WE'RE GOING TO HAVE TO START FROM SCRATCH.
THAT'S NOT ENTIRELY THE CASE.
I KEPT w@rldtr33.net RUNNING ON AN ISOLATED NETWORK. I'VE JUST PUT IT BACK ONLINE.
YOU...YOU WHAT?
IF THE UNDERNET EVER CAME BACK, I KNEW WE'D NEED w@rldtr33.
FUCK.
I NEED YOU TO FLY TO PENNSYLVANIA. WE'LL MEET EVERYONE THERE AND ASSESS HOW BAD IT IS.
YOU SOUND WEIRDLY CALM. DO YOU REMEMBER WHAT HAPPENED LAST TIME?

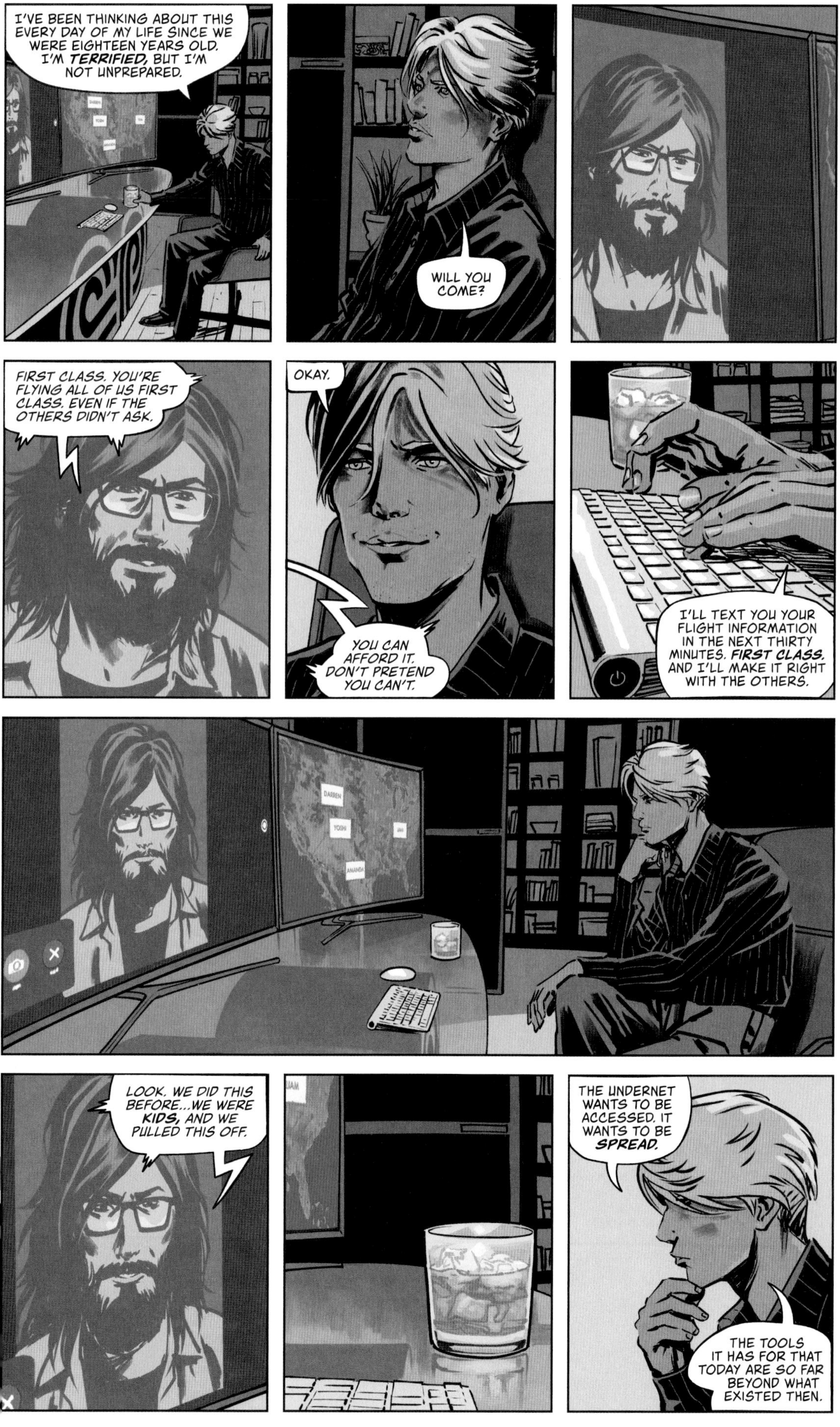
I'VE BEEN THINKING ABOUT THIS EVERY DAY OF MY LIFE SINCE WE WERE EIGHTEEN YEARS OLD. I'M TERRIFIED, BUT I'M NOT UNPREPARED.
WILL YOU COME?
FIRST CLASS. YOU'RE FLYING ALL OF US FIRST CLASS. EVEN IF THE OTHERS DIDN'T ASK.
OKAY.
YOU CAN AFFORD IT. DON'T PRETEND YOU CAN'T.
I'LL TEXT YOU YOUR FLIGHT INFORMATION IN THE NEXT THIRTY MINUTES. FIRST CLASS. AND I'LL MAKE IT RIGHT WITH THE OTHERS.
DARREN
YOSHI
AMANDA
LOOK. WE DID THIS BEFORE...WE WERE KIDS, AND WE PULLED THIS OFF.
THE UNDERNET WANTS TO BE ACCESSED. IT WANTS TO BE SPREAD.
THE TOOLS IT HAS FOR THAT TODAY ARE SO FAR BEYOND WHAT EXISTED THEN.

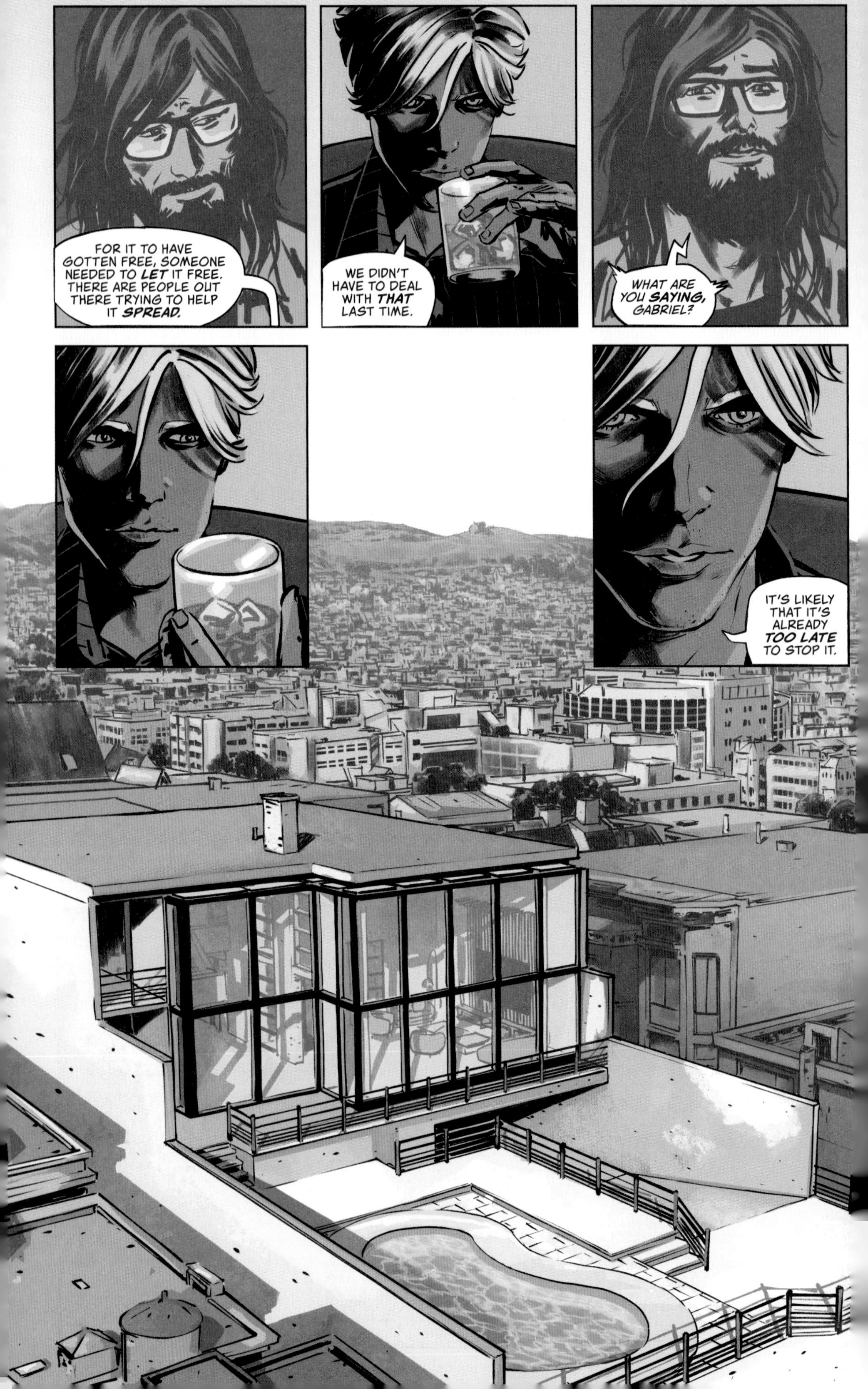
FOR IT TO HAVE GOTTEN FREE, SOMEONE NEEDED TO LET IT FREE. THERE ARE PEOPLE OUT THERE TRYING TO HELP IT SPREAD.
WE DIDN'T HAVE TO DEAL WITH THAT LAST TIME.
WHAT ARE YOU SAYING, GABRIEL?
IT'S LIKELY THAT IT'S ALREADY TOO LATE TO STOP IT.

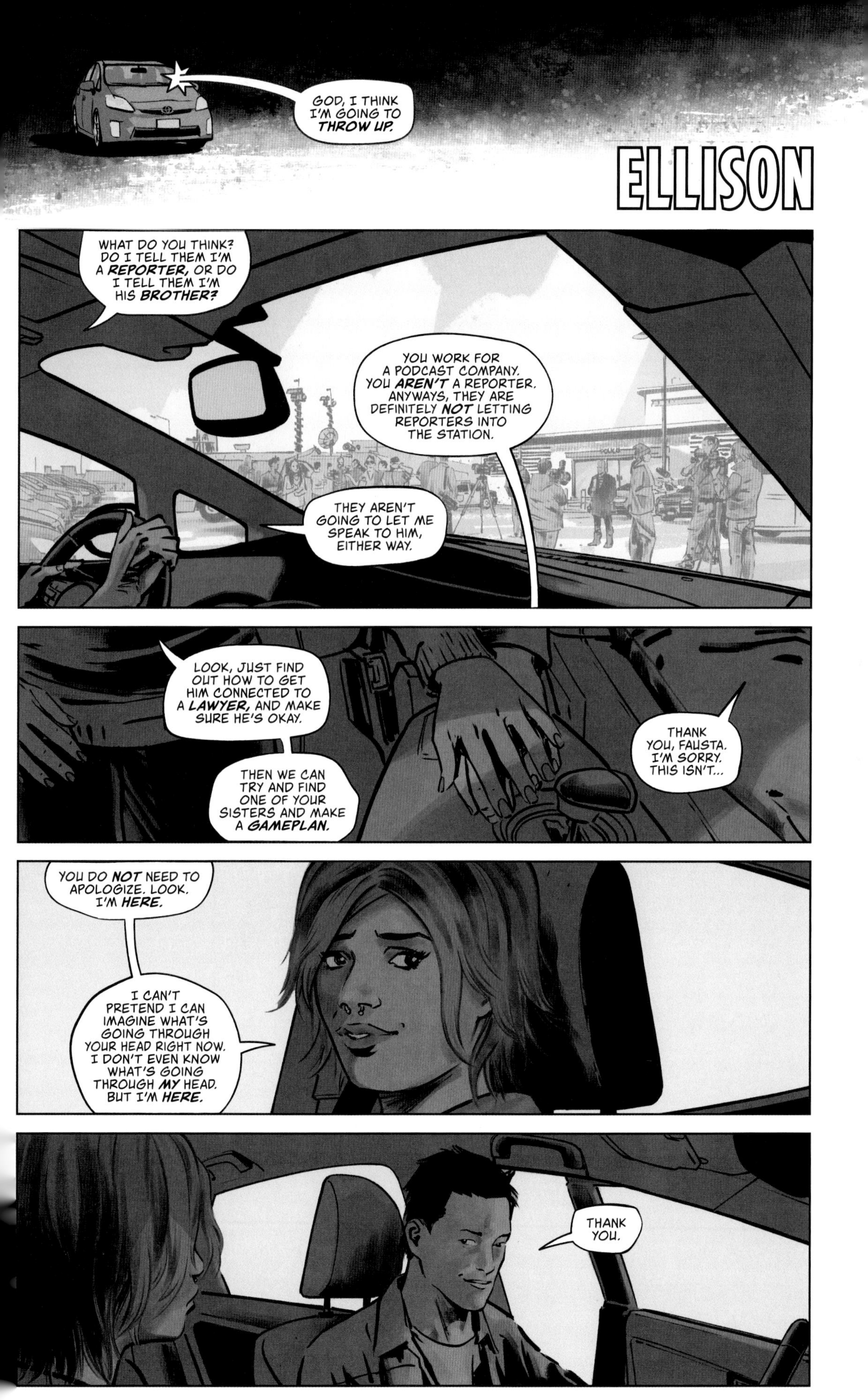
GOD, I THINK I'M GOING TO THROW UP.
ELLISON
WHAT DO YOU THINK? DO I TELL THEM I'M A REPORTER, OR DO I TELL THEM I'M HIS BROTHER?
YOU WORK FOR A PODCAST COMPANY. YOU AREN'T A REPORTER. ANYWAYS, THEY ARE DEFINITELY NOT LETTING REPORTERS INTO THE STATION.
THEY AREN'T GOING TO LET ME SPEAK TO HIM, EITHER WAY.
LOOK, JUST FIND OUT HOW TO GET HIM CONNECTED TO A LAWYER, AND MAKE SURE HE'S OKAY.
THEN WE CAN TRY AND FIND ONE OF YOUR SISTERS AND MAKE A GAMEPLAN.
THANK YOU, FAUSTA. I'M SORRY. THIS ISN'T...
YOU DO NOT NEED TO APOLOGIZE. LOOK. I'M HERE.
I CAN'T PRETEND I CAN IMAGINE WHAT'S GOING THROUGH YOUR HEAD RIGHT NOW. I DON'T EVEN KNOW WHAT'S GOING THROUGH MY HEAD. BUT I'M HERE.
THANK YOU.

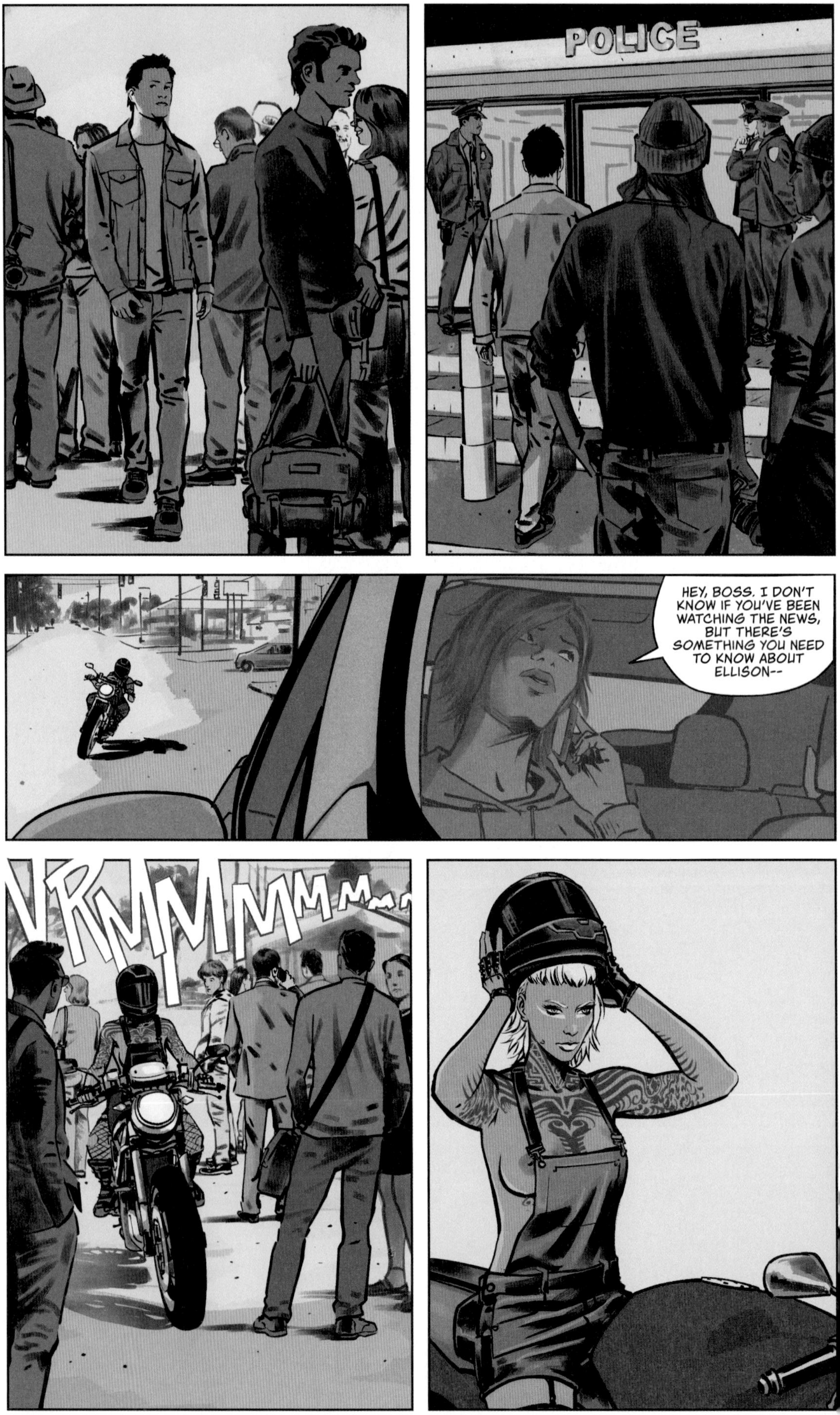
POLICE
HEY, BOSS. I DON'T KNOW IF YOU'VE BEEN WATCHING THE NEWS, BUT THERE'S SOMETHING YOU NEED TO KNOW ABOUT ELLISON--
VRMMMMMM

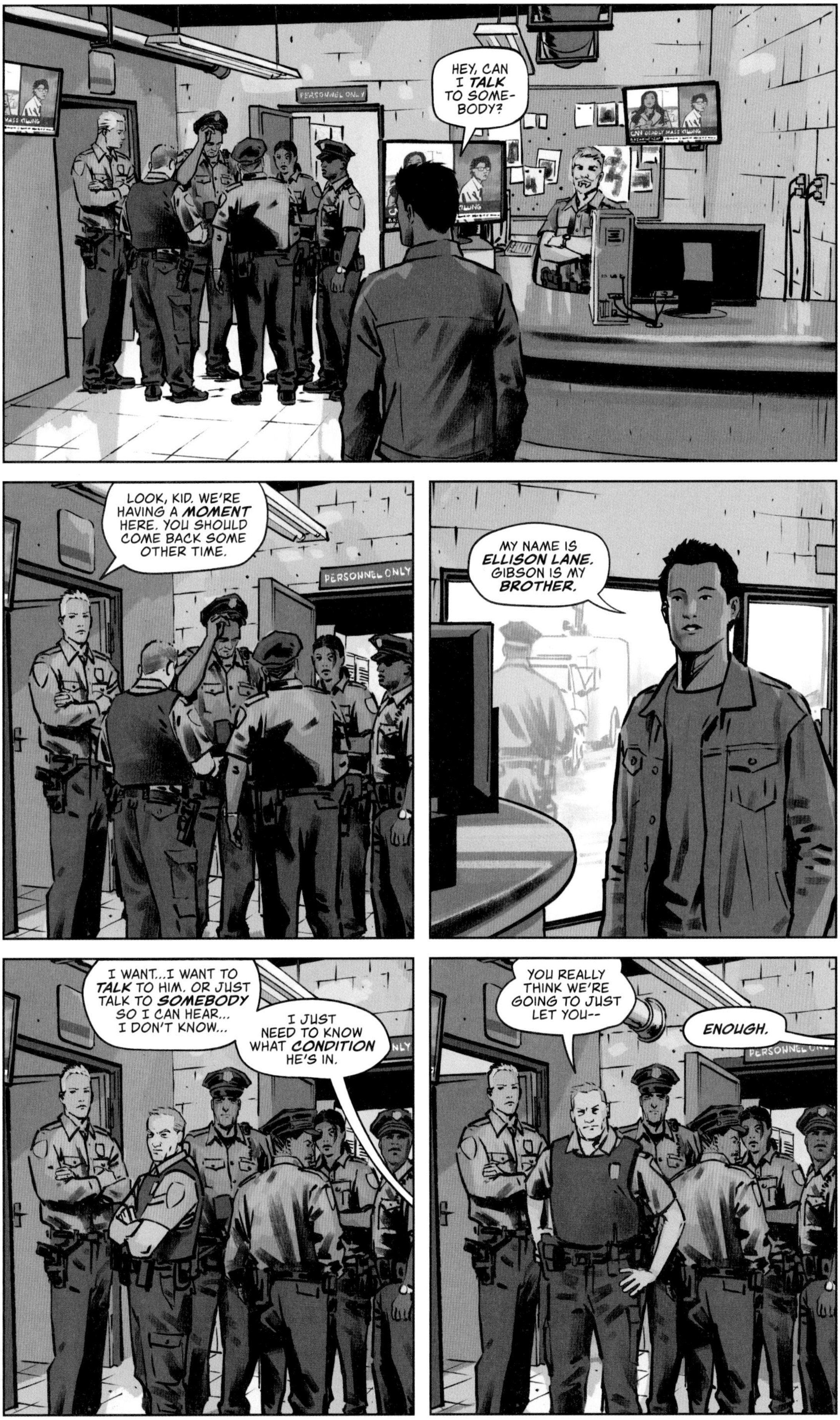
PERSONNEL ONLY
HEY, CAN I *TALK* TO SOMEBODY?
LOOK, KID. WE'RE HAVING A *MOMENT* HERE. YOU SHOULD COME BACK SOME OTHER TIME.
PERSONNEL ONLY
MY NAME IS *ELLISON LANE.* GIBSON IS MY *BROTHER.*
I WANT...I WANT TO *TALK* TO HIM. OR JUST TALK TO *SOMEBODY* SO I CAN HEAR... I DON'T KNOW...
I JUST NEED TO KNOW WHAT *CONDITION* HE'S IN.
YOU REALLY THINK WE'RE GOING TO JUST LET YOU--
ENOUGH.

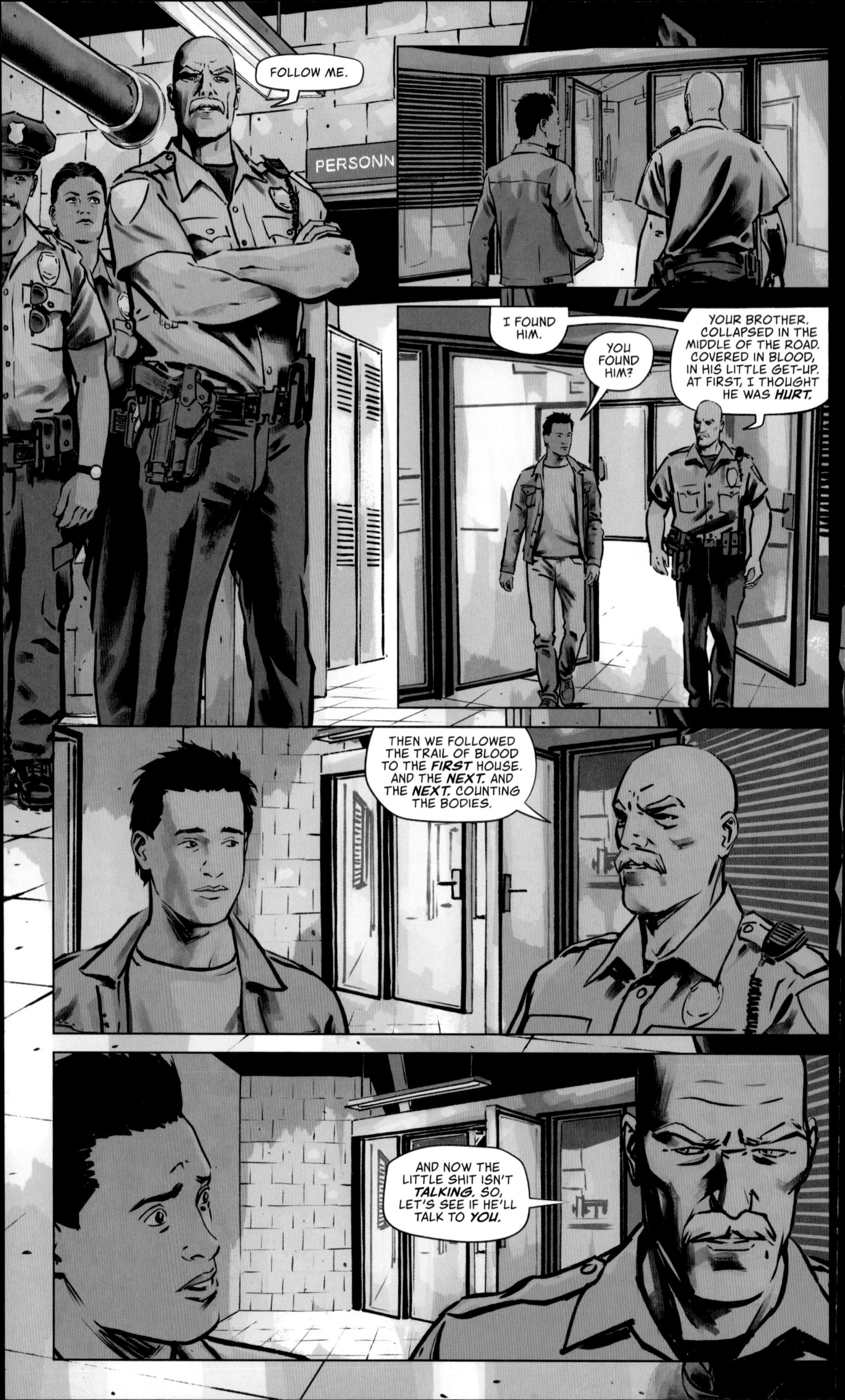
PERSONN
FOLLOW ME.
I FOUND HIM.
YOU FOUND HIM?
YOUR BROTHER. COLLAPSED IN THE MIDDLE OF THE ROAD. COVERED IN BLOOD, IN HIS LITTLE GET-UP. AT FIRST, I THOUGHT HE WAS HURT.
THEN WE FOLLOWED THE TRAIL OF BLOOD TO THE FIRST HOUSE. AND THE NEXT. AND THE NEXT. COUNTING THE BODIES.
AND NOW THE LITTLE SHIT ISN'T TALKING. SO, LET'S SEE IF HE'LL TALK TO YOU.

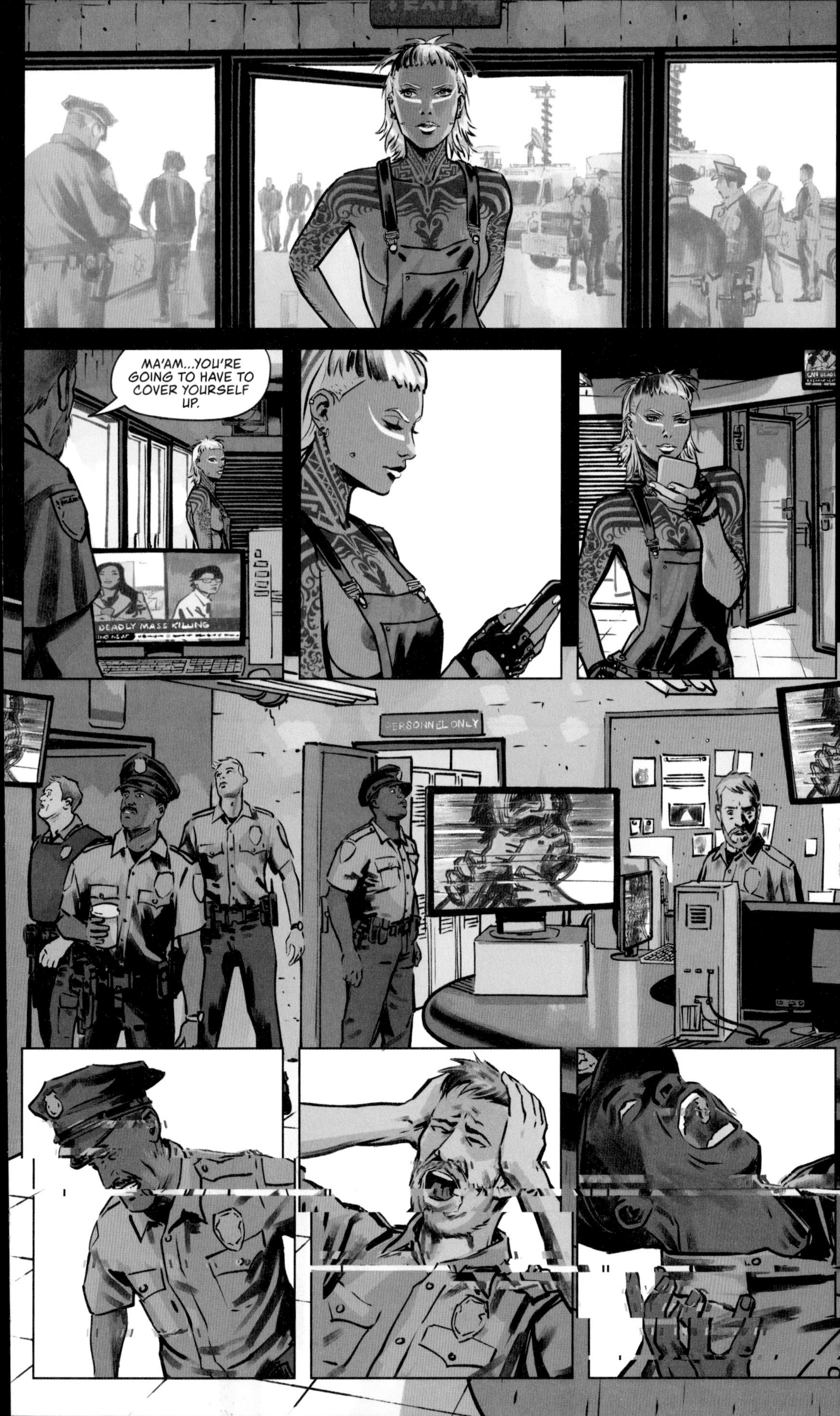
MA'AM...YOU'RE GOING TO HAVE TO COVER YOURSELF UP.
DEADLY MASS KILLING
PERSONNEL ONLY

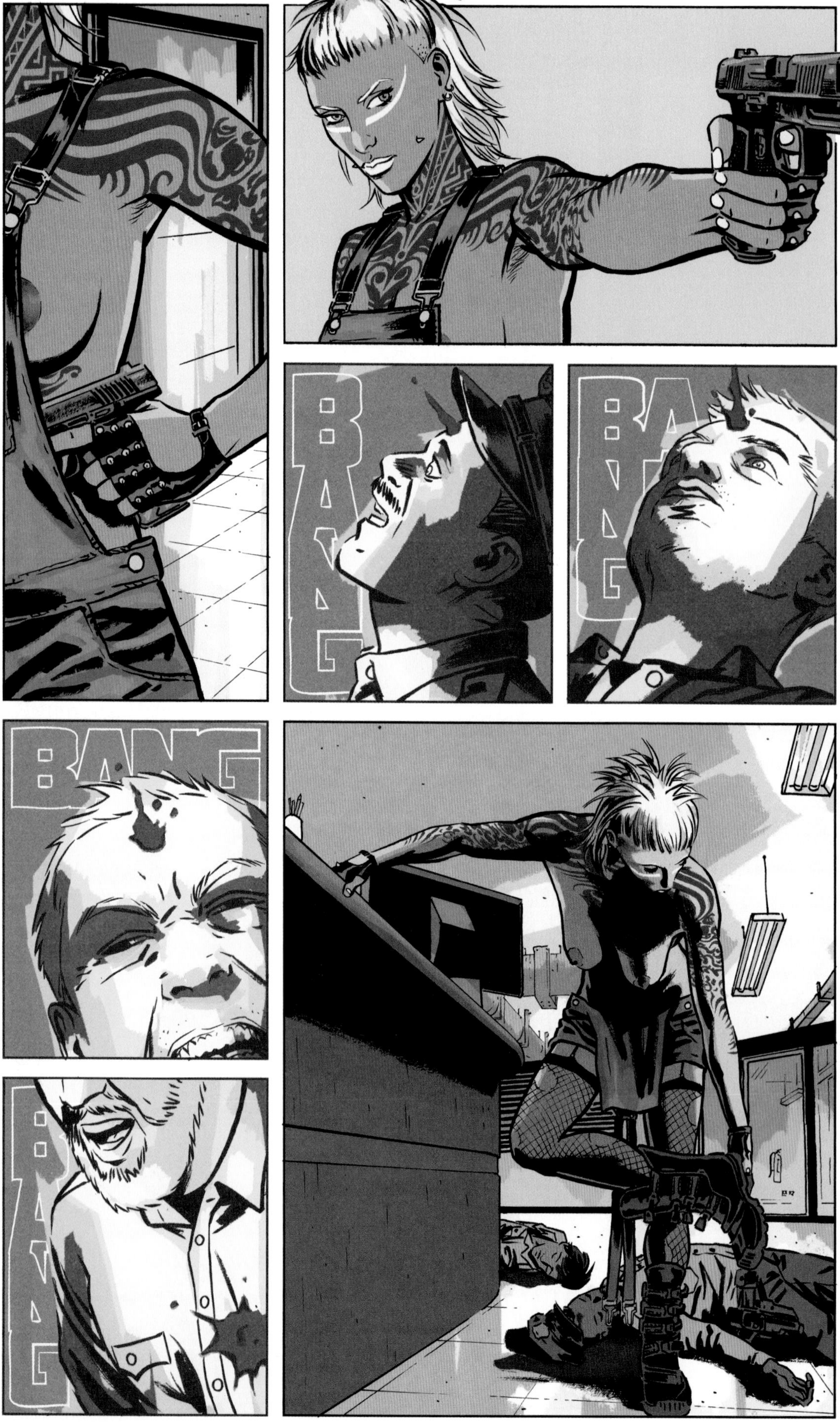
BANG
BANG
BANG
BANG

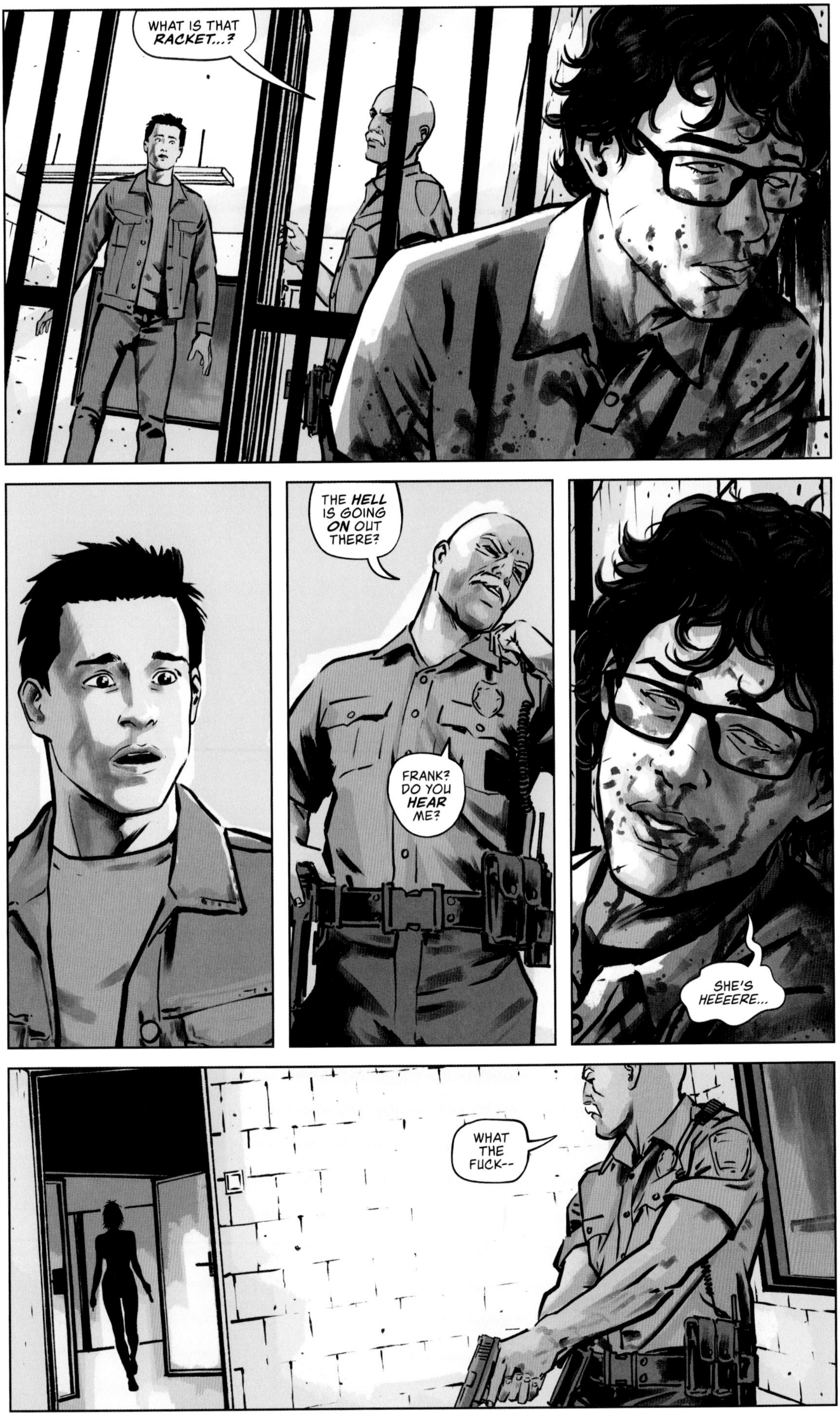
WHAT IS THAT RACKET...?
THE HELL IS GOING ON OUT THERE?
FRANK? DO YOU HEAR ME?
SHE'S HEEEERE...
WHAT THE FUCK--

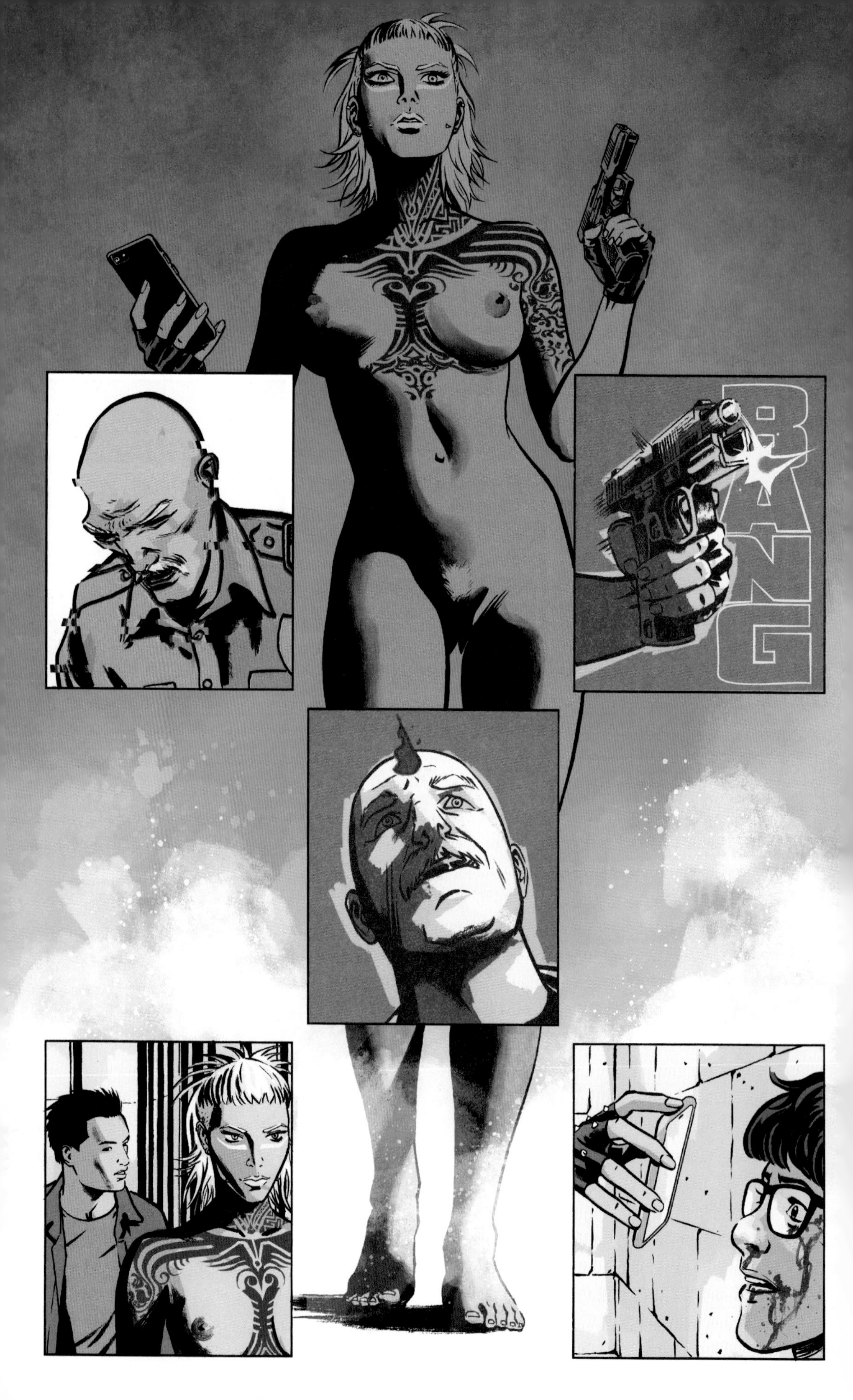
BANG

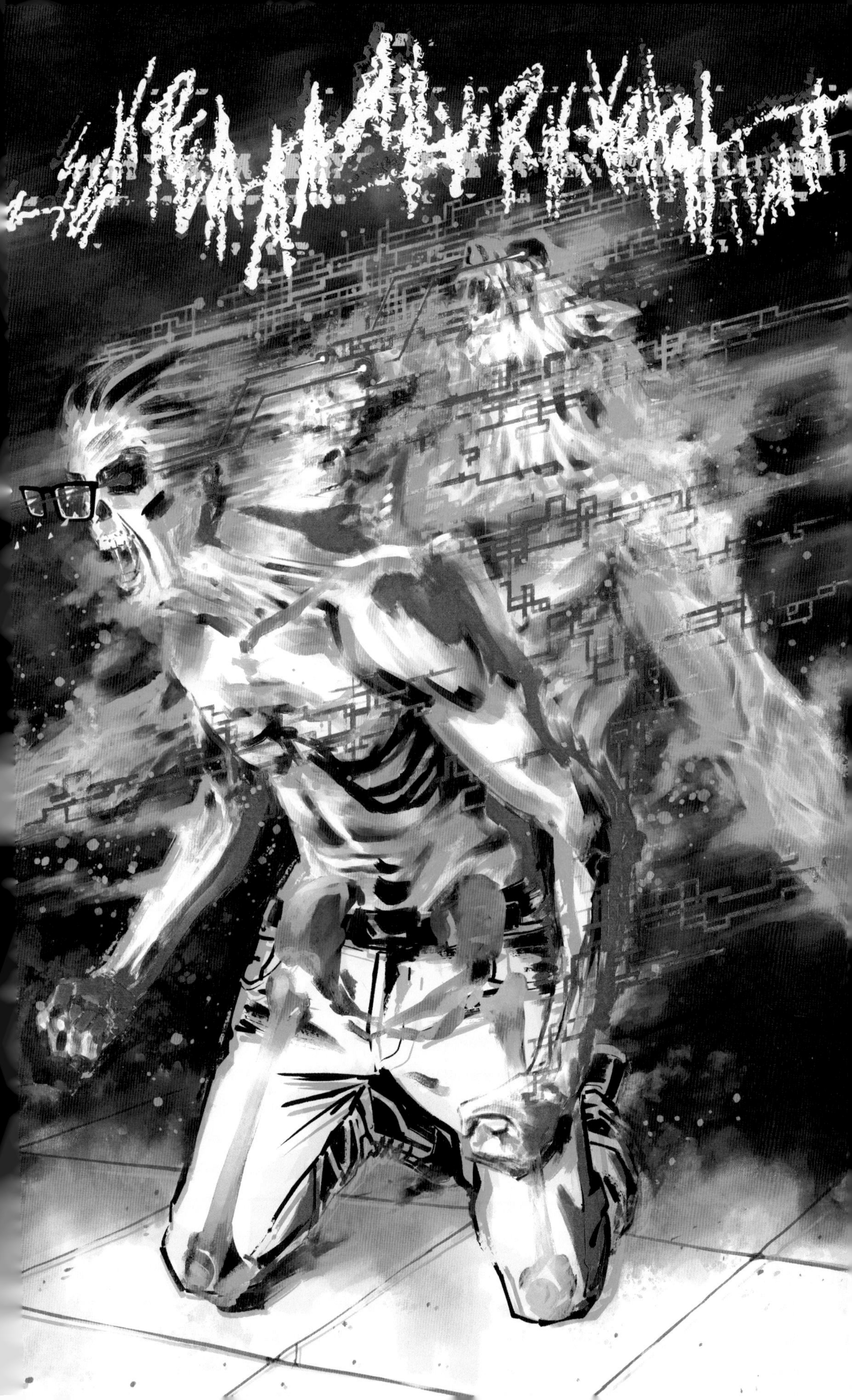

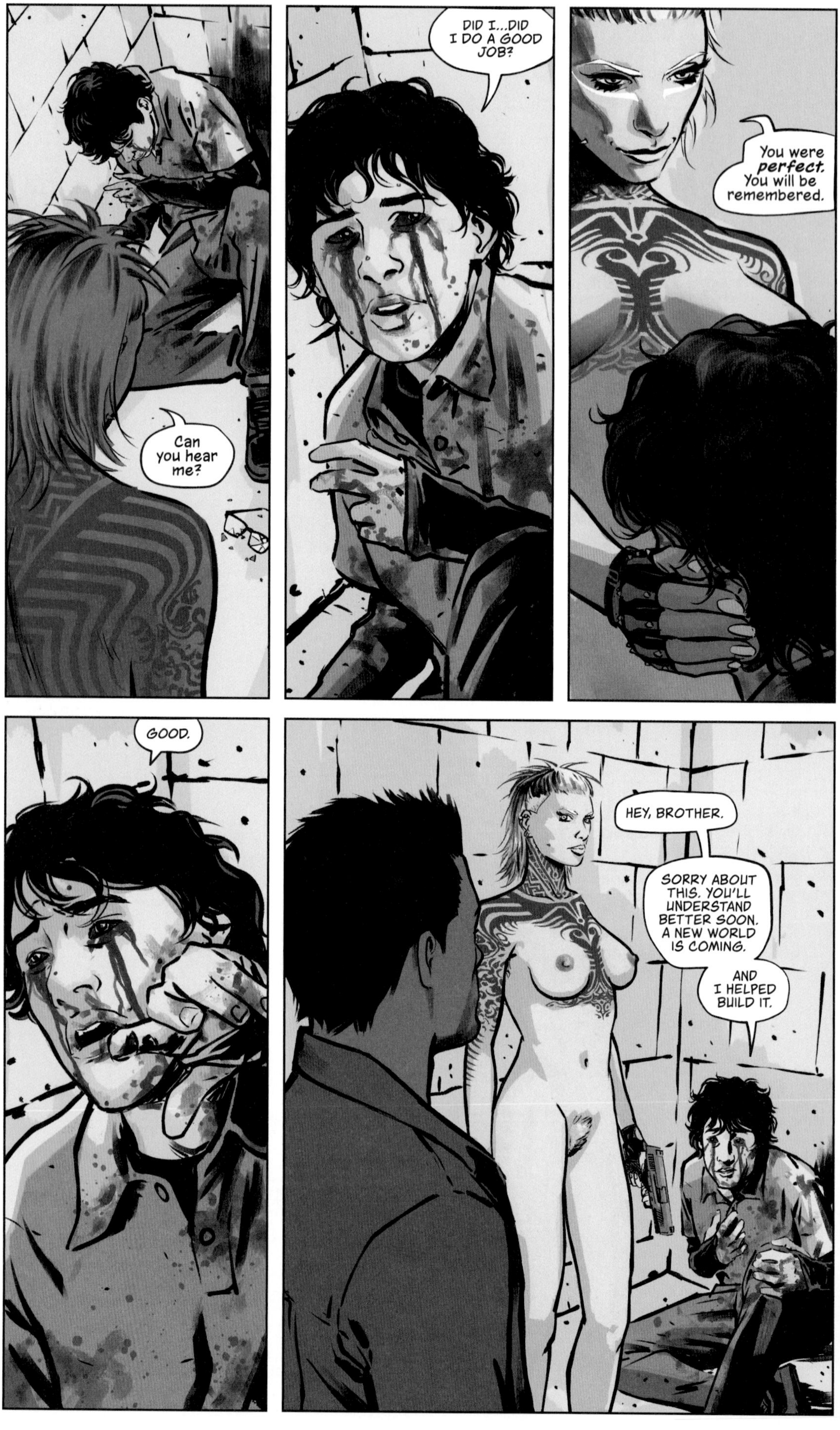
Can you hear me?
DID I...DID I DO A GOOD JOB?
You were *perfect.* You will be remembered.
GOOD.
HEY, BROTHER.
SORRY ABOUT THIS. YOU'LL UNDERSTAND BETTER SOON. A NEW WORLD IS COMING.
AND I HELPED BUILD IT.

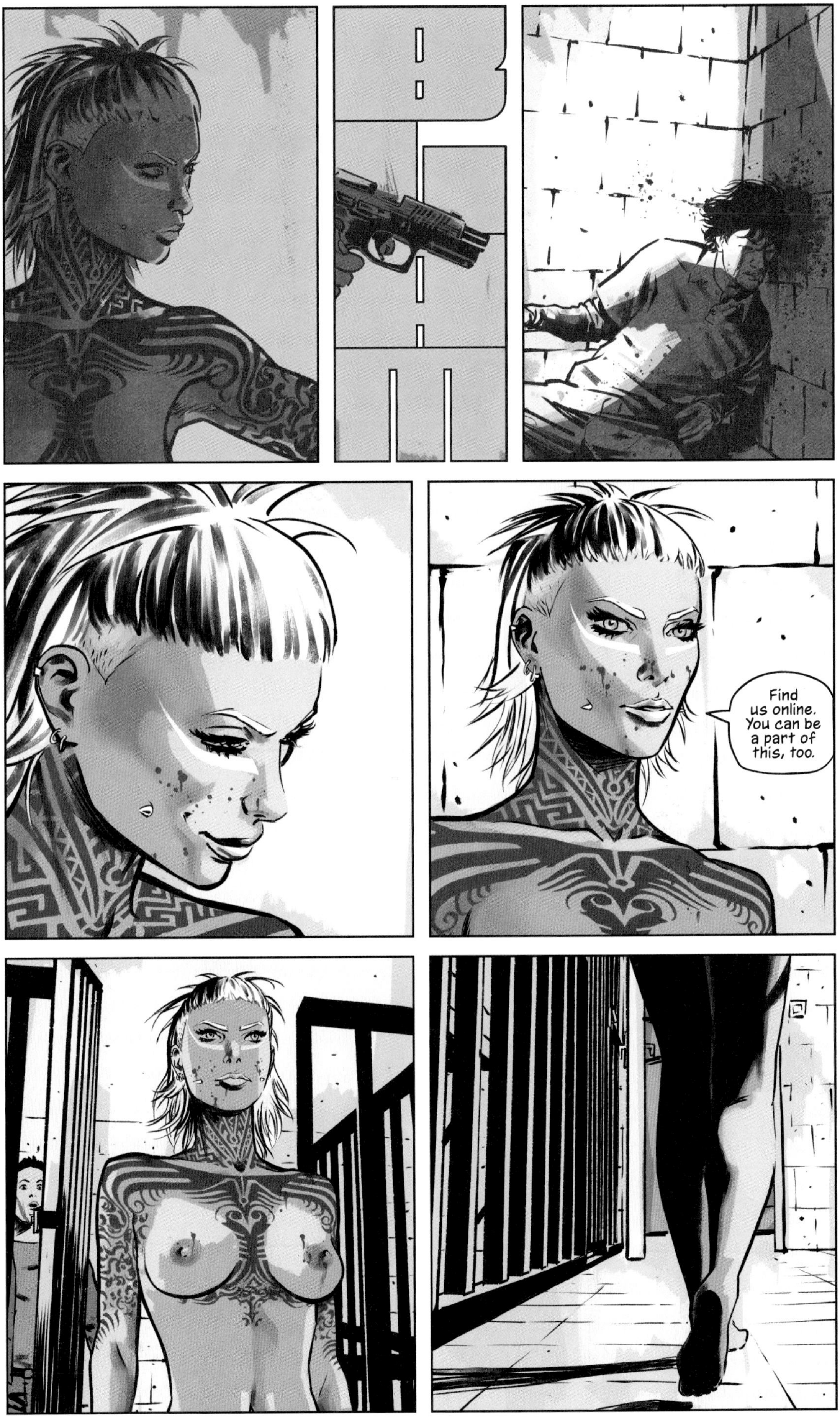
Find us online. You can be a part of this, too.

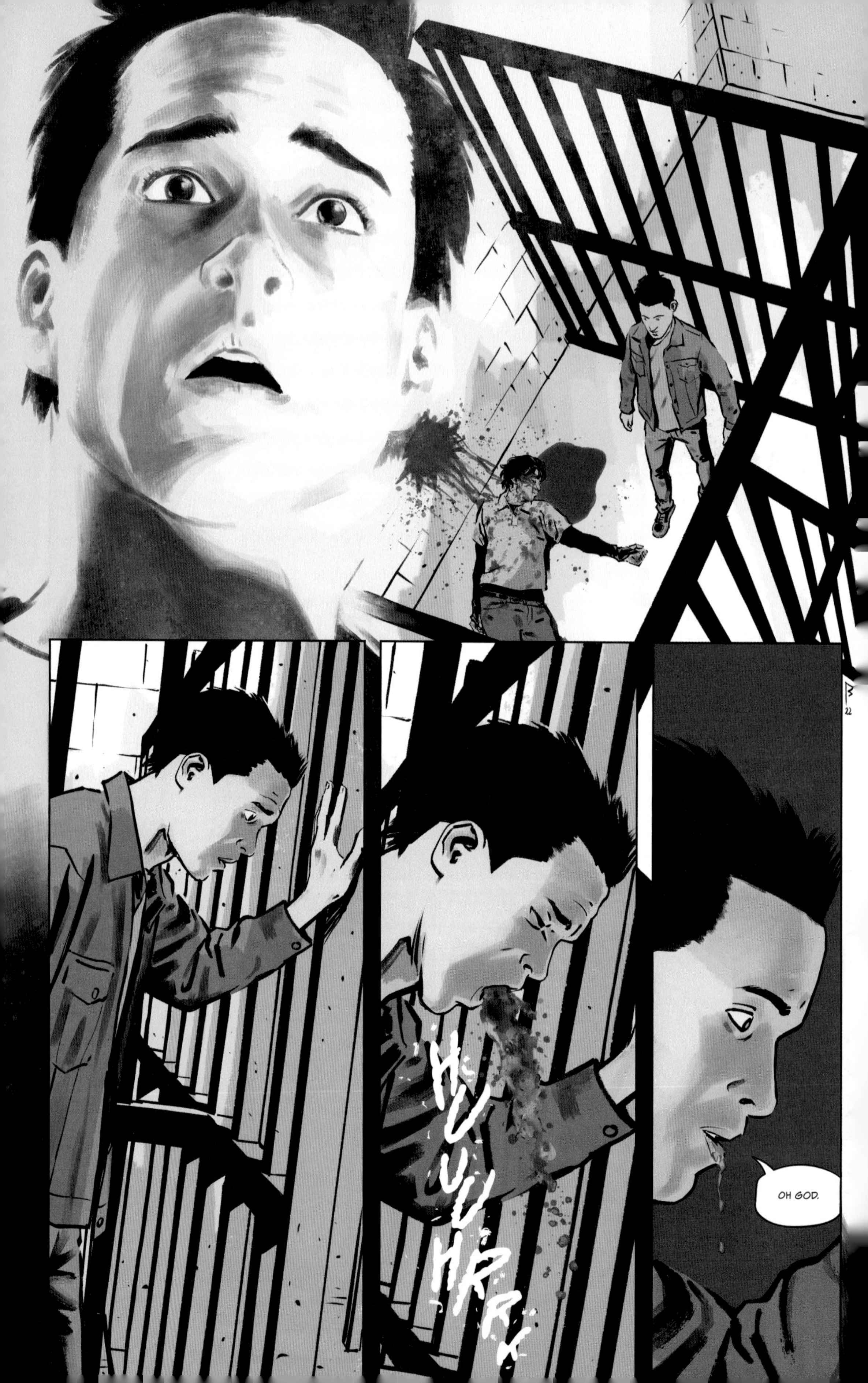
HUUUHRRK
OH GOD.

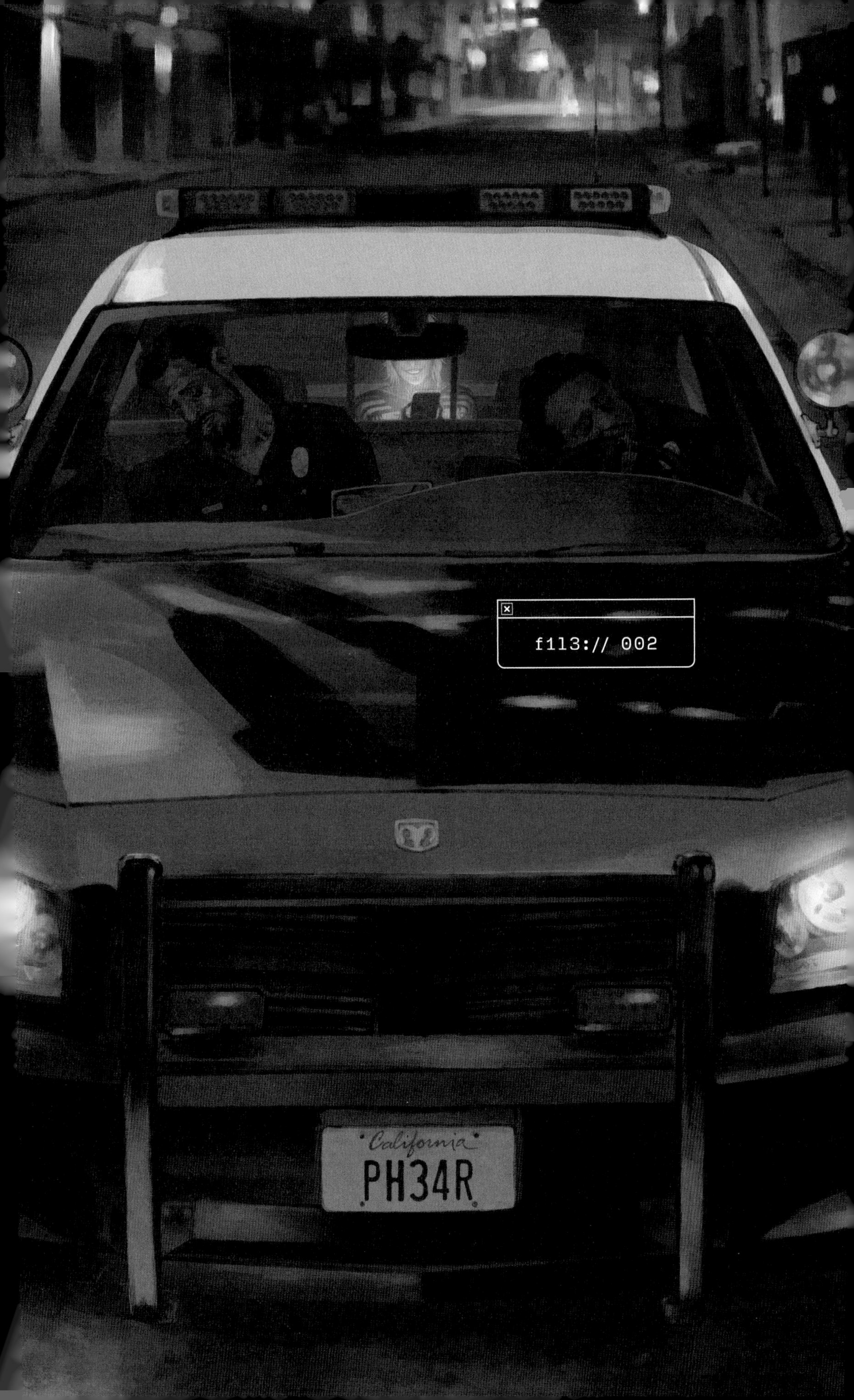
f113:// 002
California
PH34R

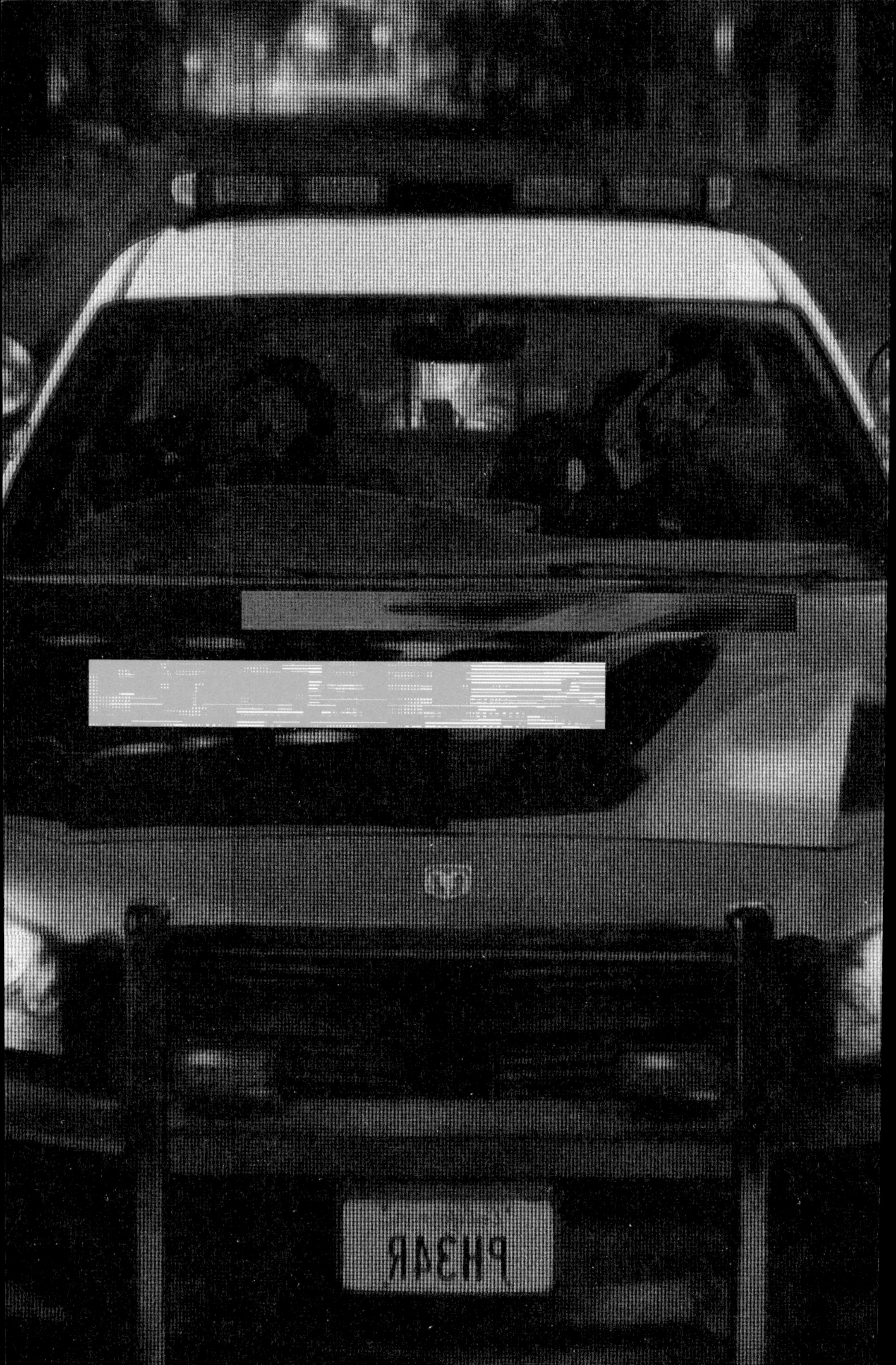

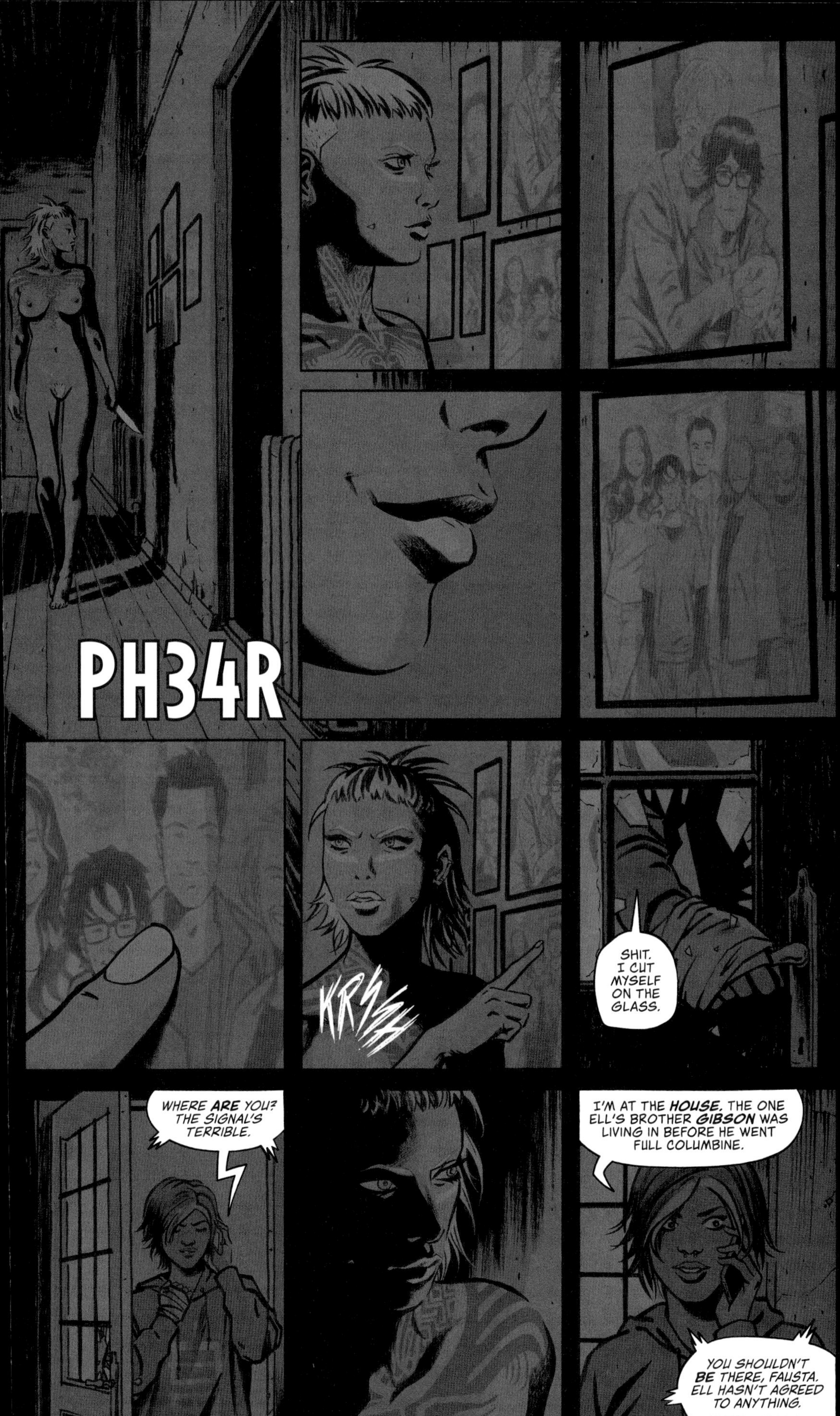
PH34R
KRSSH
SHIT. I CUT MYSELF ON THE GLASS.
WHERE ARE YOU? THE SIGNAL'S TERRIBLE.
I'M AT THE HOUSE. THE ONE ELL'S BROTHER GIBSON WAS LIVING IN BEFORE HE WENT FULL COLUMBINE.
YOU SHOULDN'T BE THERE, FAUSTA. ELL HASN'T AGREED TO ANYTHING.

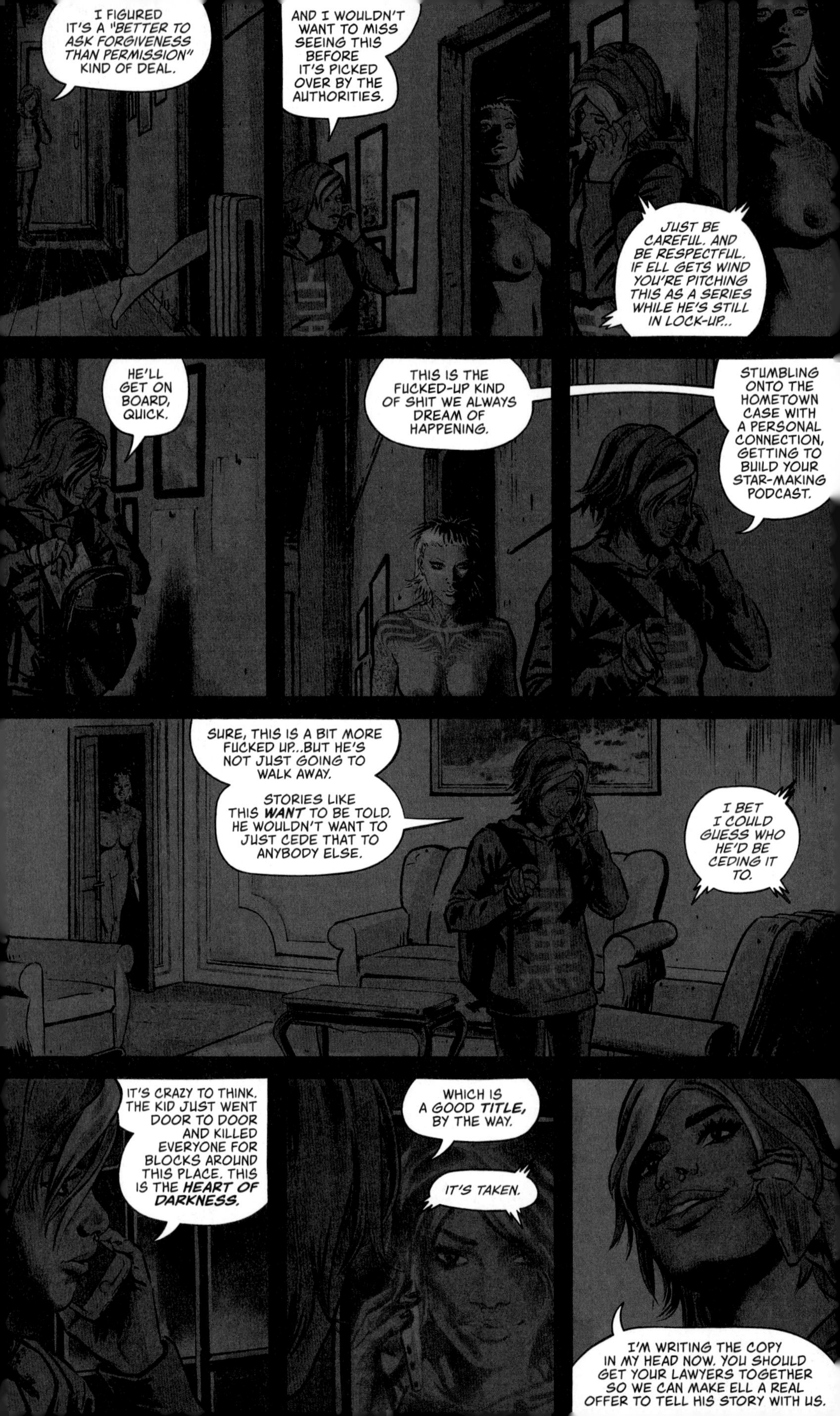
I FIGURED IT'S A "BETTER TO ASK FORGIVENESS THAN PERMISSION" KIND OF DEAL.
AND I WOULDN'T WANT TO MISS SEEING THIS BEFORE IT'S PICKED OVER BY THE AUTHORITIES.
JUST BE CAREFUL. AND BE RESPECTFUL. IF ELL GETS WIND YOU'RE PITCHING THIS AS A SERIES WHILE HE'S STILL IN LOCK-UP...
HE'LL GET ON BOARD, QUICK.
THIS IS THE FUCKED-UP KIND OF SHIT WE ALWAYS DREAM OF HAPPENING.
STUMBLING ONTO THE HOMETOWN CASE WITH A PERSONAL CONNECTION, GETTING TO BUILD YOUR STAR-MAKING PODCAST.
SURE, THIS IS A BIT MORE FUCKED UP...BUT HE'S NOT JUST GOING TO WALK AWAY.
STORIES LIKE THIS WANT TO BE TOLD. HE WOULDN'T WANT TO JUST CEDE THAT TO ANYBODY ELSE.
I BET I COULD GUESS WHO HE'D BE CEDING IT TO.
IT'S CRAZY TO THINK. THE KID JUST WENT DOOR TO DOOR AND KILLED EVERYONE FOR BLOCKS AROUND THIS PLACE. THIS IS THE HEART OF DARKNESS.
WHICH IS A GOOD TITLE, BY THE WAY.
IT'S TAKEN.
I'M WRITING THE COPY IN MY HEAD NOW. YOU SHOULD GET YOUR LAWYERS TOGETHER SO WE CAN MAKE ELL A REAL OFFER TO TELL HIS STORY WITH US.

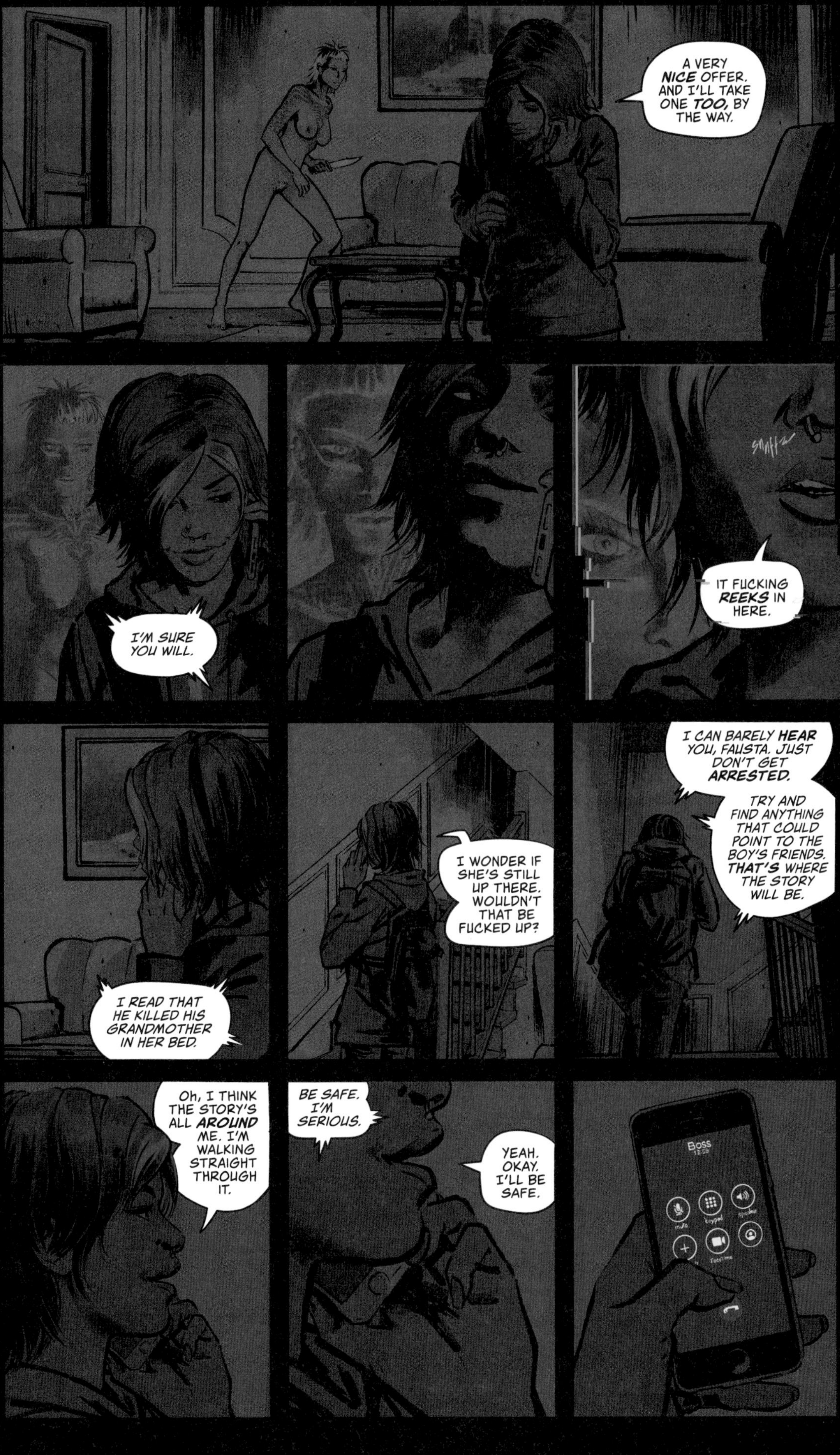
A VERY NICE OFFER. AND I'LL TAKE ONE TOO, BY THE WAY.
I'M SURE YOU WILL.
IT FUCKING REEKS IN HERE.
I READ THAT HE KILLED HIS GRANDMOTHER IN HER BED.
I WONDER IF SHE'S STILL UP THERE. WOULDN'T THAT BE FUCKED UP?
I CAN BARELY HEAR YOU, FAUSTA. JUST DON'T GET ARRESTED.
TRY AND FIND ANYTHING THAT COULD POINT TO THE BOY'S FRIENDS. THAT'S WHERE THE STORY WILL BE.
Oh, I THINK THE STORY'S ALL AROUND ME. I'M WALKING STRAIGHT THROUGH IT.
BE SAFE. I'M SERIOUS.
YEAH. OKAY. I'LL BE SAFE.
Boss

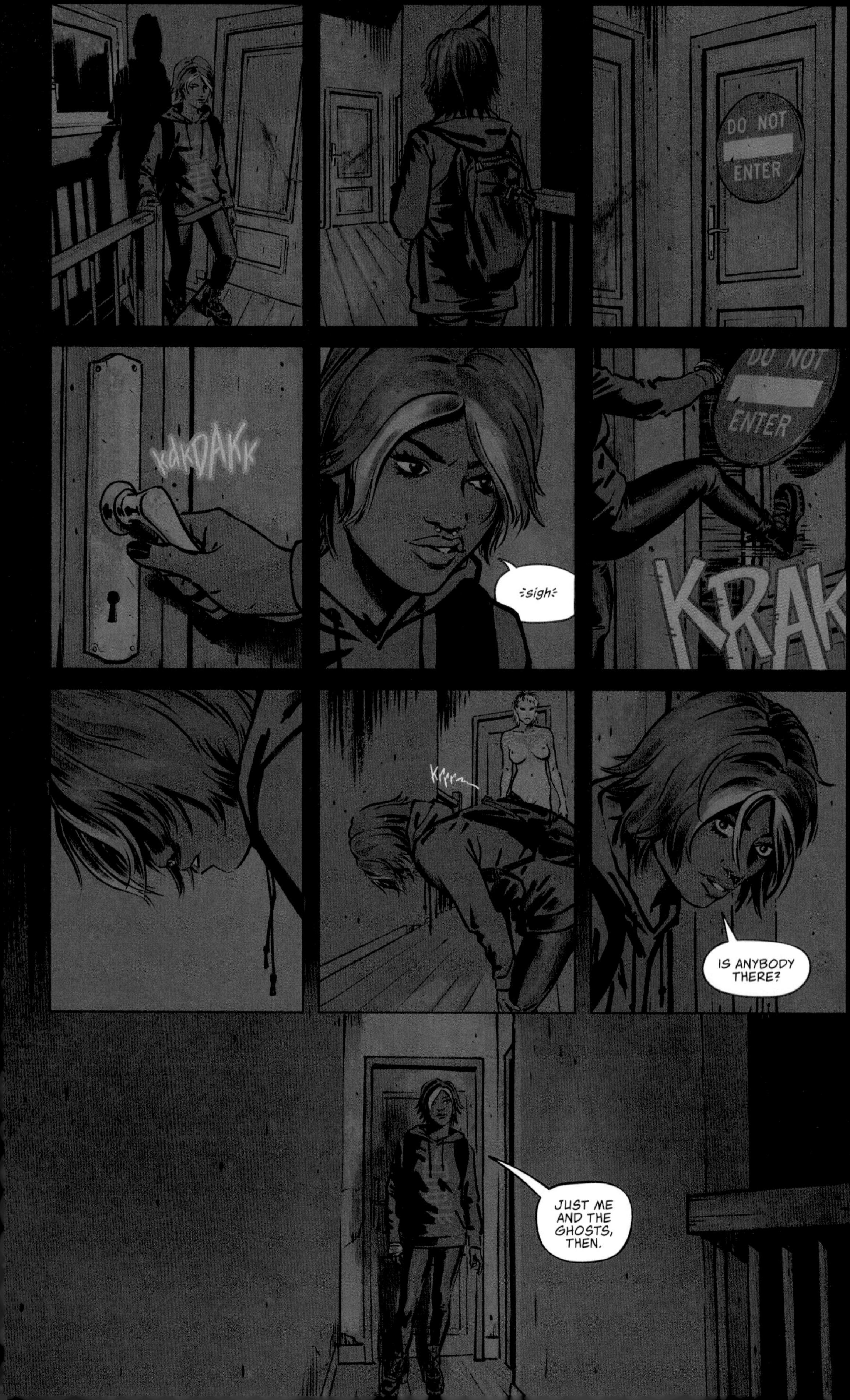
DO NOT ENTER
kakDAKk
sigh
DO NOT ENTER
KRAK
Krrrr
IS ANYBODY THERE?
JUST ME AND THE GHOSTS, THEN.

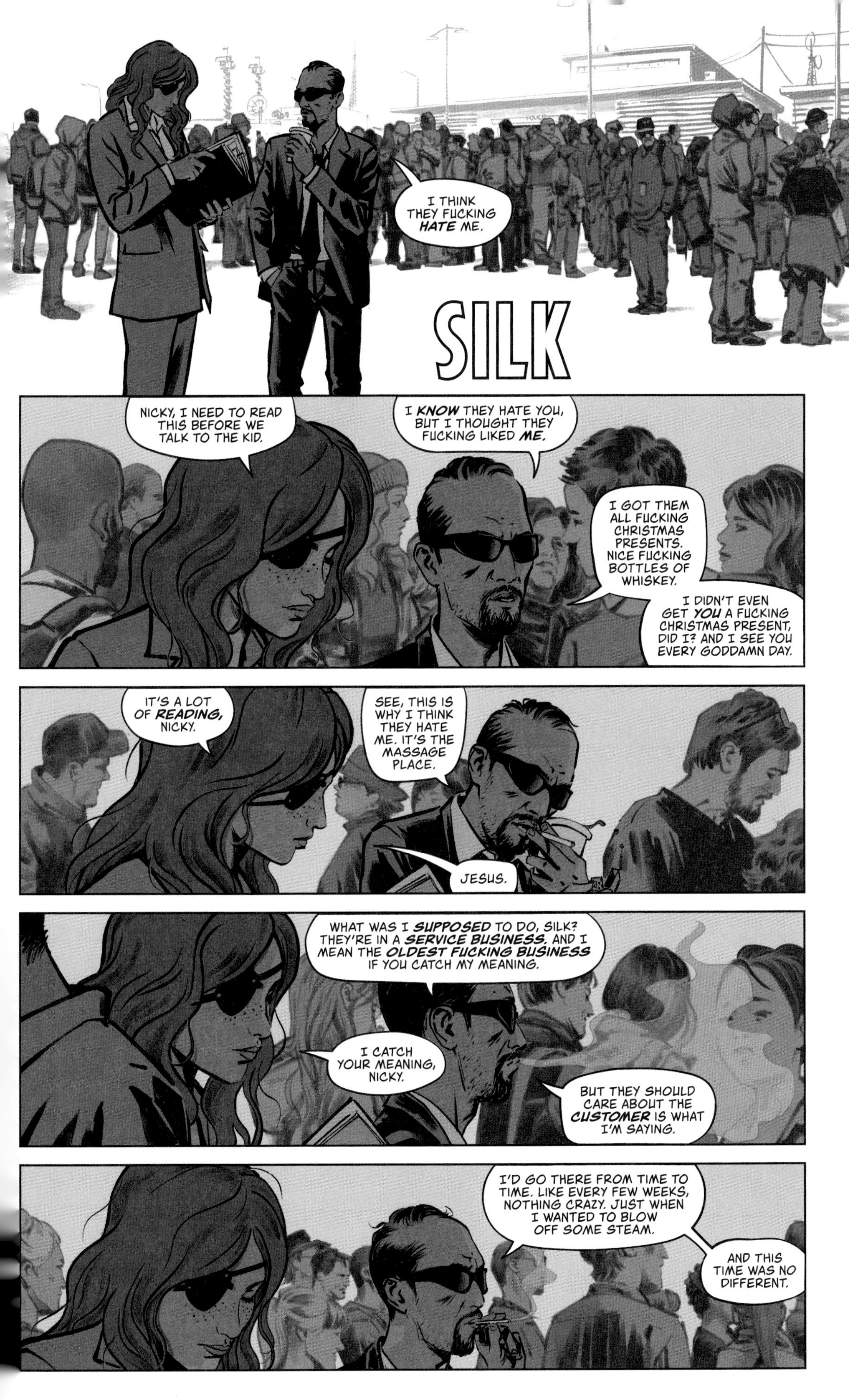
I THINK THEY FUCKING HATE ME.
SILK
NICKY, I NEED TO READ THIS BEFORE WE TALK TO THE KID.
I KNOW THEY HATE YOU, BUT I THOUGHT THEY FUCKING LIKED ME.
I GOT THEM ALL FUCKING CHRISTMAS PRESENTS. NICE FUCKING BOTTLES OF WHISKEY.
I DIDN'T EVEN GET YOU A FUCKING CHRISTMAS PRESENT, DID I? AND I SEE YOU EVERY GODDAMN DAY.
IT'S A LOT OF READING, NICKY.
SEE, THIS IS WHY I THINK THEY HATE ME. IT'S THE MASSAGE PLACE.
JESUS.
WHAT WAS I SUPPOSED TO DO, SILK? THEY'RE IN A SERVICE BUSINESS. AND I MEAN THE OLDEST FUCKING BUSINESS IF YOU CATCH MY MEANING.
I CATCH YOUR MEANING, NICKY.
BUT THEY SHOULD CARE ABOUT THE CUSTOMER IS WHAT I'M SAYING.
I'D GO THERE FROM TIME TO TIME. LIKE EVERY FEW WEEKS, NOTHING CRAZY. JUST WHEN I WANTED TO BLOW OFF SOME STEAM.
AND THIS TIME WAS NO DIFFERENT.

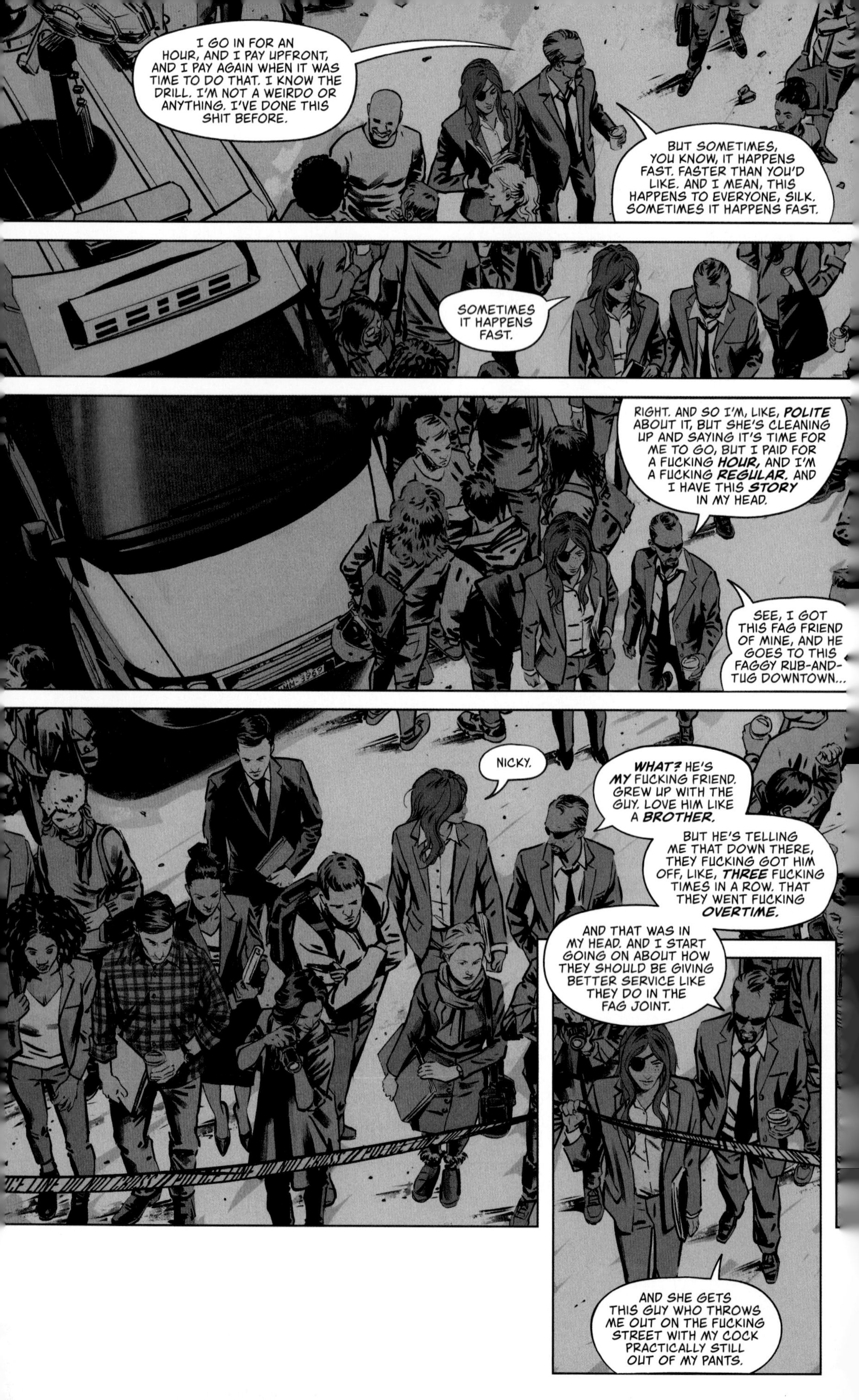

I GO IN FOR AN HOUR, AND I PAY UPFRONT, AND I PAY AGAIN WHEN IT WAS TIME TO DO THAT. I KNOW THE DRILL. I'M NOT A WEIRDO OR ANYTHING. I'VE DONE THIS SHIT BEFORE.
BUT SOMETIMES, YOU KNOW, IT HAPPENS FAST. FASTER THAN YOU'D LIKE. AND I MEAN, THIS HAPPENS TO EVERYONE, SILK. SOMETIMES IT HAPPENS FAST.
SOMETIMES IT HAPPENS FAST.
RIGHT. AND SO I'M, LIKE, **POLITE** ABOUT IT, BUT SHE'S CLEANING UP AND SAYING IT'S TIME FOR ME TO GO, BUT I PAID FOR A FUCKING **HOUR,** AND I'M A FUCKING **REGULAR.** AND I HAVE THIS **STORY** IN MY HEAD.
SEE, I GOT THIS FAG FRIEND OF MINE, AND HE GOES TO THIS FAGGY RUB-AND-TUG DOWNTOWN...
NICKY.
WHAT? HE'S **MY** FUCKING FRIEND. GREW UP WITH THE GUY. LOVE HIM LIKE A **BROTHER.**
BUT HE'S TELLING ME THAT DOWN THERE, THEY FUCKING GOT HIM OFF, LIKE, **THREE** FUCKING TIMES IN A ROW. THAT THEY WENT FUCKING **OVERTIME.**
AND THAT WAS IN MY HEAD. AND I START GOING ON ABOUT HOW THEY SHOULD BE GIVING BETTER SERVICE LIKE THEY DO IN THE FAG JOINT.
AND SHE GETS THIS GUY WHO THROWS ME OUT ON THE FUCKING STREET WITH MY COCK PRACTICALLY STILL OUT OF MY PANTS.

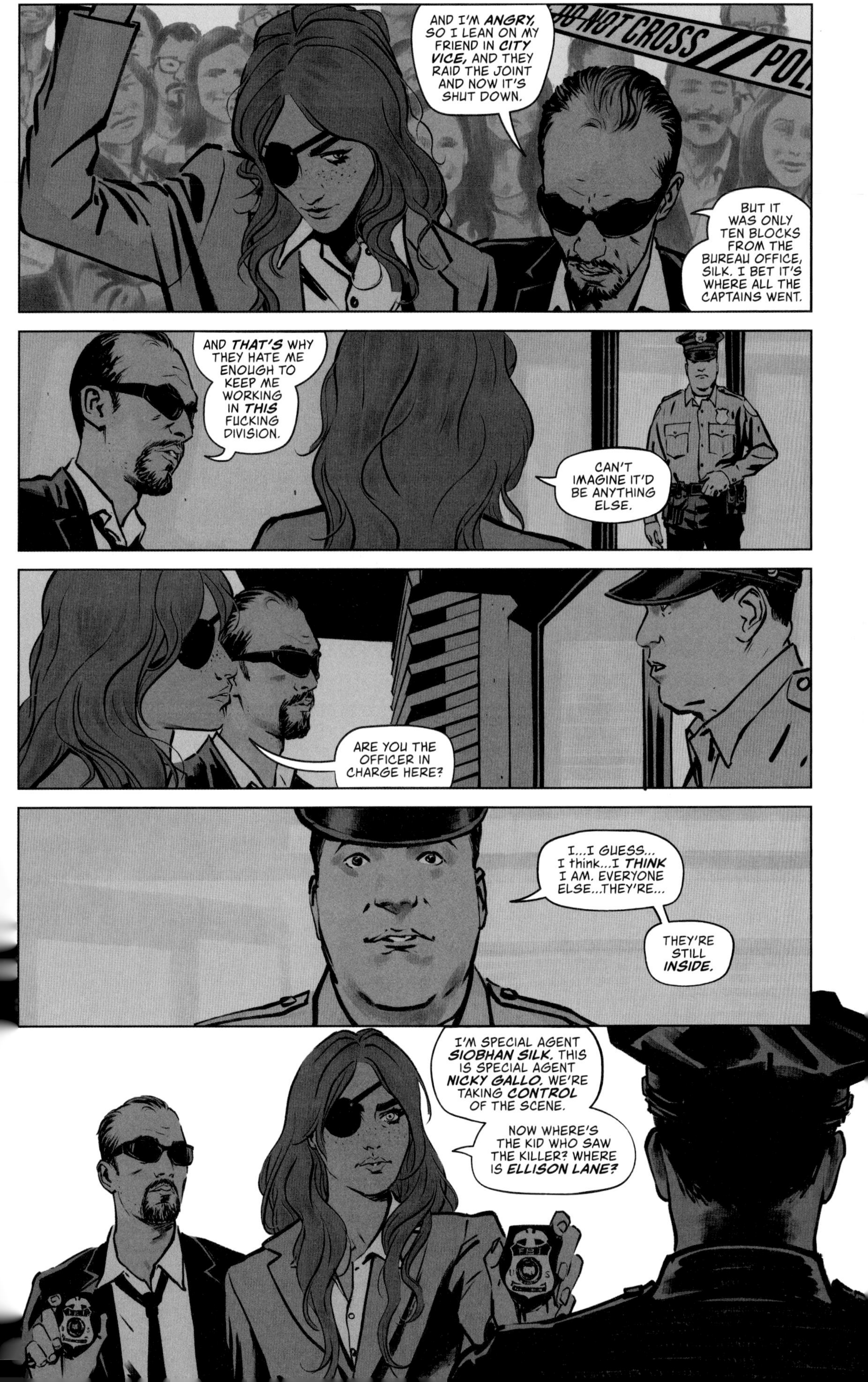
DO NOT CROSS
POL
AND I'M ANGRY, SO I LEAN ON MY FRIEND IN CITY VICE, AND THEY RAID THE JOINT AND NOW IT'S SHUT DOWN.
BUT IT WAS ONLY TEN BLOCKS FROM THE BUREAU OFFICE, SILK. I BET IT'S WHERE ALL THE CAPTAINS WENT.
AND THAT'S WHY THEY HATE ME ENOUGH TO KEEP ME WORKING IN THIS FUCKING DIVISION.
CAN'T IMAGINE IT'D BE ANYTHING ELSE.
ARE YOU THE OFFICER IN CHARGE HERE?
I...I GUESS... I think...I THINK I AM. EVERYONE ELSE...THEY'RE...
THEY'RE STILL INSIDE.
I'M SPECIAL AGENT SIOBHAN SILK. THIS IS SPECIAL AGENT NICKY GALLO. WE'RE TAKING CONTROL OF THE SCENE.
NOW WHERE'S THE KID WHO SAW THE KILLER? WHERE IS ELLISON LANE?

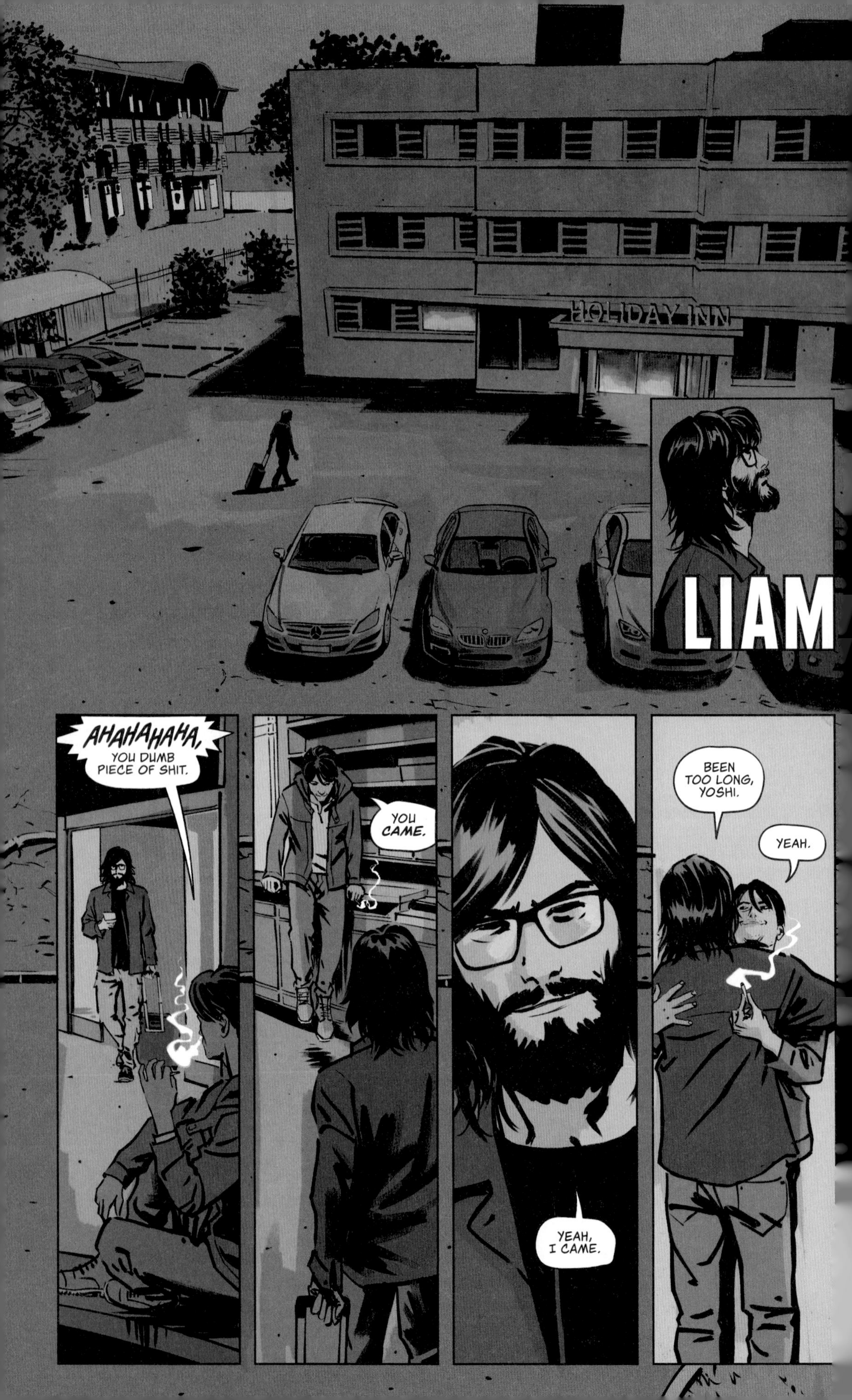
HOLIDAY INN
LIAM
AHAHAHAHA, YOU DUMB PIECE OF SHIT.
YOU CAME.
YEAH, I CAME.
BEEN TOO LONG, YOSHI.
YEAH.

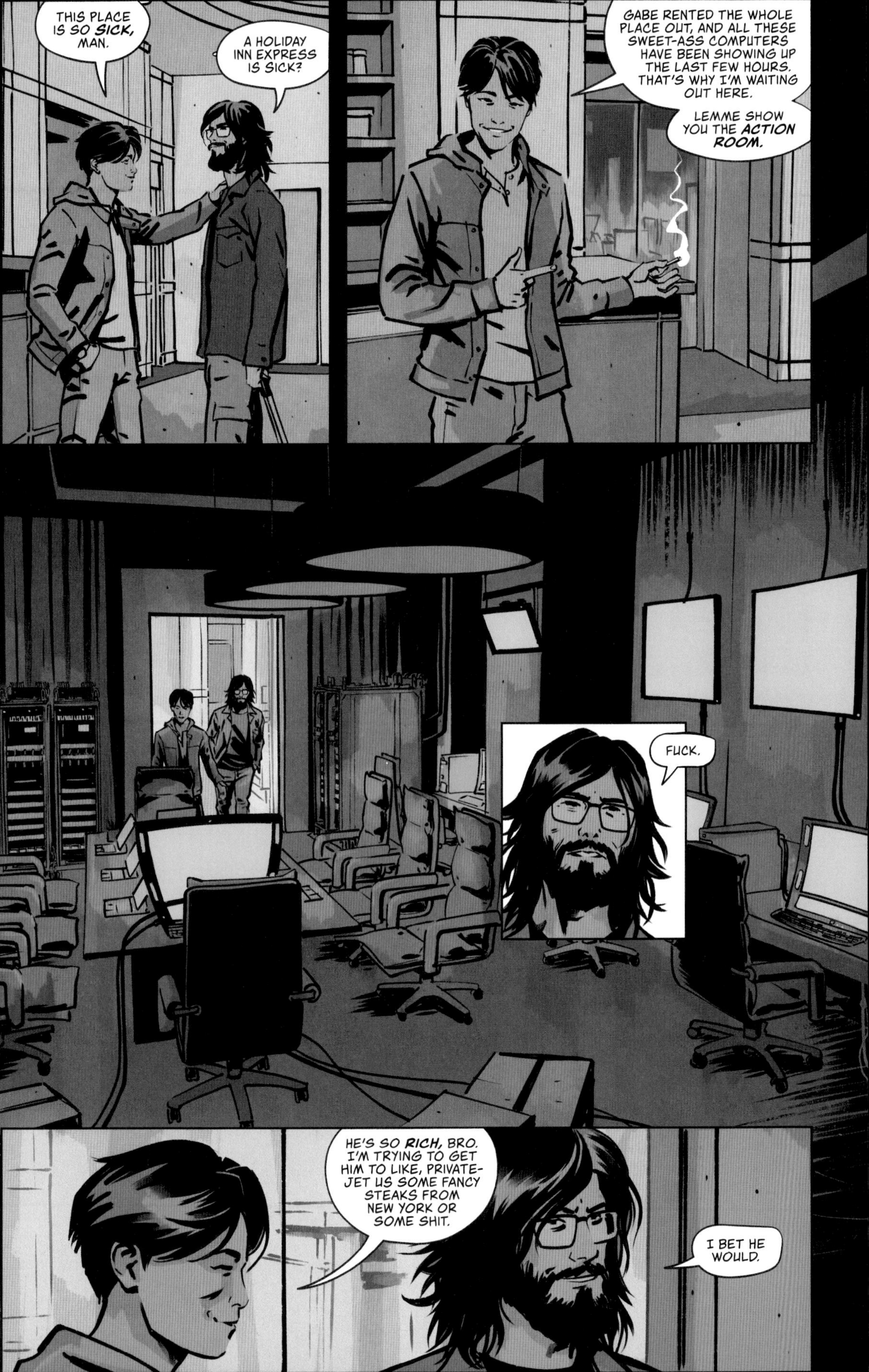
THIS PLACE IS SO SICK, MAN.
A HOLIDAY INN EXPRESS IS SICK?
GABE RENTED THE WHOLE PLACE OUT, AND ALL THESE SWEET-ASS COMPUTERS HAVE BEEN SHOWING UP THE LAST FEW HOURS. THAT'S WHY I'M WAITING OUT HERE.
LEMME SHOW YOU THE ACTION ROOM.
FUCK.
HE'S SO RICH, BRO. I'M TRYING TO GET HIM TO LIKE, PRIVATE-JET US SOME FANCY STEAKS FROM NEW YORK OR SOME SHIT.
I BET HE WOULD.

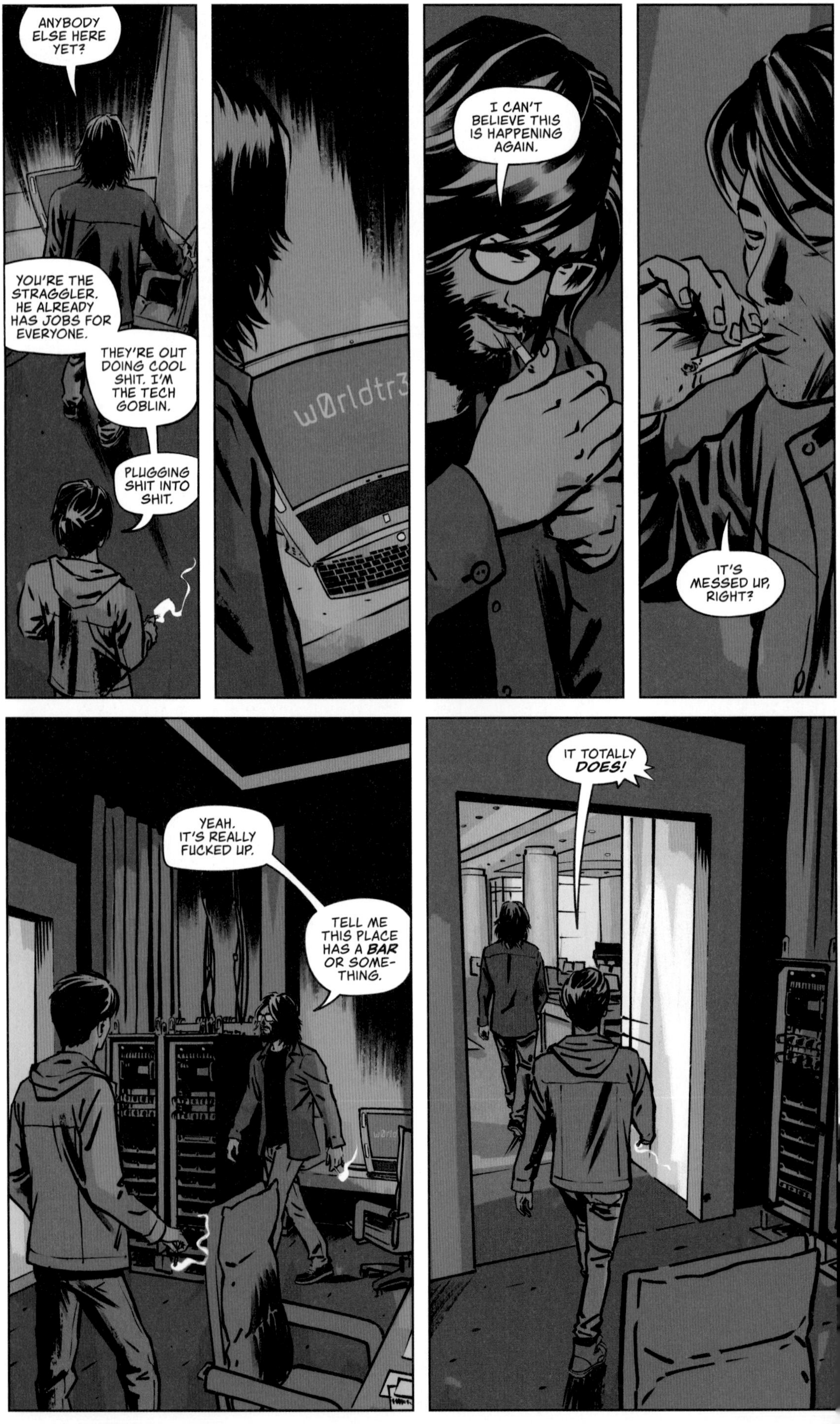
ANYBODY ELSE HERE YET?
YOU'RE THE STRAGGLER. HE ALREADY HAS JOBS FOR EVERYONE.
THEY'RE OUT DOING COOL SHIT. I'M THE TECH GOBLIN.
PLUGGING SHIT INTO SHIT.
w0rldtr3
I CAN'T BELIEVE THIS IS HAPPENING AGAIN.
IT'S MESSED UP, RIGHT?
YEAH. IT'S REALLY FUCKED UP.
TELL ME THIS PLACE HAS A **BAR** OR SOME-THING.
IT TOTALLY **DOES!**

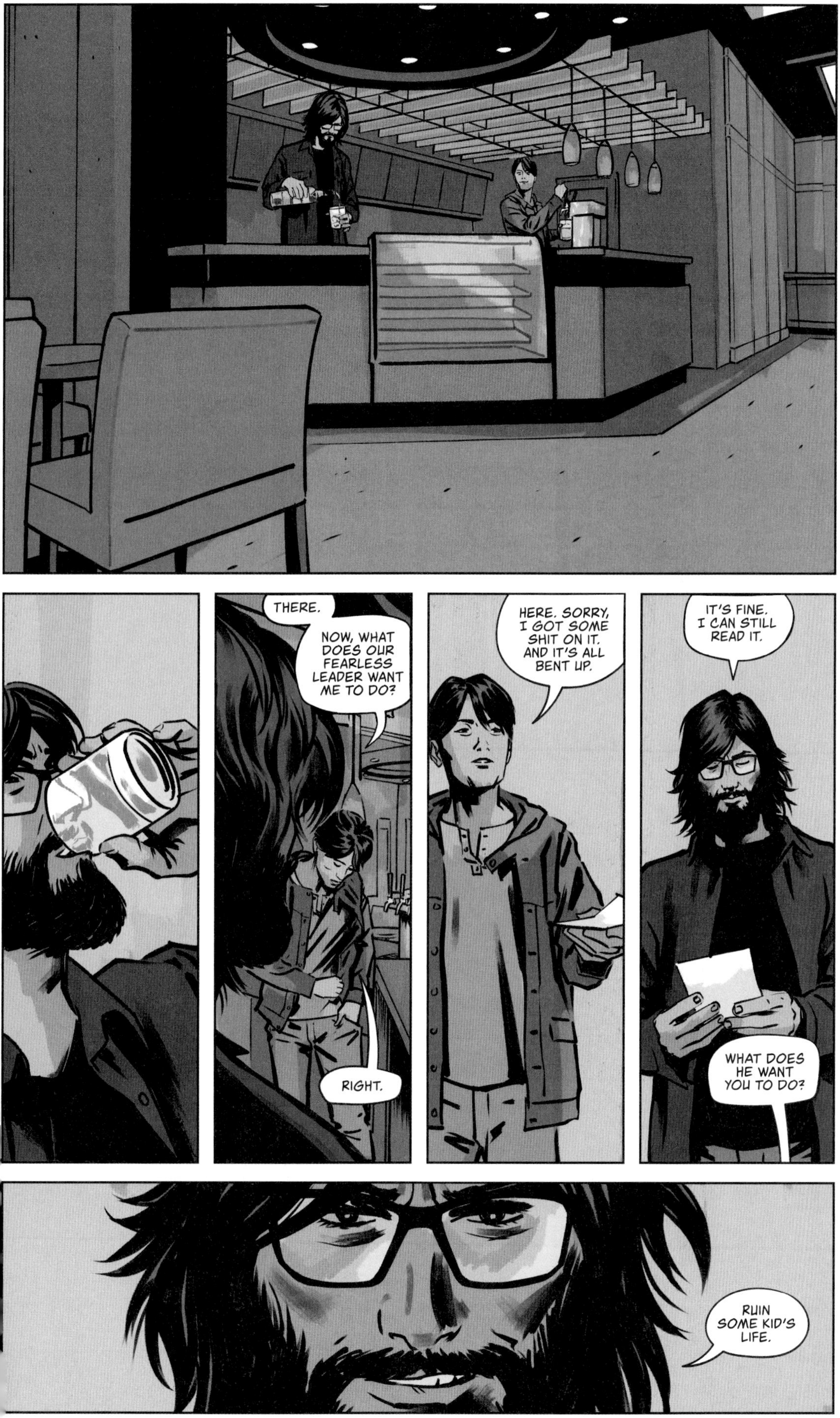
THERE.
NOW, WHAT DOES OUR FEARLESS LEADER WANT ME TO DO?
RIGHT.
HERE. SORRY, I GOT SOME SHIT ON IT. AND IT'S ALL BENT UP.
IT'S FINE. I CAN STILL READ IT.
WHAT DOES HE WANT YOU TO DO?
RUIN SOME KID'S LIFE.

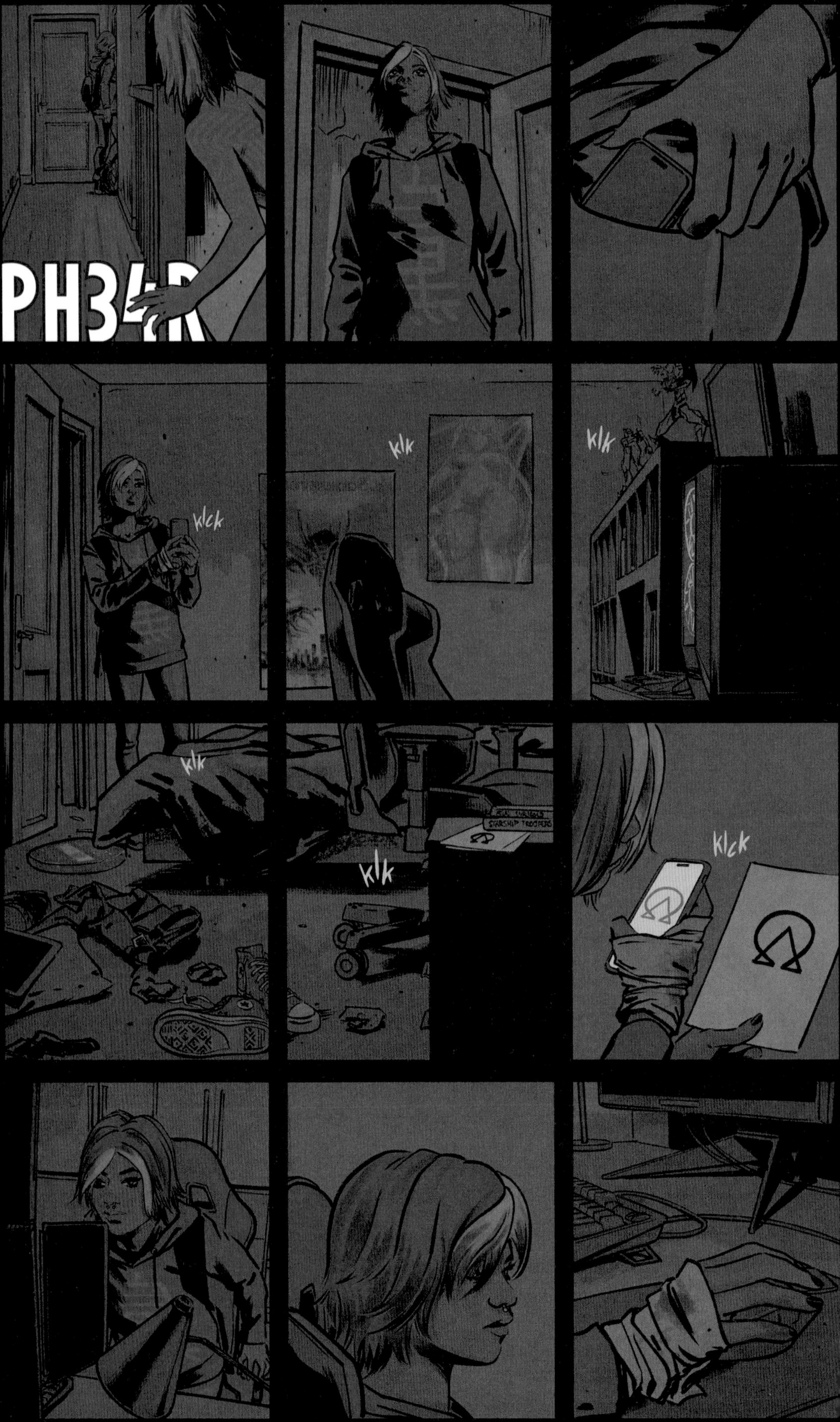
PH34R
klick
klk
klk
klk
STARSHIP TROOPERS
klk
klck

Connect
M1LL10N5
M1LL10N5
****
Connect
kdAk
Connecting
deeeeet-DOOTDEETDOOTOO
Connecting
ding-daah-
Connecting
Connection Established
Accessing Undernet
WHAT THE FUCK...
UNNGH...
SOMETHING... SOMETHING'S WRONG...
Oh...OH GOD...

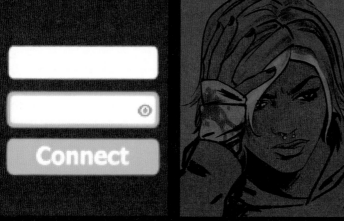

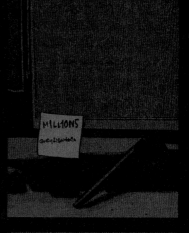

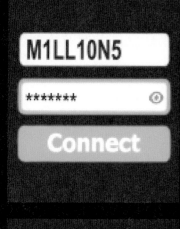

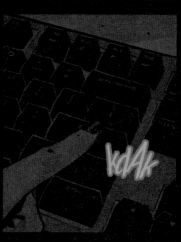

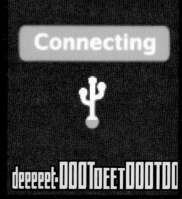

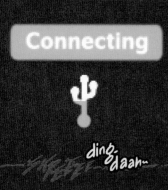

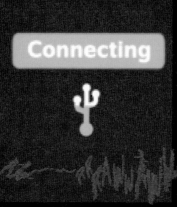

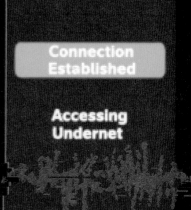

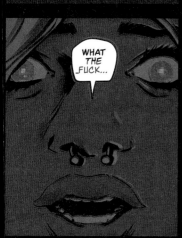

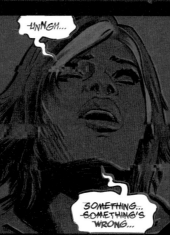

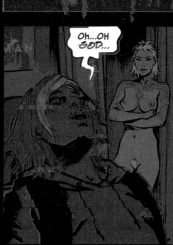

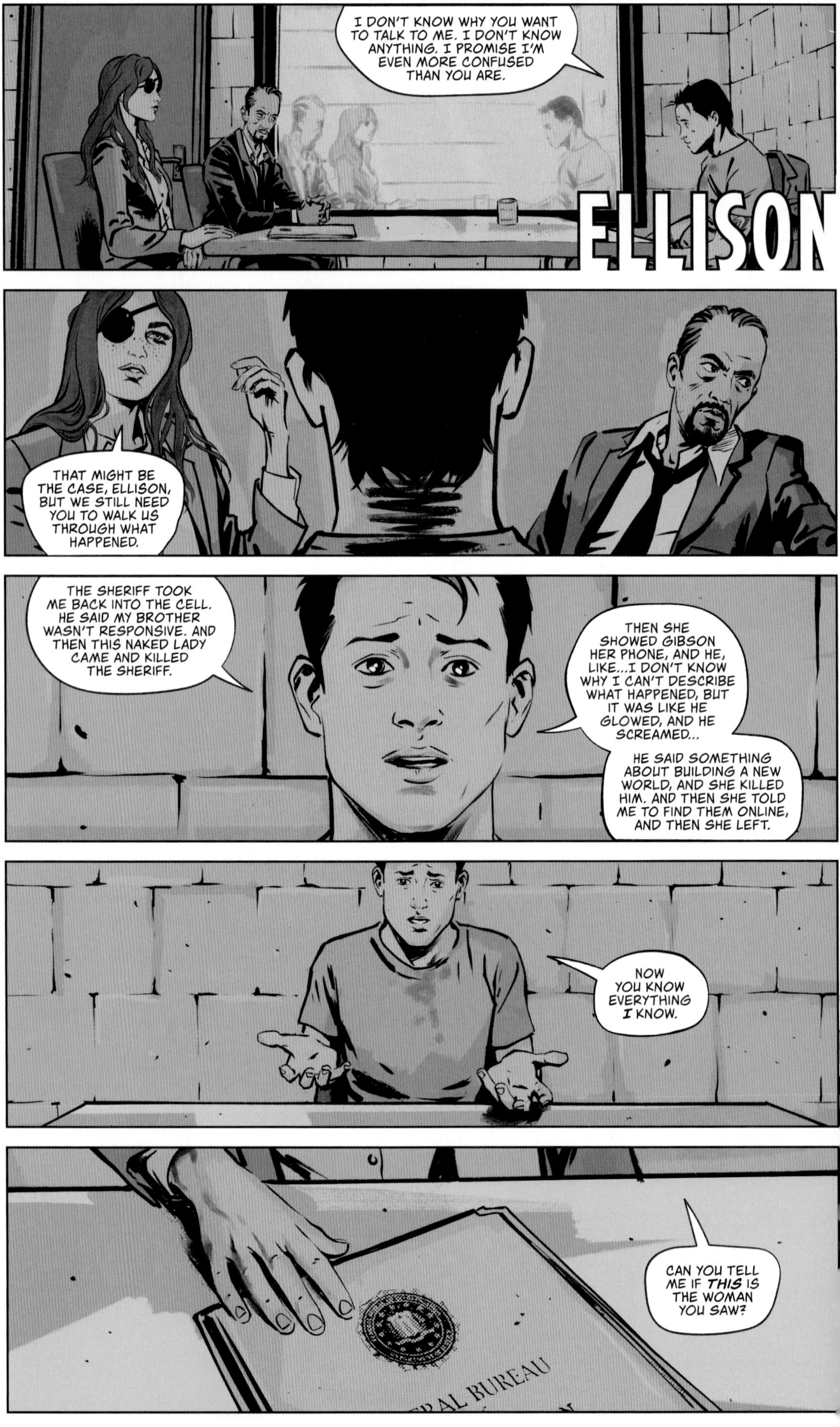
I DON'T KNOW WHY YOU WANT TO TALK TO ME. I DON'T KNOW ANYTHING. I PROMISE I'M EVEN MORE CONFUSED THAN YOU ARE.
ELLISON
THAT MIGHT BE THE CASE, ELLISON, BUT WE STILL NEED YOU TO WALK US THROUGH WHAT HAPPENED.
THE SHERIFF TOOK ME BACK INTO THE CELL. HE SAID MY BROTHER WASN'T RESPONSIVE. AND THEN THIS NAKED LADY CAME AND KILLED THE SHERIFF.
THEN SHE SHOWED GIBSON HER PHONE, AND HE, LIKE...I DON'T KNOW WHY I CAN'T DESCRIBE WHAT HAPPENED, BUT IT WAS LIKE HE GLOWED, AND HE SCREAMED...
HE SAID SOMETHING ABOUT BUILDING A NEW WORLD, AND SHE KILLED HIM. AND THEN SHE TOLD ME TO FIND THEM ONLINE, AND THEN SHE LEFT.
NOW YOU KNOW EVERYTHING *I* KNOW.
CAN YOU TELL ME IF *THIS* IS THE WOMAN YOU SAW?
RAL BUREAU

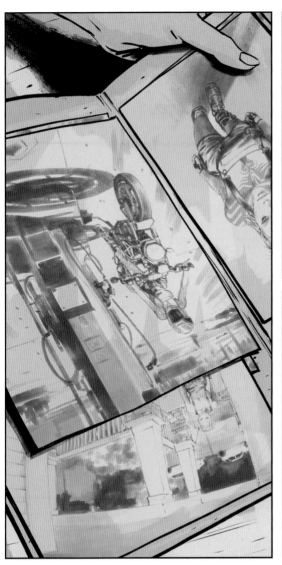

YES. THAT'S HER.

DO YOU KNOW WHO SHE IS?

OH, YEAH. SHE'S A FRIEND OF OURS. WE'RE BIG INTO *NAKED MURDER LADIES* AT THE FBI.

NICKY. *QUIET.*

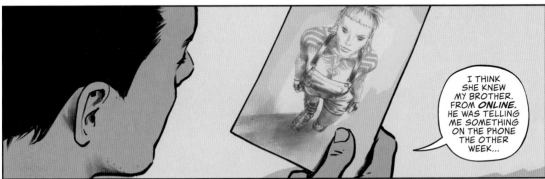

I THINK SHE KNEW MY BROTHER, FROM *ONLINE.* HE WAS TELLING ME SOMETHING ON THE PHONE THE OTHER WEEK...

STOP TALKING.

THE FUCK ARE *YOU?*

WE'RE IN THE *MIDDLE* OF SOMETHING HERE...

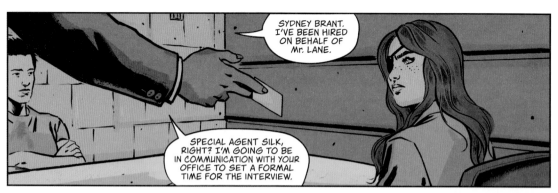

SYDNEY BRANT, I'VE BEEN HIRED ON BEHALF OF MR. LANE.

SPECIAL AGENT SILK, RIGHT? I'M GOING TO BE IN COMMUNICATION WITH YOUR OFFICE TO SET A FORMAL TIME FOR THE INTERVIEW.

Oh, YOU GOT TO BE FUCKING *KIDDING* ME.

I DIDN'T *HIRE* A LAWYER.

I'VE BEEN HIRED ON YOUR BEHALF. YOU CAN FIRE ME, BUT I SUGGEST YOU DO THAT LATER ONCE WE'VE ASSESSED YOUR SITUATION.

I'M VERY EXPENSIVE, AND I'VE ALREADY BEEN PAID.

Okay?

THIS IS AN ACTIVE SITUATION. A COP-KILLER IS ON THE LOOSE. THIS IS THE ONLY PERSON WHO SAW HER AND LIVED. WE NEED TO KNOW WHAT HE KNOWS.

HE WON'T LEAVE THE COUNTY UNTIL YOU'VE HAD YOUR INTERVIEW. I'LL BE IN TOUCH IN THE NEXT TWENTY-FOUR HOURS.

FINE.

I CAN GO?

YES, YOU CAN GO.

OKAY.

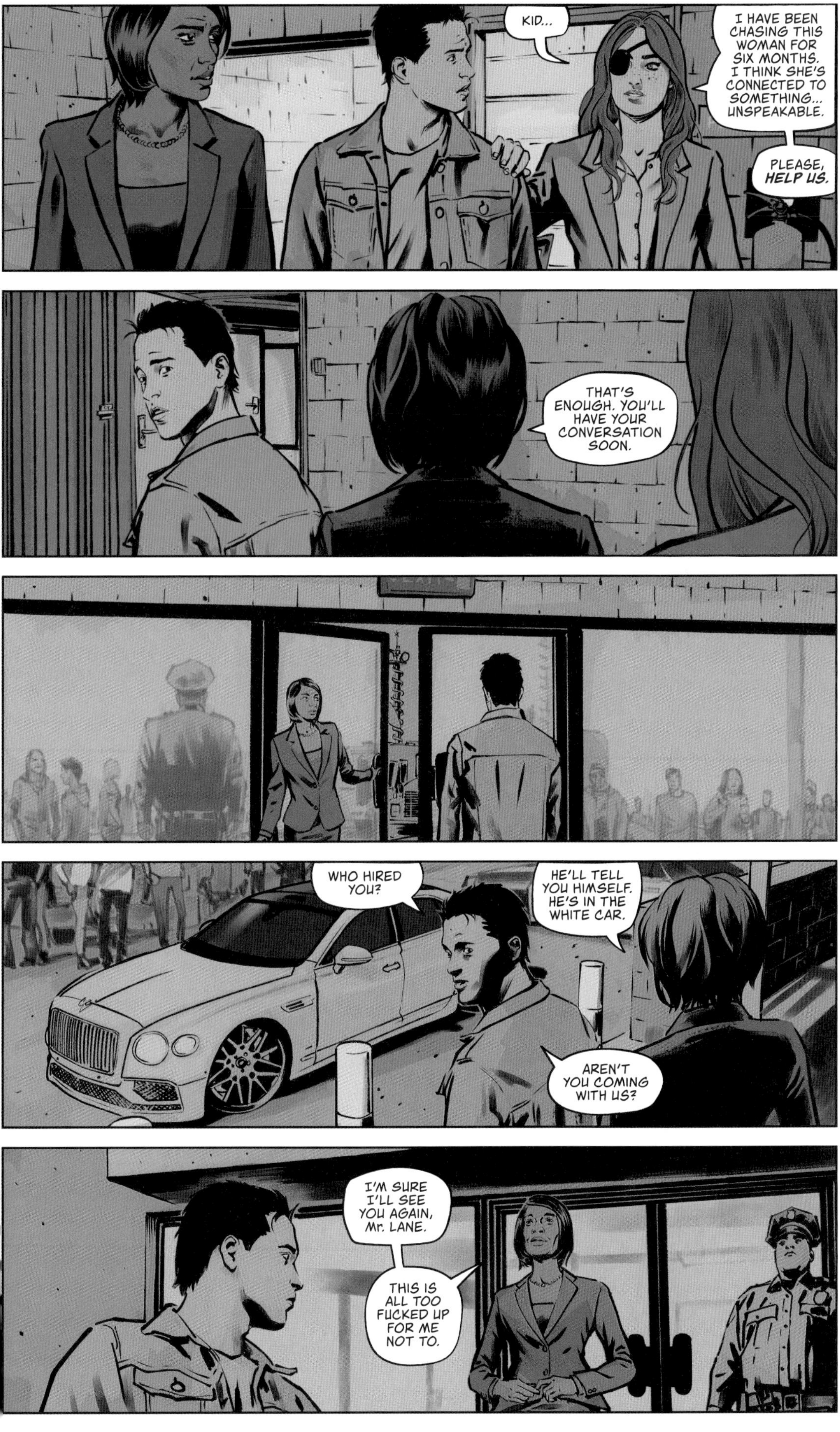
KID...
I HAVE BEEN CHASING THIS WOMAN FOR SIX MONTHS. I THINK SHE'S CONNECTED TO SOMETHING... UNSPEAKABLE.
PLEASE, HELP US.
THAT'S ENOUGH. YOU'LL HAVE YOUR CONVERSATION SOON.
WHO HIRED YOU?
HE'LL TELL YOU HIMSELF. HE'S IN THE WHITE CAR.
AREN'T YOU COMING WITH US?
I'M SURE I'LL SEE YOU AGAIN, Mr. LANE.
THIS IS ALL TOO FUCKED UP FOR ME NOT TO.

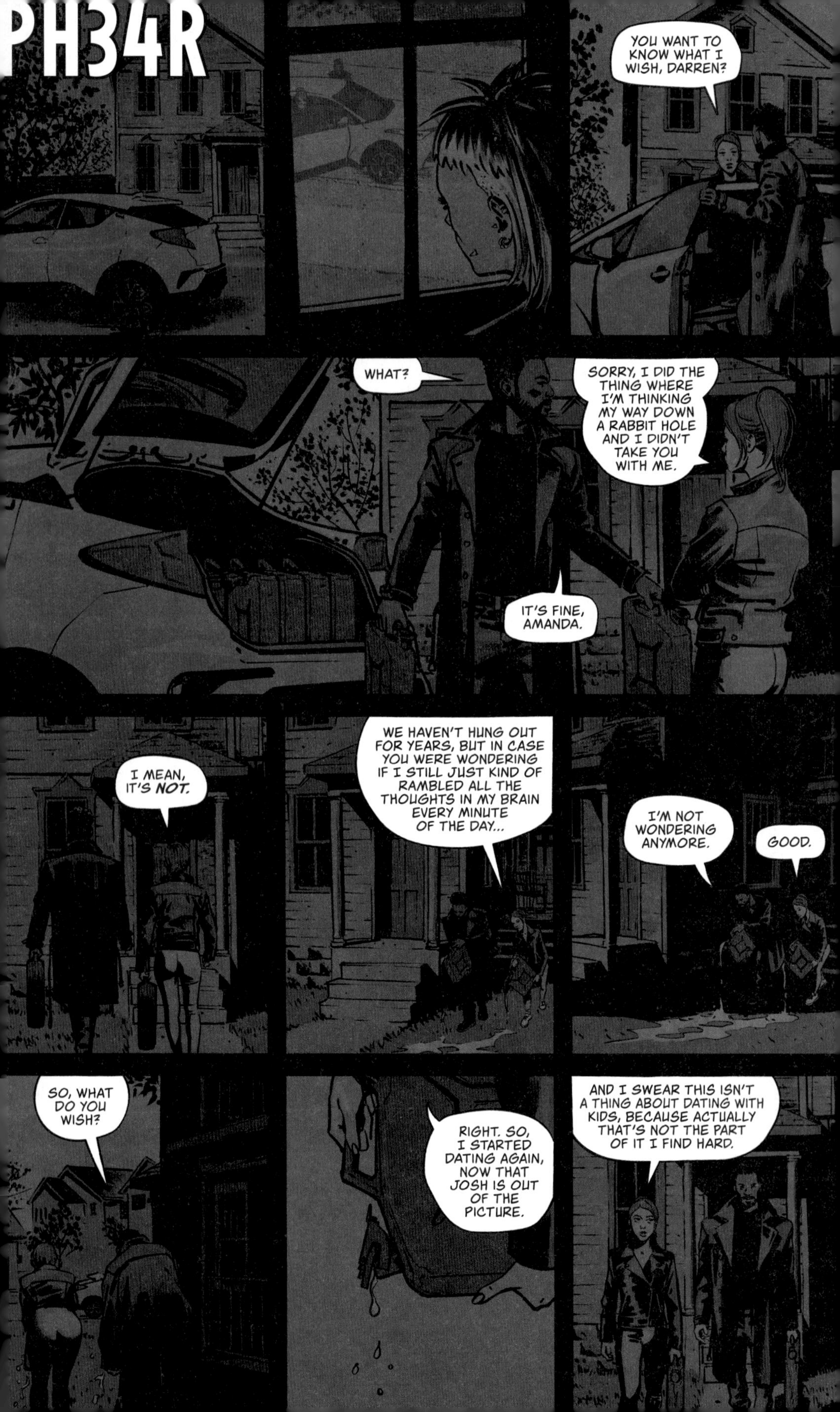
YOU WANT TO KNOW WHAT I WISH, DARREN?
WHAT?
SORRY, I DID THE THING WHERE I'M THINKING MY WAY DOWN A RABBIT HOLE AND I DIDN'T TAKE YOU WITH ME.
IT'S FINE, AMANDA.
I MEAN, IT'S *NOT.*
WE HAVEN'T HUNG OUT FOR YEARS, BUT IN CASE YOU WERE WONDERING IF I STILL JUST KIND OF RAMBLED ALL THE THOUGHTS IN MY BRAIN EVERY MINUTE OF THE DAY...
I'M NOT WONDERING ANYMORE.
GOOD.
SO, WHAT DO YOU WISH?
RIGHT. SO, I STARTED DATING AGAIN, NOW THAT JOSH IS OUT OF THE PICTURE.
AND I SWEAR THIS ISN'T A THING ABOUT DATING WITH KIDS, BECAUSE ACTUALLY THAT'S NOT THE PART OF IT I FIND HARD.

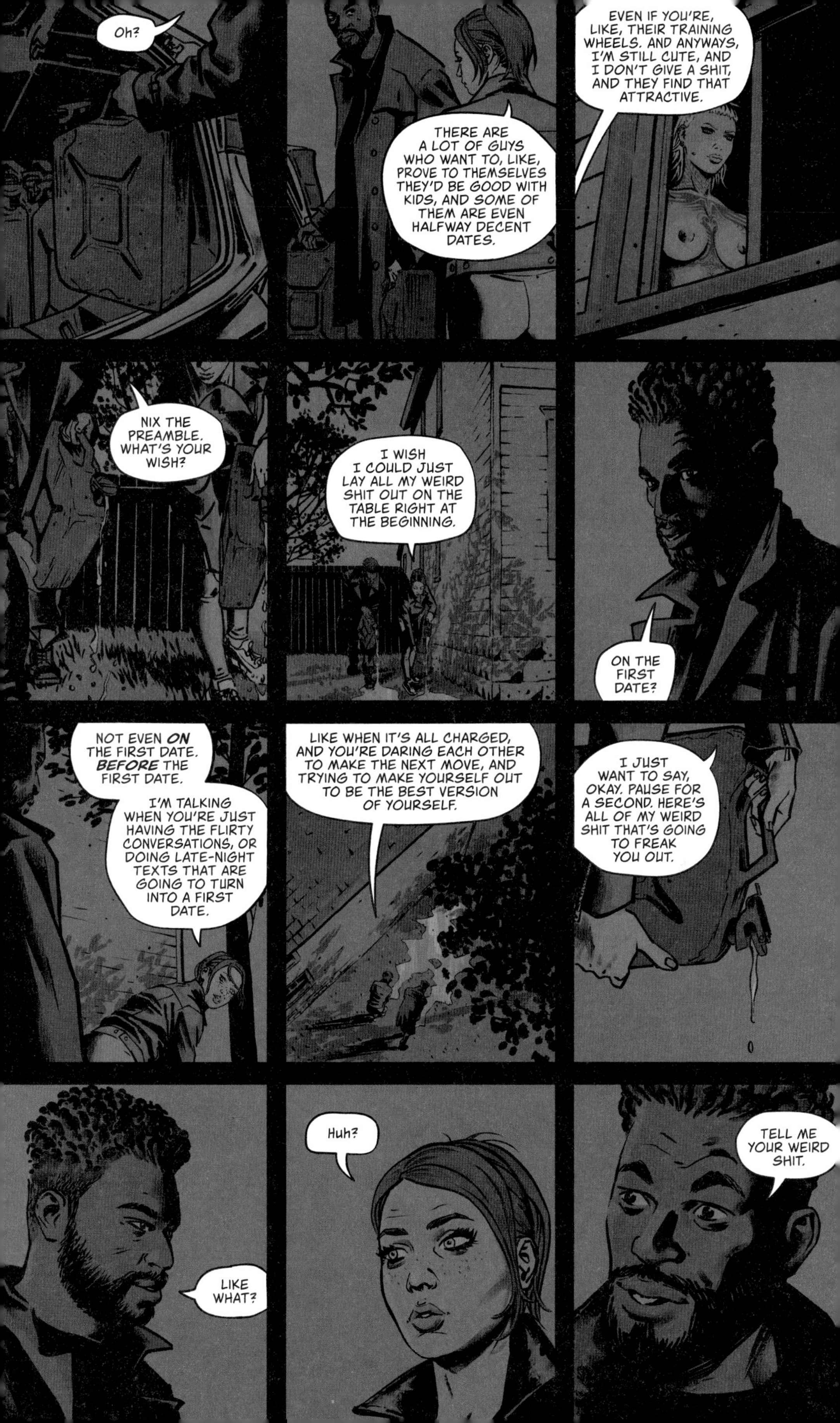
Oh?
THERE ARE A LOT OF GUYS WHO WANT TO, LIKE, PROVE TO THEMSELVES THEY'D BE GOOD WITH KIDS, AND SOME OF THEM ARE EVEN HALFWAY DECENT DATES.
EVEN IF YOU'RE, LIKE, THEIR TRAINING WHEELS. AND ANYWAYS, I'M STILL CUTE, AND I DON'T GIVE A SHIT, AND THEY FIND THAT ATTRACTIVE.
NIX THE PREAMBLE. WHAT'S YOUR WISH?
I WISH I COULD JUST LAY ALL MY WEIRD SHIT OUT ON THE TABLE RIGHT AT THE BEGINNING.
ON THE FIRST DATE?
NOT EVEN ON THE FIRST DATE. BEFORE THE FIRST DATE.
I'M TALKING WHEN YOU'RE JUST HAVING THE FLIRTY CONVERSATIONS, OR DOING LATE-NIGHT TEXTS THAT ARE GOING TO TURN INTO A FIRST DATE.
LIKE WHEN IT'S ALL CHARGED, AND YOU'RE DARING EACH OTHER TO MAKE THE NEXT MOVE, AND TRYING TO MAKE YOURSELF OUT TO BE THE BEST VERSION OF YOURSELF.
I JUST WANT TO SAY, OKAY. PAUSE FOR A SECOND. HERE'S ALL OF MY WEIRD SHIT THAT'S GOING TO FREAK YOU OUT.
LIKE WHAT?
Huh?
TELL ME YOUR WEIRD SHIT.

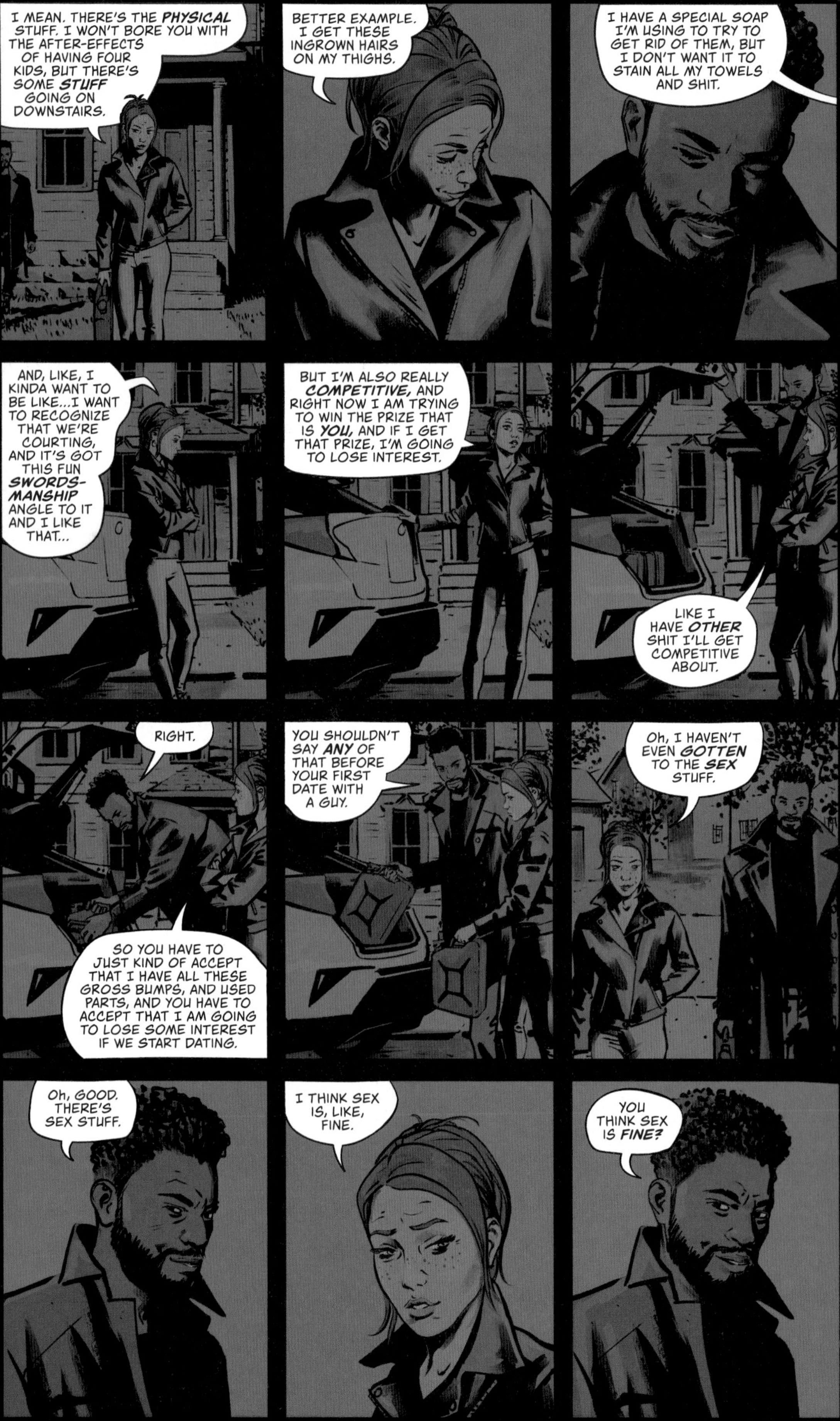
I MEAN. THERE'S THE PHYSICAL STUFF. I WON'T BORE YOU WITH THE AFTER-EFFECTS OF HAVING FOUR KIDS, BUT THERE'S SOME STUFF GOING ON DOWNSTAIRS.
BETTER EXAMPLE. I GET THESE INGROWN HAIRS ON MY THIGHS.
I HAVE A SPECIAL SOAP I'M USING TO TRY TO GET RID OF THEM, BUT I DON'T WANT IT TO STAIN ALL MY TOWELS AND SHIT.
AND, LIKE, I KINDA WANT TO BE LIKE...I WANT TO RECOGNIZE THAT WE'RE COURTING, AND IT'S GOT THIS FUN SWORDS-MANSHIP ANGLE TO IT AND I LIKE THAT...
BUT I'M ALSO REALLY COMPETITIVE, AND RIGHT NOW I AM TRYING TO WIN THE PRIZE THAT IS YOU, AND IF I GET THAT PRIZE, I'M GOING TO LOSE INTEREST.
LIKE I HAVE OTHER SHIT I'LL GET COMPETITIVE ABOUT.
RIGHT.
SO YOU HAVE TO JUST KIND OF ACCEPT THAT I HAVE ALL THESE GROSS BUMPS, AND USED PARTS, AND YOU HAVE TO ACCEPT THAT I AM GOING TO LOSE SOME INTEREST IF WE START DATING.
YOU SHOULDN'T SAY ANY OF THAT BEFORE YOUR FIRST DATE WITH A GUY.
Oh, I HAVEN'T EVEN GOTTEN TO THE SEX STUFF.
Oh, GOOD. THERE'S SEX STUFF.
I THINK SEX IS, LIKE, FINE.
YOU THINK SEX IS FINE?

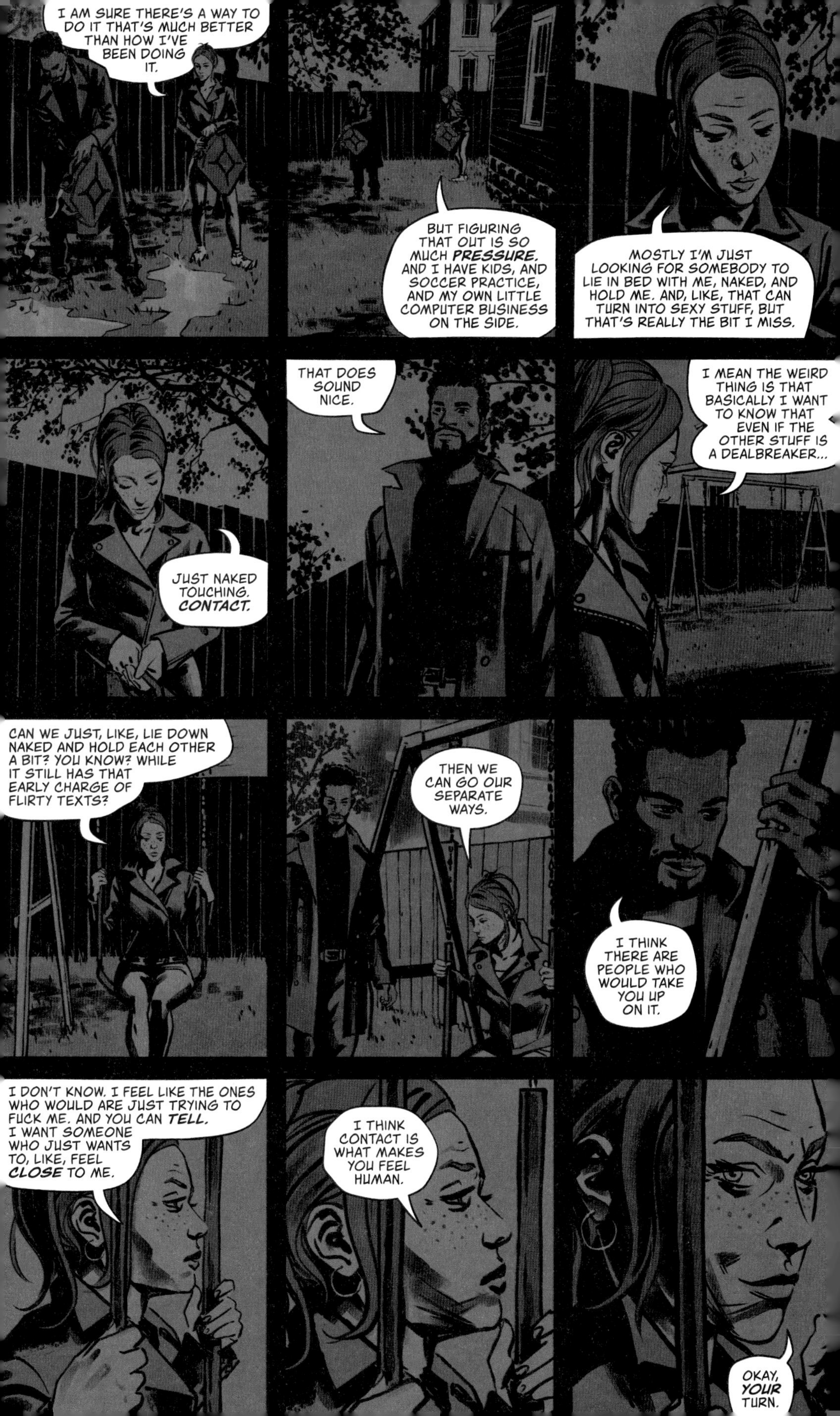
I AM SURE THERE'S A WAY TO DO IT THAT'S MUCH BETTER THAN HOW I'VE BEEN DOING IT.
BUT FIGURING THAT OUT IS SO MUCH **PRESSURE.** AND I HAVE KIDS, AND SOCCER PRACTICE, AND MY OWN LITTLE COMPUTER BUSINESS ON THE SIDE.
MOSTLY I'M JUST LOOKING FOR SOMEBODY TO LIE IN BED WITH ME, NAKED, AND HOLD ME. AND, LIKE, THAT CAN TURN INTO SEXY STUFF, BUT THAT'S REALLY THE BIT I MISS.
JUST NAKED TOUCHING. ***CONTACT.***
THAT DOES SOUND NICE.
I MEAN THE WEIRD THING IS THAT BASICALLY I WANT TO KNOW THAT EVEN IF THE OTHER STUFF IS A DEALBREAKER...
CAN WE JUST, LIKE, LIE DOWN NAKED AND HOLD EACH OTHER A BIT? YOU KNOW? WHILE IT STILL HAS THAT EARLY CHARGE OF FLIRTY TEXTS?
THEN WE CAN GO OUR SEPARATE WAYS.
I THINK THERE ARE PEOPLE WHO WOULD TAKE YOU UP ON IT.
I DON'T KNOW. I FEEL LIKE THE ONES WHO WOULD ARE JUST TRYING TO FUCK ME. AND YOU CAN ***TELL.*** I WANT SOMEONE WHO JUST WANTS TO, LIKE, FEEL ***CLOSE*** TO ME.
I THINK CONTACT IS WHAT MAKES YOU FEEL HUMAN.
OKAY, ***YOUR*** TURN.

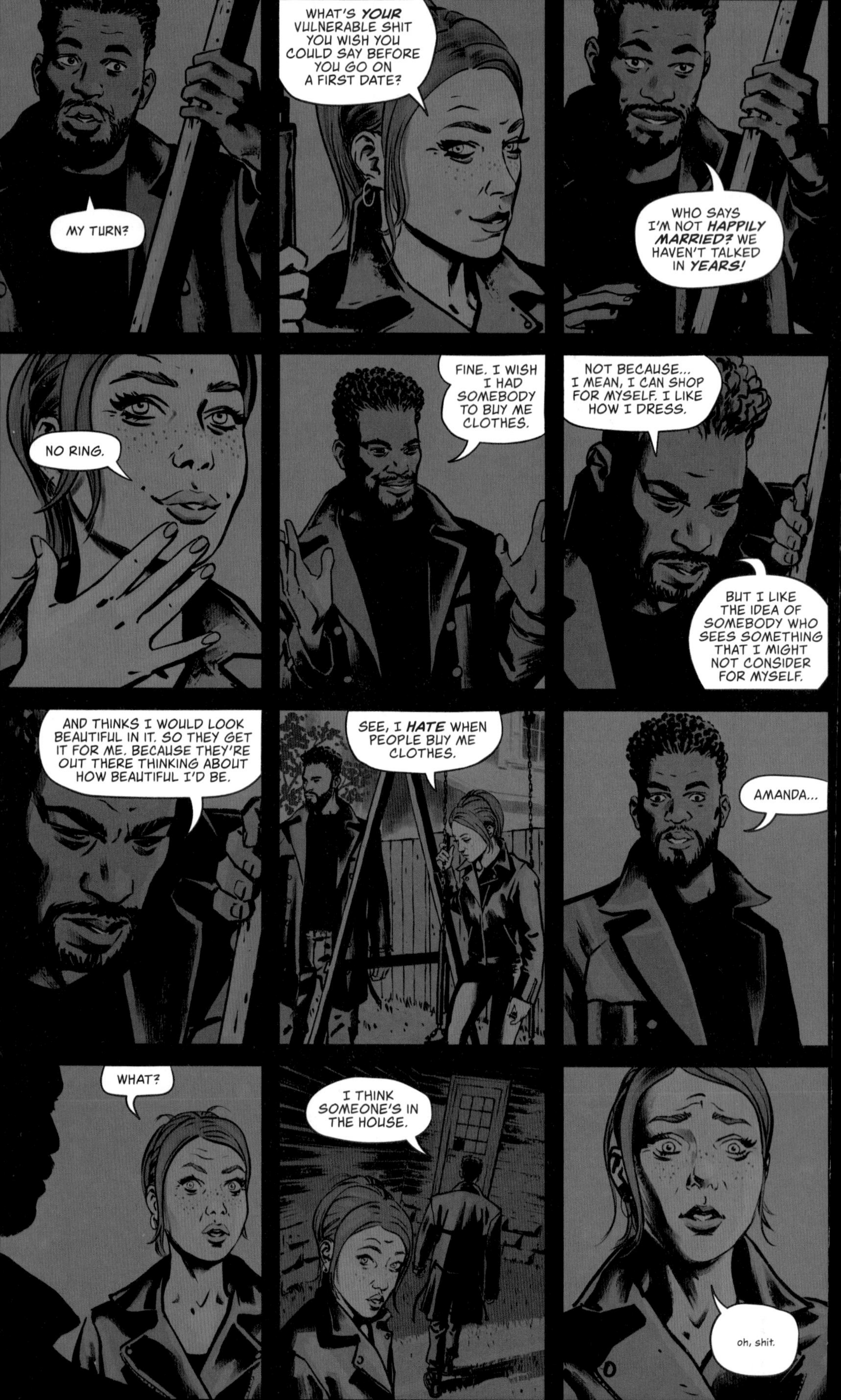
MY TURN?
WHAT'S YOUR VULNERABLE SHIT YOU WISH YOU COULD SAY BEFORE YOU GO ON A FIRST DATE?
WHO SAYS I'M NOT HAPPILY MARRIED? WE HAVEN'T TALKED IN YEARS!
NO RING.
FINE. I WISH I HAD SOMEBODY TO BUY ME CLOTHES.
NOT BECAUSE... I MEAN, I CAN SHOP FOR MYSELF. I LIKE HOW I DRESS.
BUT I LIKE THE IDEA OF SOMEBODY WHO SEES SOMETHING THAT I MIGHT NOT CONSIDER FOR MYSELF.
AND THINKS I WOULD LOOK BEAUTIFUL IN IT. SO THEY GET IT FOR ME. BECAUSE THEY'RE OUT THERE THINKING ABOUT HOW BEAUTIFUL I'D BE.
SEE, I HATE WHEN PEOPLE BUY ME CLOTHES.
AMANDA...
WHAT?
I THINK SOMEONE'S IN THE HOUSE.
oh, shit.

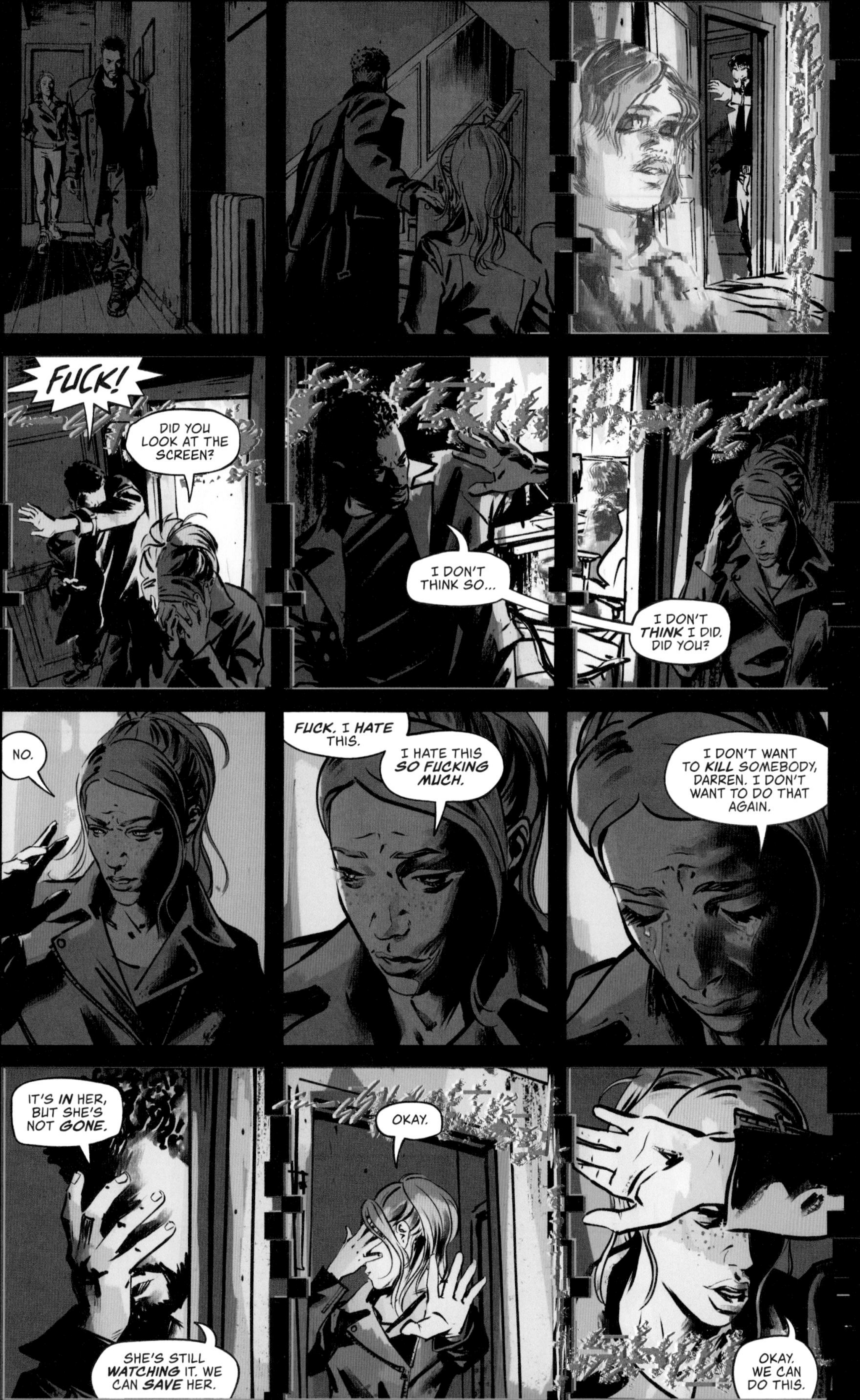

FUCK!
DID YOU LOOK AT THE SCREEN?
I DON'T THINK SO...
I DON'T THINK I DID. DID YOU?
NO.
FUCK. I HATE THIS.
I HATE THIS SO FUCKING MUCH.
I DON'T WANT TO KILL SOMEBODY, DARREN. I DON'T WANT TO DO THAT AGAIN.
IT'S IN HER, BUT SHE'S NOT GONE.
SHE'S STILL WATCHING IT. WE CAN SAVE HER.
OKAY.
OKAY. WE CAN DO THIS.

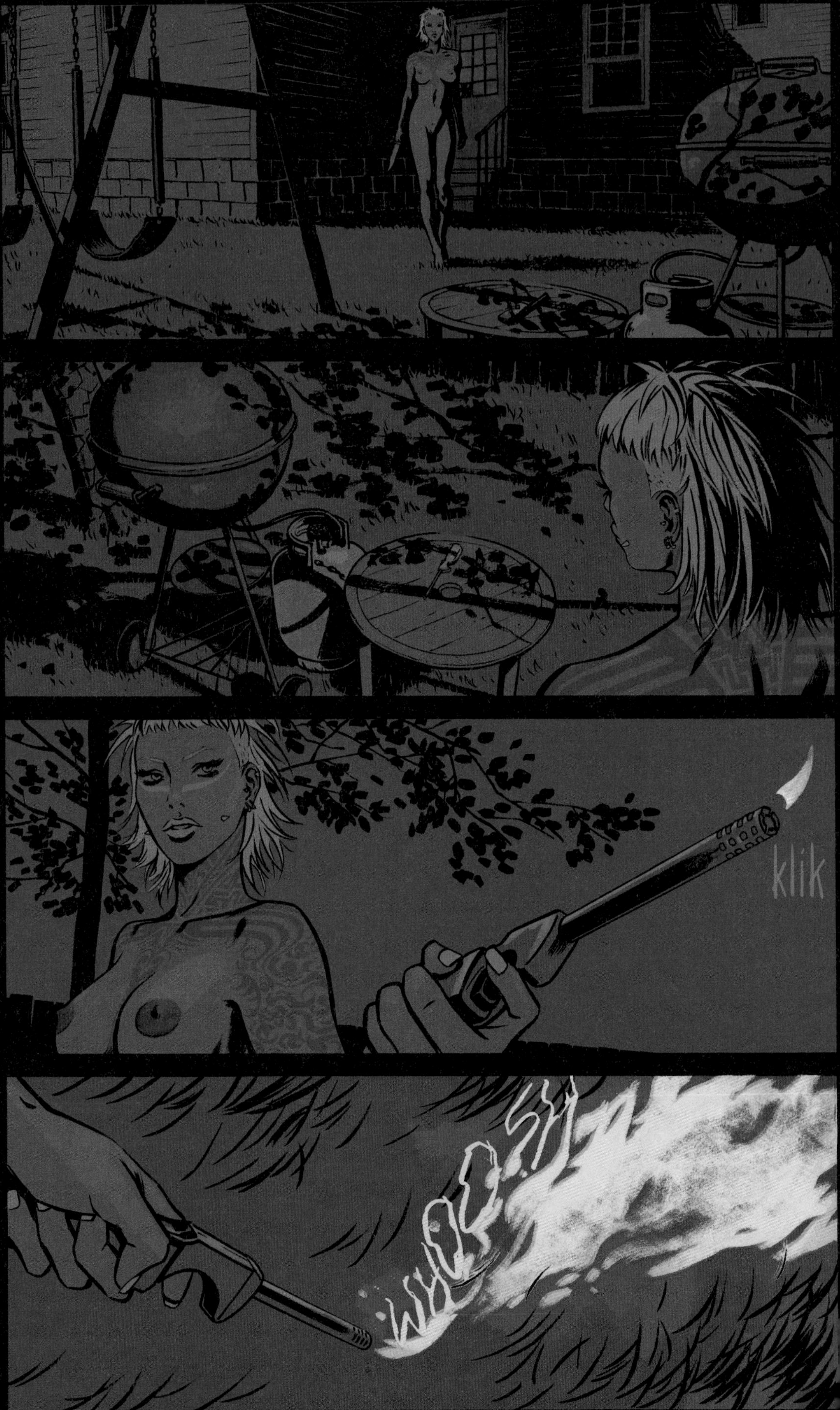
klik
WHOOSH

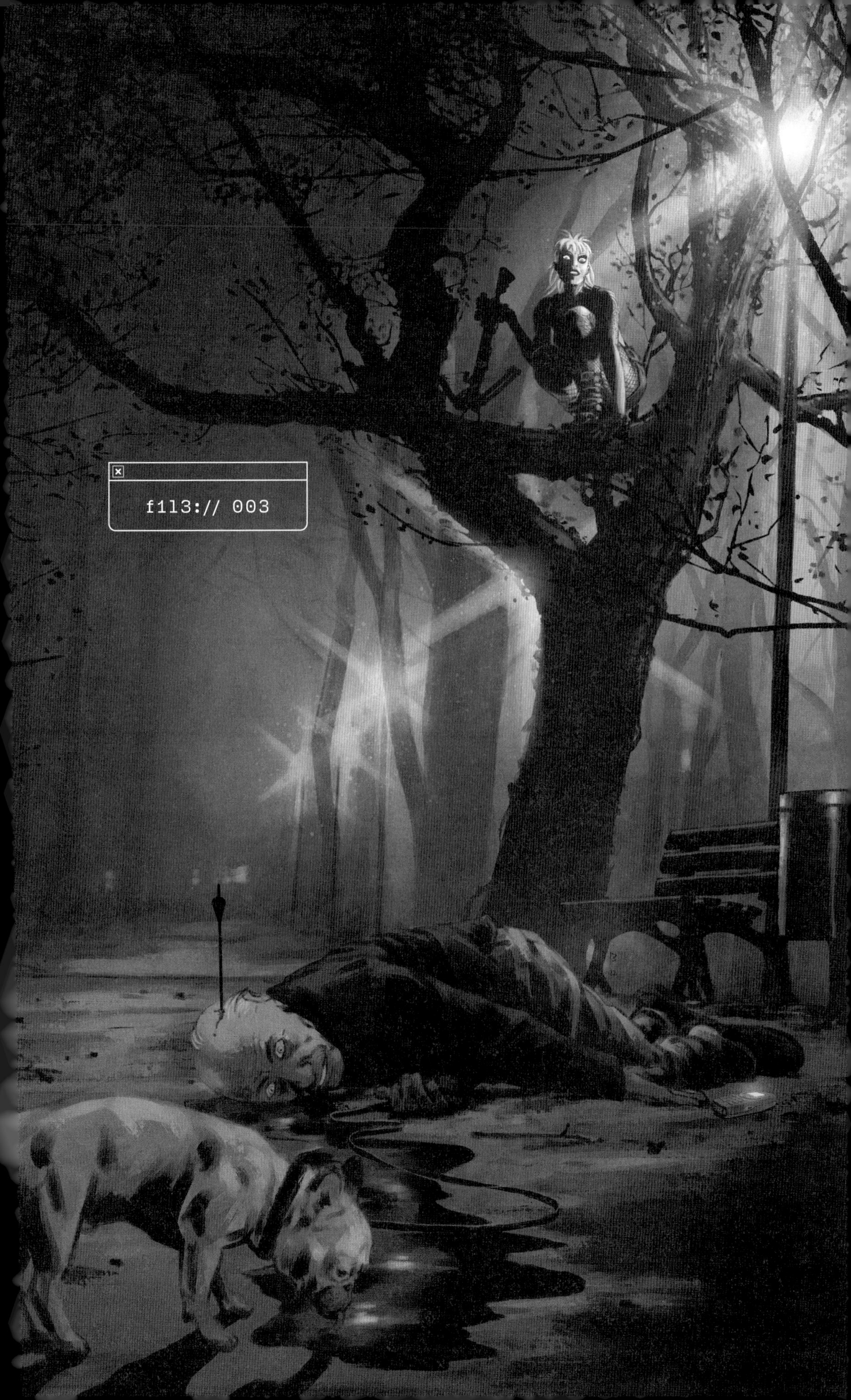
f113:// 003

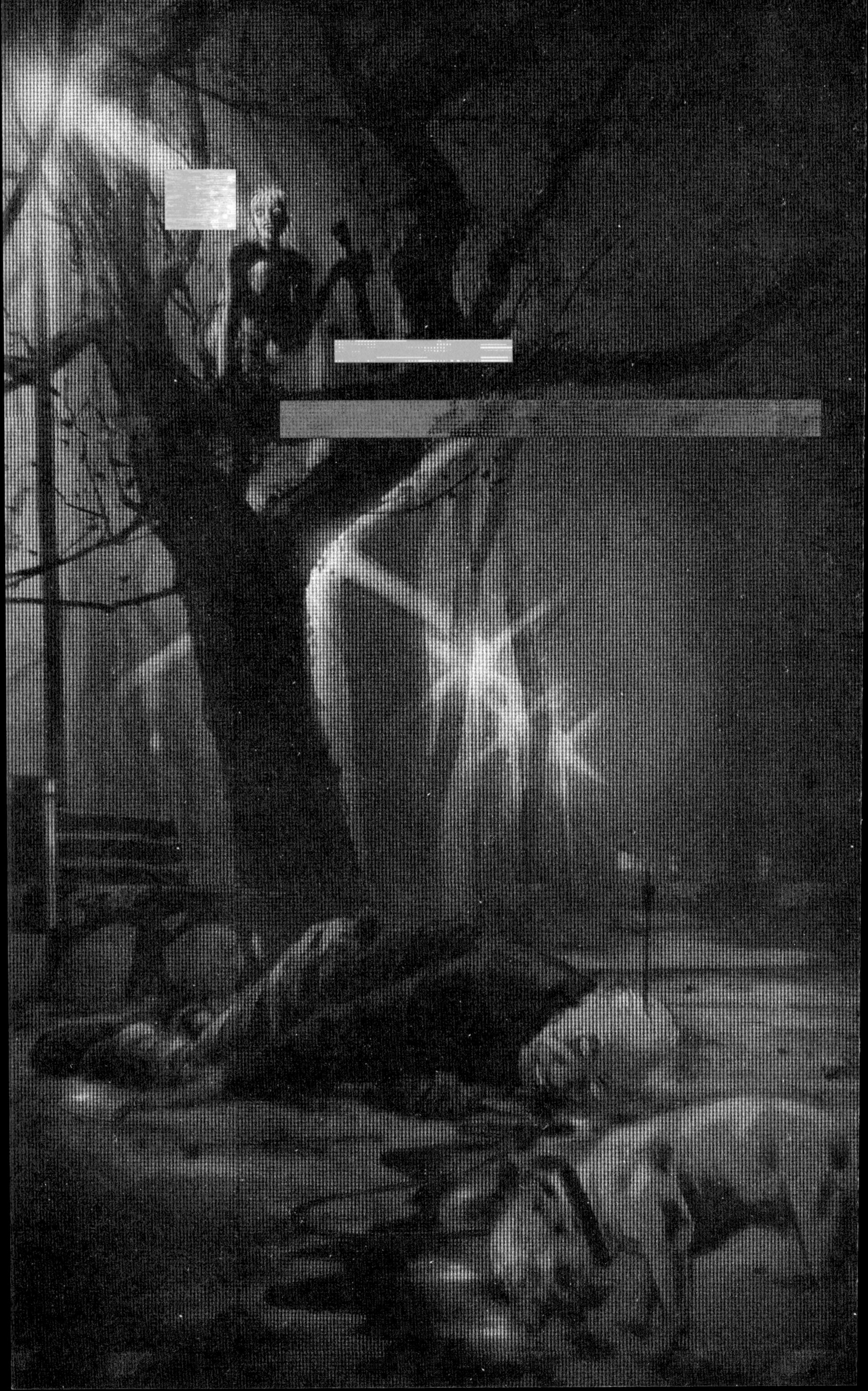

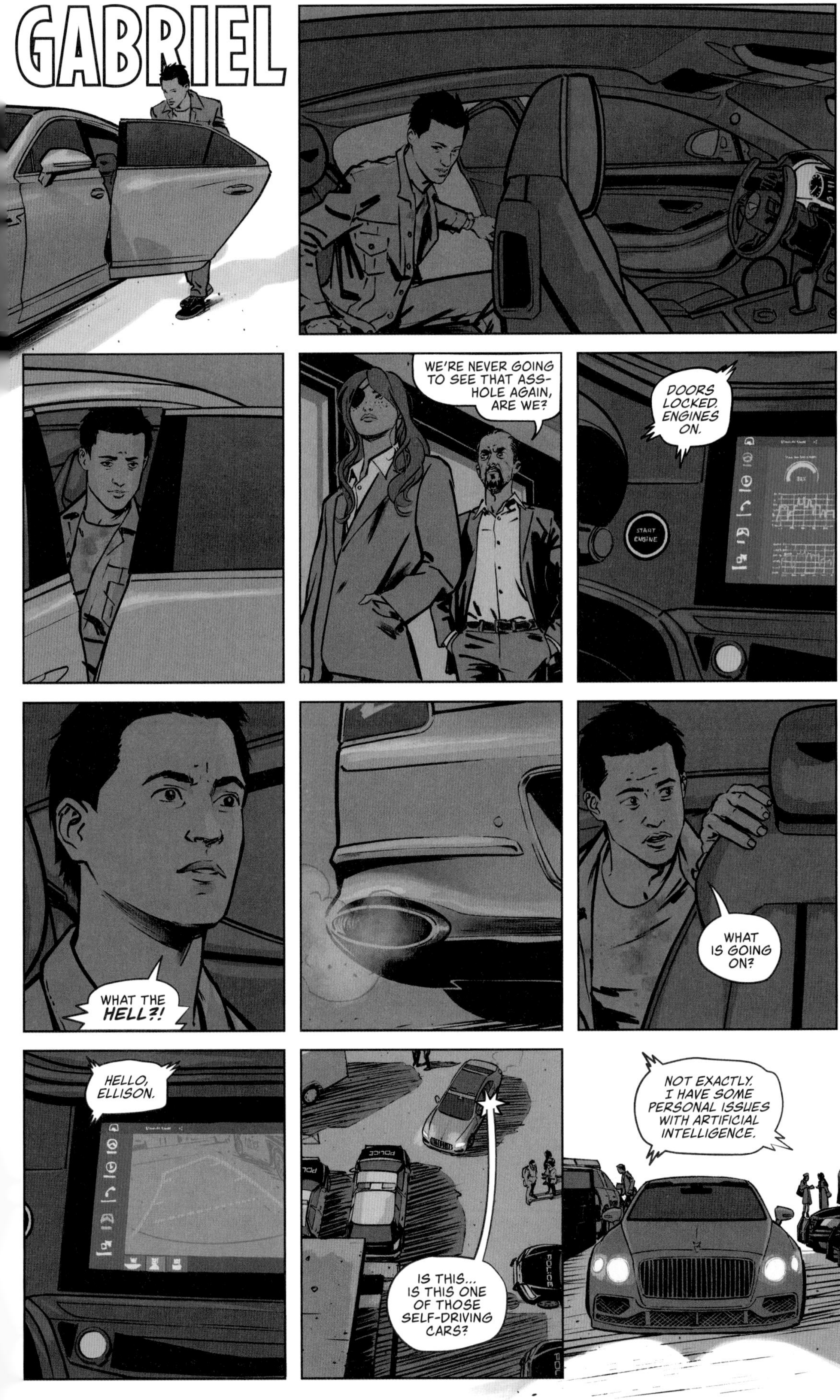
GABRIEL
WE'RE NEVER GOING TO SEE THAT ASS-HOLE AGAIN, ARE WE?
DOORS LOCKED. ENGINES ON.
START ENGINE
WHAT THE HELL?!
WHAT IS GOING ON?
HELLO, ELLISON.
IS THIS... IS THIS ONE OF THOSE SELF-DRIVING CARS?
NOT EXACTLY. I HAVE SOME PERSONAL ISSUES WITH ARTIFICIAL INTELLIGENCE.
POLICE

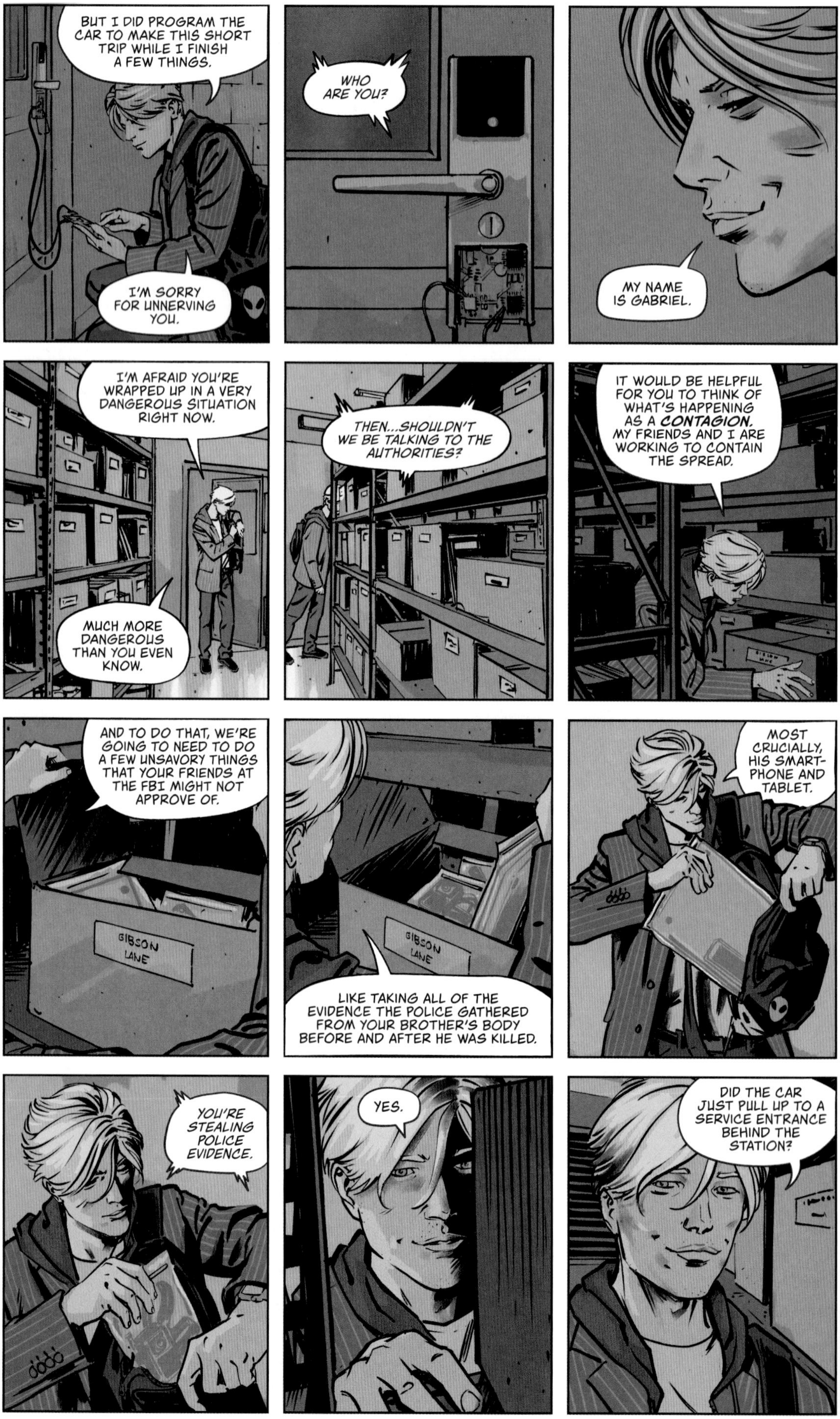
BUT I DID PROGRAM THE CAR TO MAKE THIS SHORT TRIP WHILE I FINISH A FEW THINGS.
I'M SORRY FOR UNNERVING YOU.
WHO ARE YOU?
MY NAME IS GABRIEL.
I'M AFRAID YOU'RE WRAPPED UP IN A VERY DANGEROUS SITUATION RIGHT NOW.
MUCH MORE DANGEROUS THAN YOU EVEN KNOW.
THEN...SHOULDN'T WE BE TALKING TO THE AUTHORITIES?
IT WOULD BE HELPFUL FOR YOU TO THINK OF WHAT'S HAPPENING AS A CONTAGION. MY FRIENDS AND I ARE WORKING TO CONTAIN THE SPREAD.
AND TO DO THAT, WE'RE GOING TO NEED TO DO A FEW UNSAVORY THINGS THAT YOUR FRIENDS AT THE FBI MIGHT NOT APPROVE OF.
GIBSON LANE
GIBSON LANE
LIKE TAKING ALL OF THE EVIDENCE THE POLICE GATHERED FROM YOUR BROTHER'S BODY BEFORE AND AFTER HE WAS KILLED.
MOST CRUCIALLY, HIS SMART-PHONE AND TABLET.
YOU'RE STEALING POLICE EVIDENCE.
YES.
DID THE CAR JUST PULL UP TO A SERVICE ENTRANCE BEHIND THE STATION?

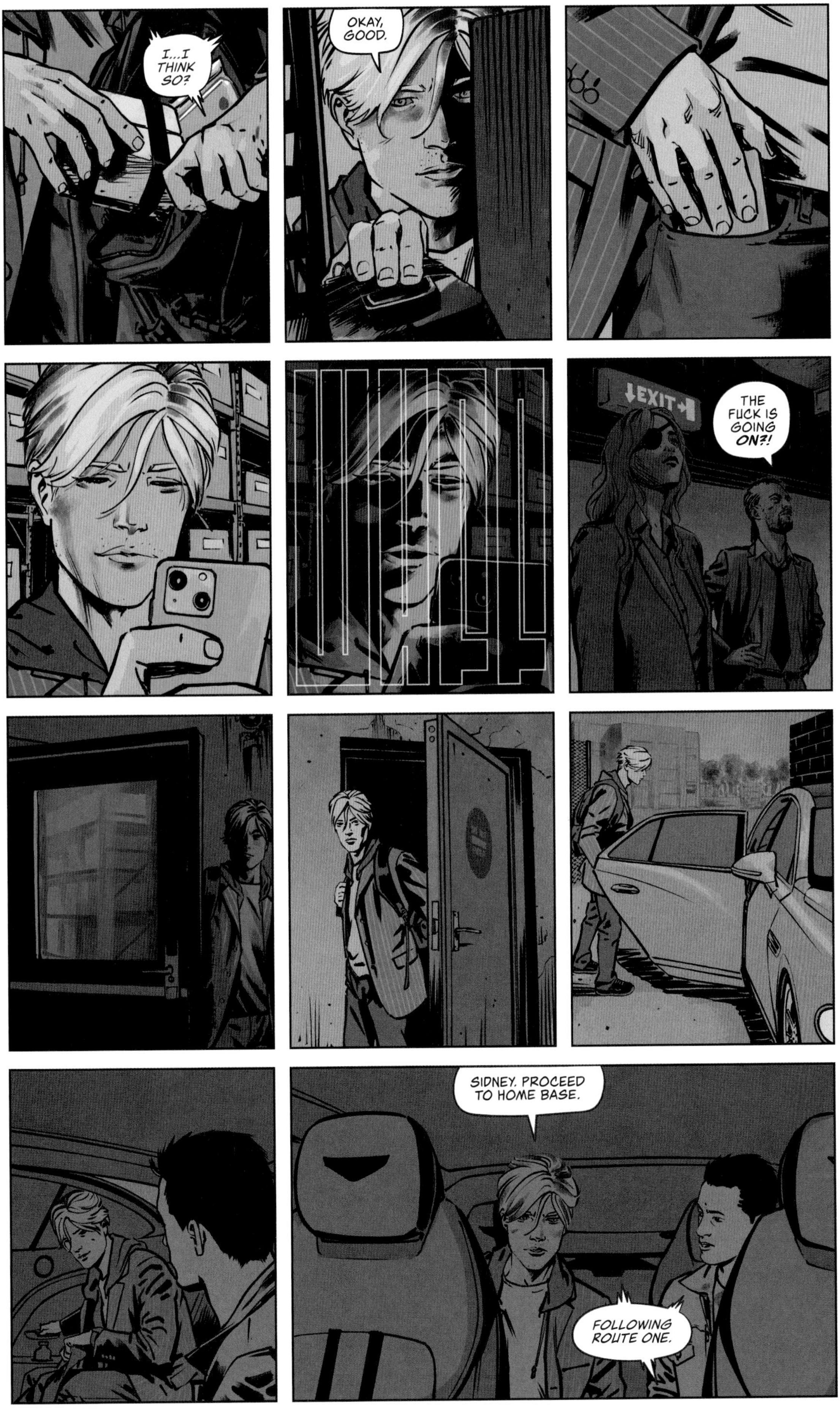
I...I THINK SO?
OKAY, GOOD.
THE FUCK IS GOING ON?!
SIDNEY. PROCEED TO HOME BASE.
FOLLOWING ROUTE ONE.

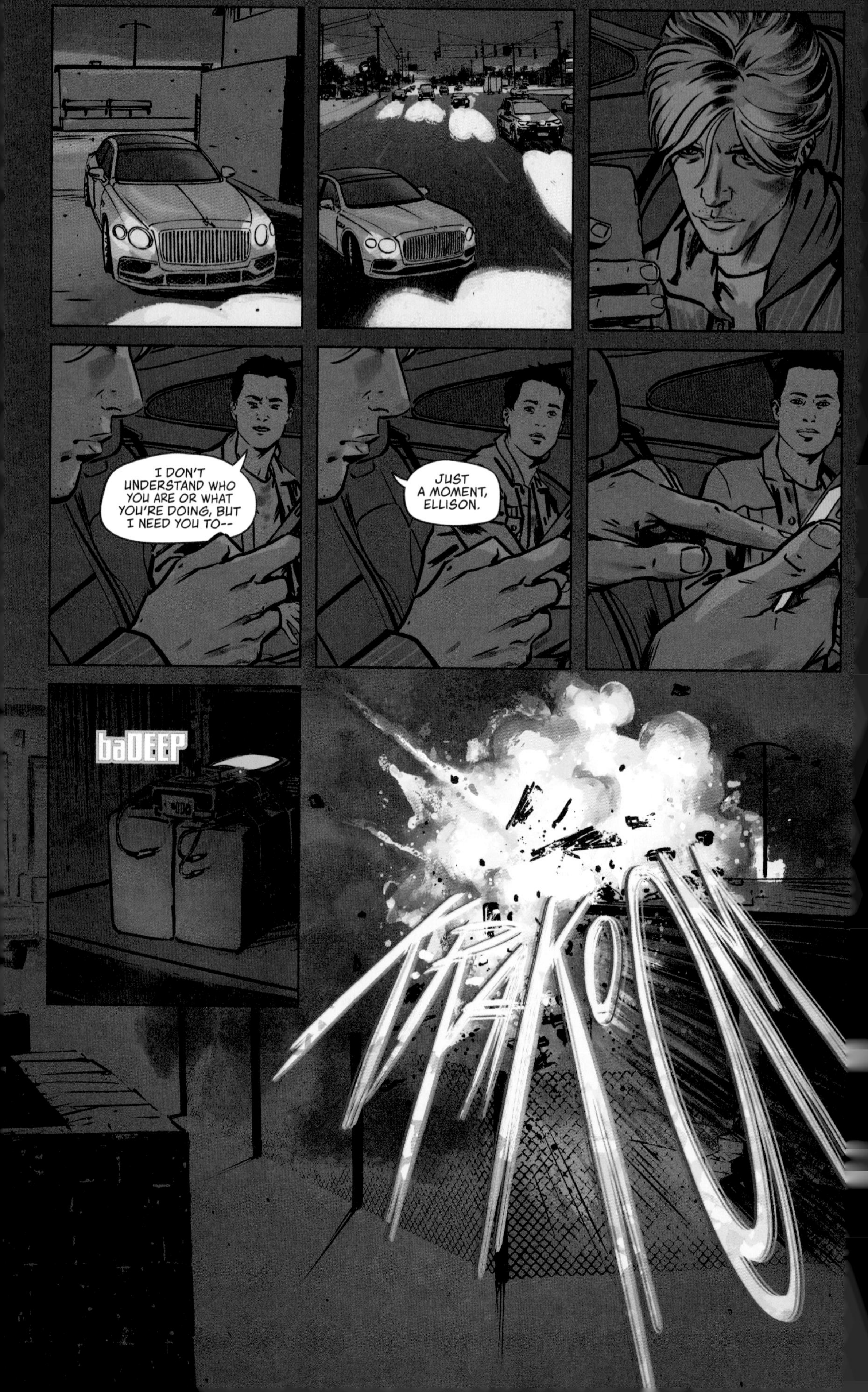
I DON'T UNDERSTAND WHO YOU ARE OR WHAT YOU'RE DOING, BUT I NEED YOU TO--
JUST A MOMENT, ELLISON.
baDEEP

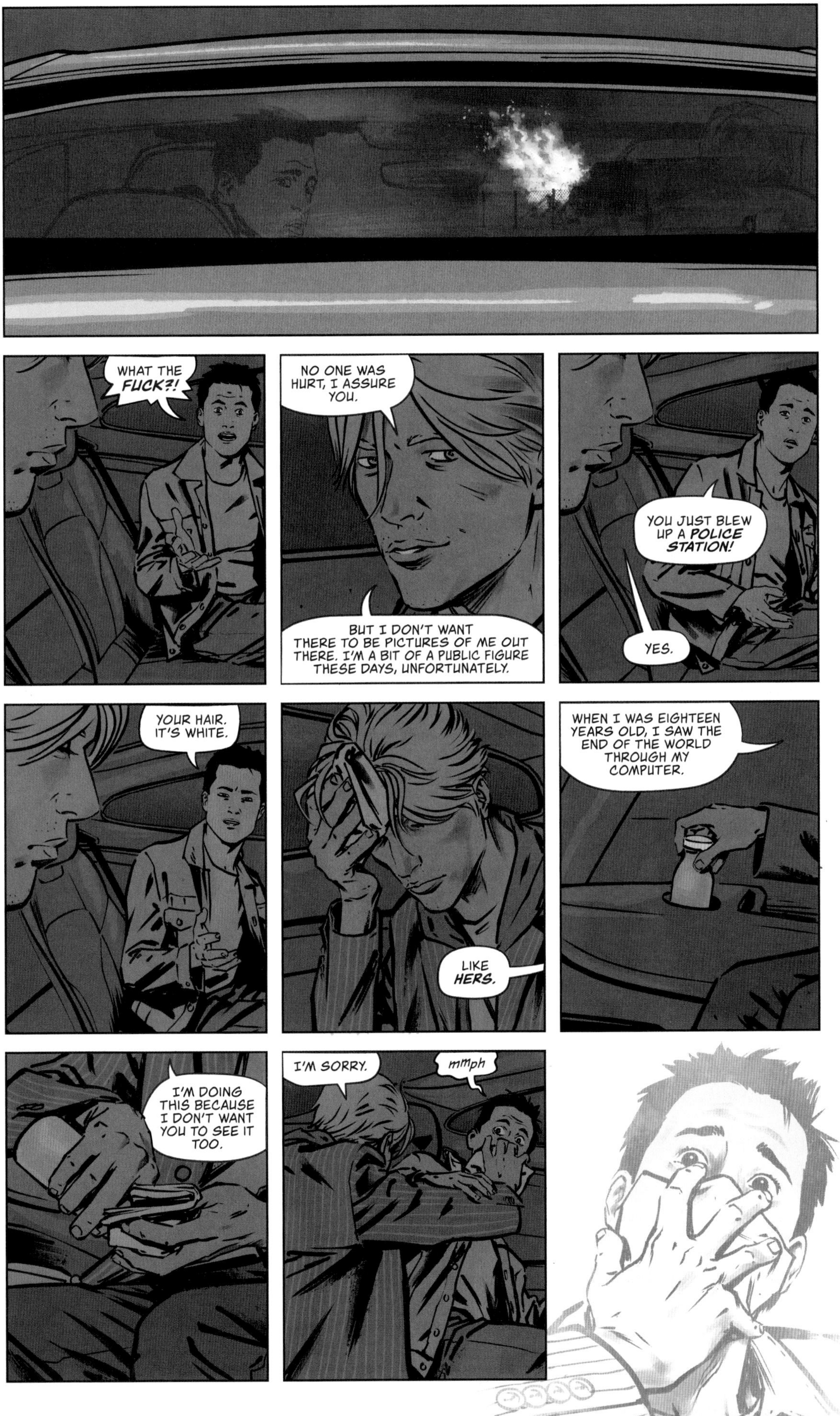
WHAT THE FUCK?!
NO ONE WAS HURT, I ASSURE YOU.
BUT I DON'T WANT THERE TO BE PICTURES OF ME OUT THERE. I'M A BIT OF A PUBLIC FIGURE THESE DAYS, UNFORTUNATELY.
YOU JUST BLEW UP A POLICE STATION!
YES.
YOUR HAIR. IT'S WHITE.
LIKE HERS.
WHEN I WAS EIGHTEEN YEARS OLD, I SAW THE END OF THE WORLD THROUGH MY COMPUTER.
I'M DOING THIS BECAUSE I DON'T WANT YOU TO SEE IT TOO.
I'M SORRY.
mmph

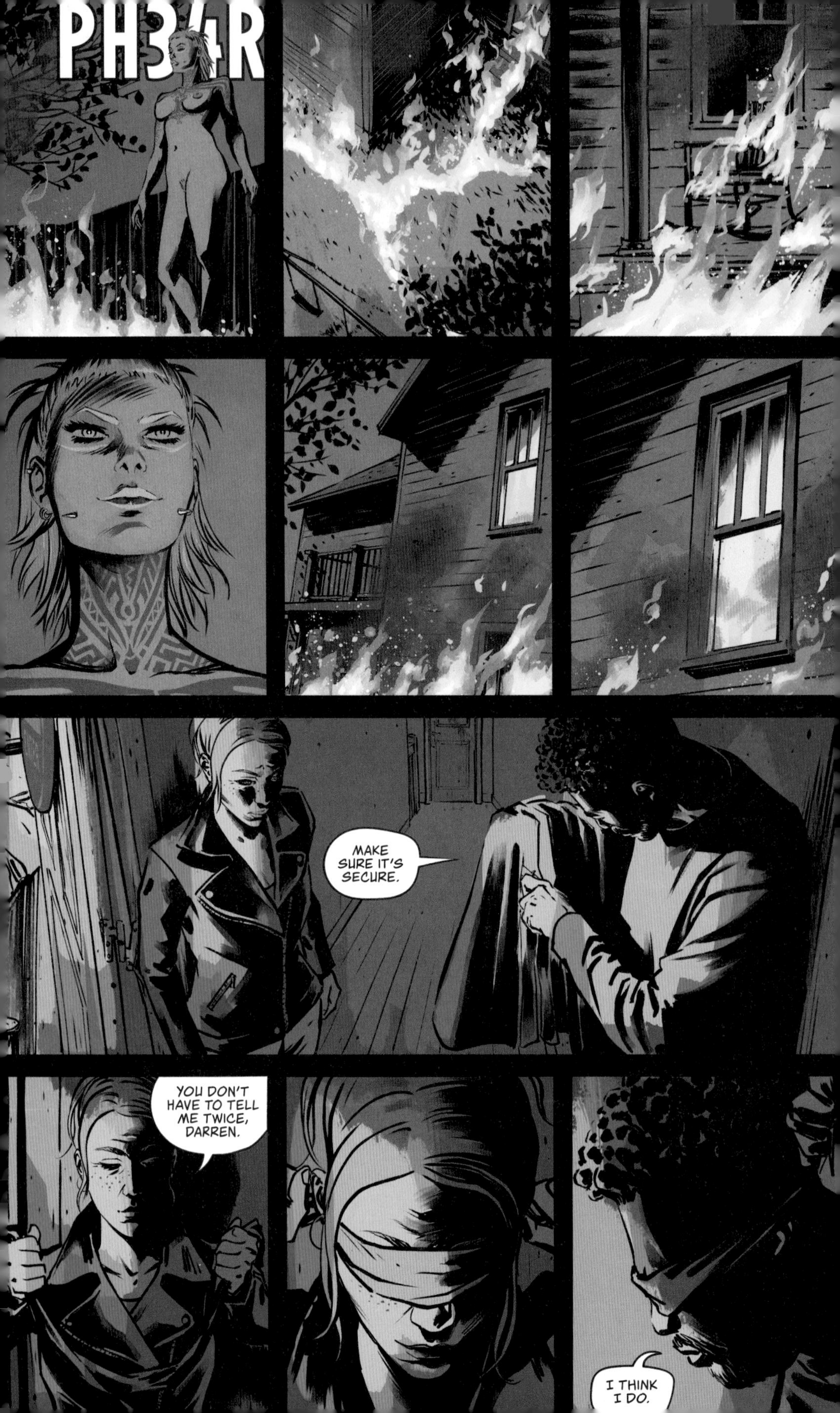
PH34R
MAKE SURE IT'S SECURE.
YOU DON'T HAVE TO TELL ME TWICE, DARREN.
I THINK I DO.

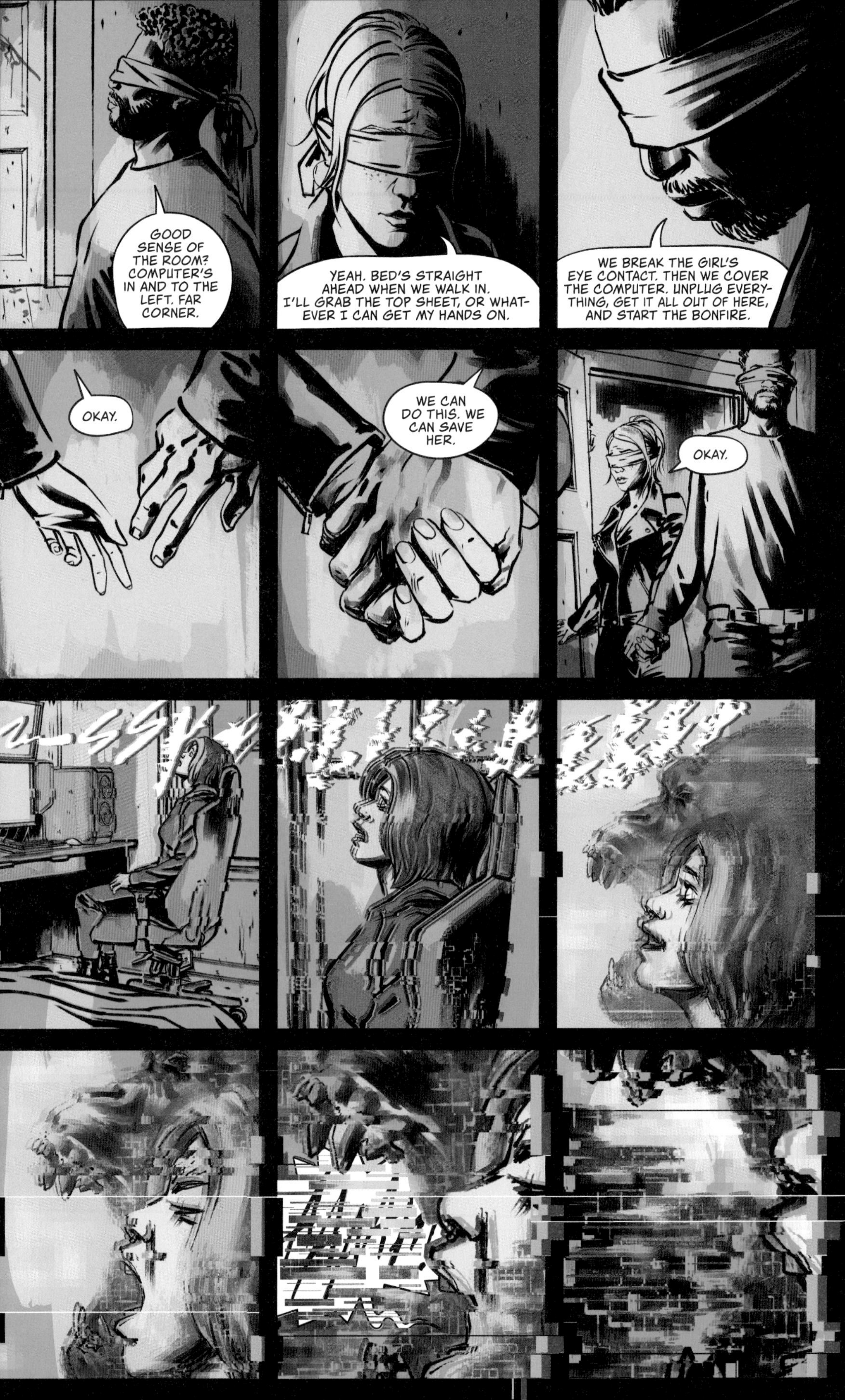
GOOD SENSE OF THE ROOM? COMPUTER'S IN AND TO THE LEFT. FAR CORNER.
YEAH. BED'S STRAIGHT AHEAD WHEN WE WALK IN. I'LL GRAB THE TOP SHEET, OR WHATEVER I CAN GET MY HANDS ON.
WE BREAK THE GIRL'S EYE CONTACT. THEN WE COVER THE COMPUTER. UNPLUG EVERYTHING, GET IT ALL OUT OF HERE, AND START THE BONFIRE.
OKAY.
WE CAN DO THIS. WE CAN SAVE HER.
OKAY.

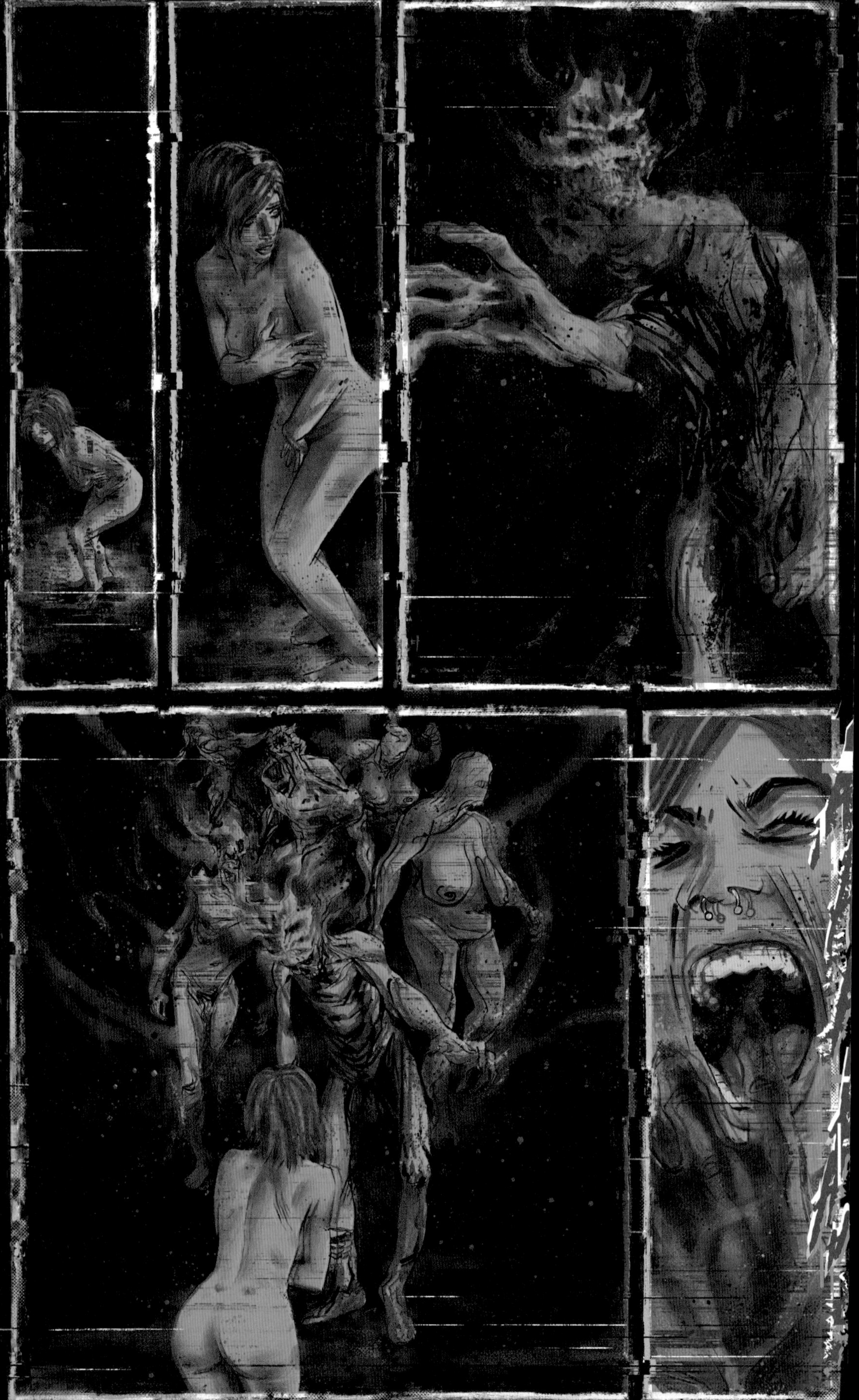

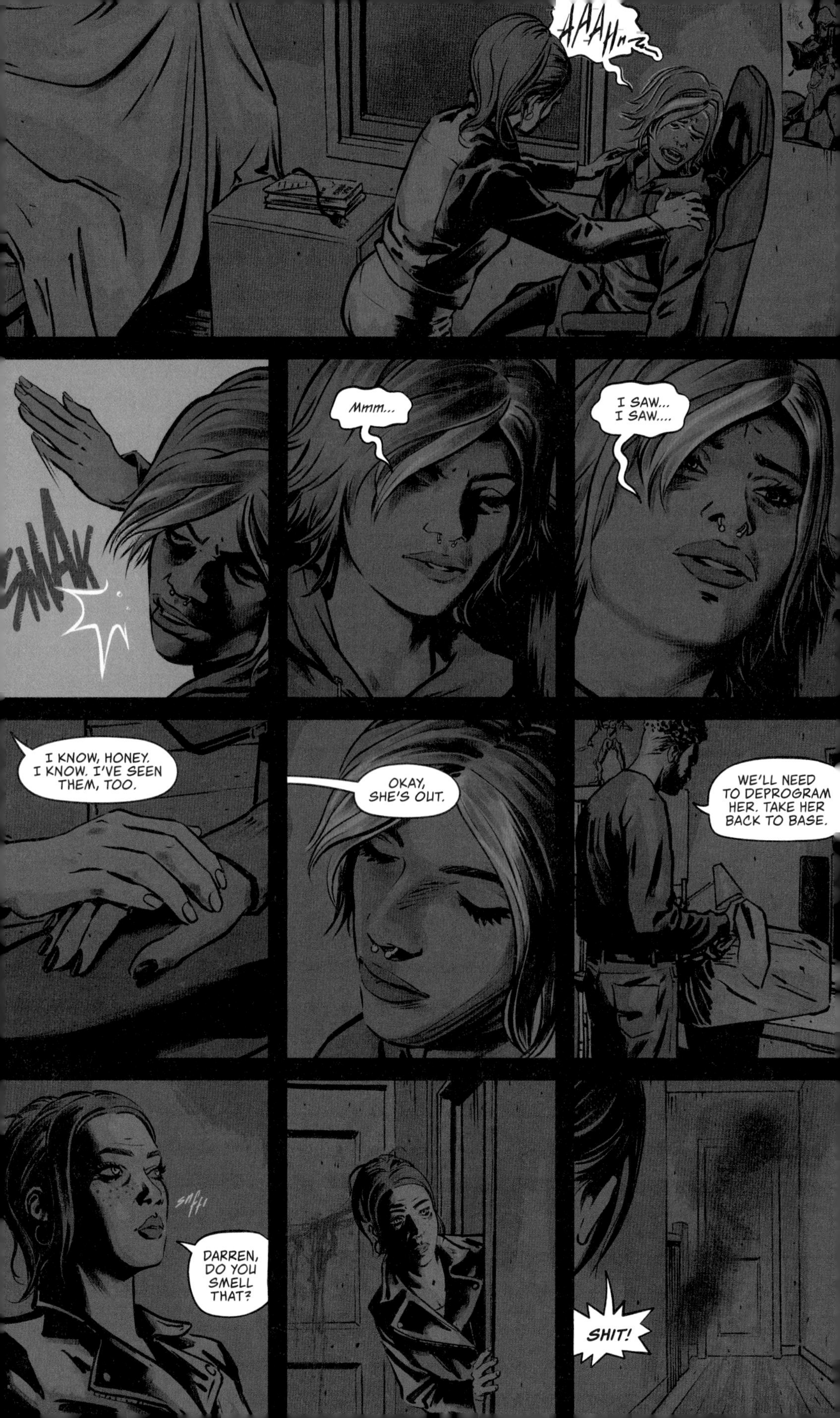
AAAHnn
SMAK
Mmm...
I SAW... I SAW....
I KNOW, HONEY. I KNOW. I'VE SEEN THEM, TOO.
OKAY, SHE'S OUT.
WE'LL NEED TO DEPROGRAM HER. TAKE HER BACK TO BASE.
SNIFF
DARREN, DO YOU SMELL THAT?
SHIT!

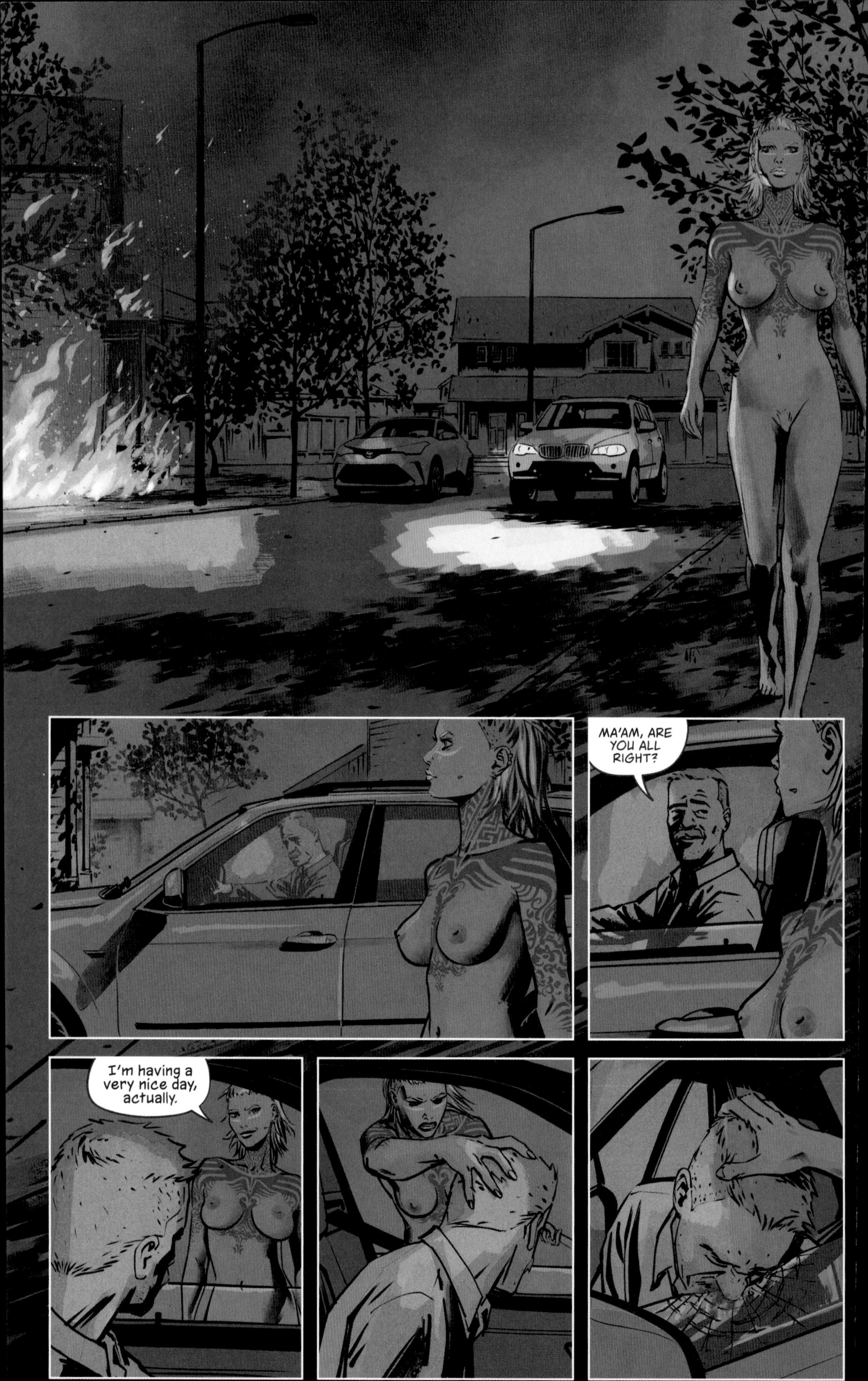
MA'AM, ARE YOU ALL RIGHT?
I'm having a very nice day, actually.

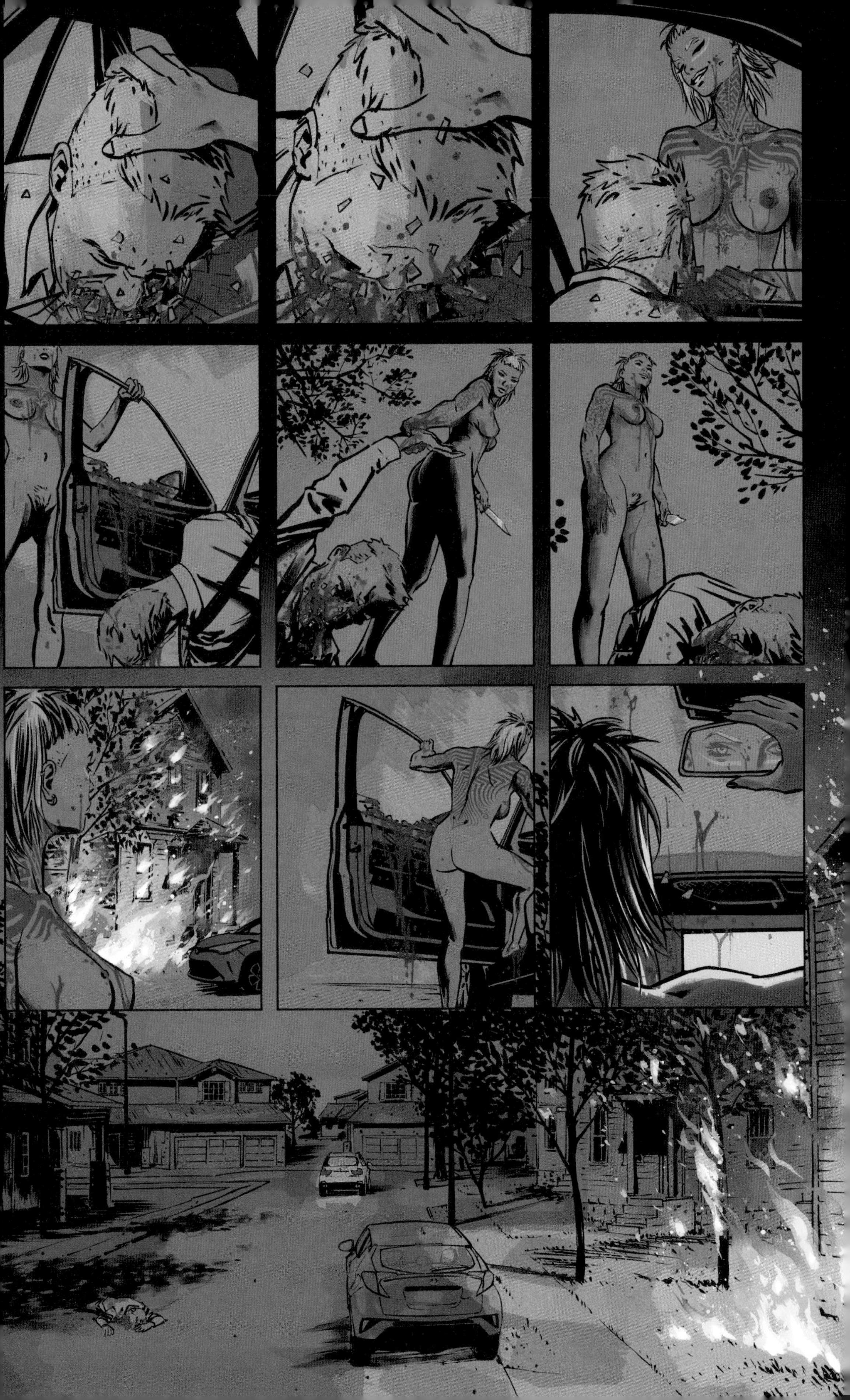

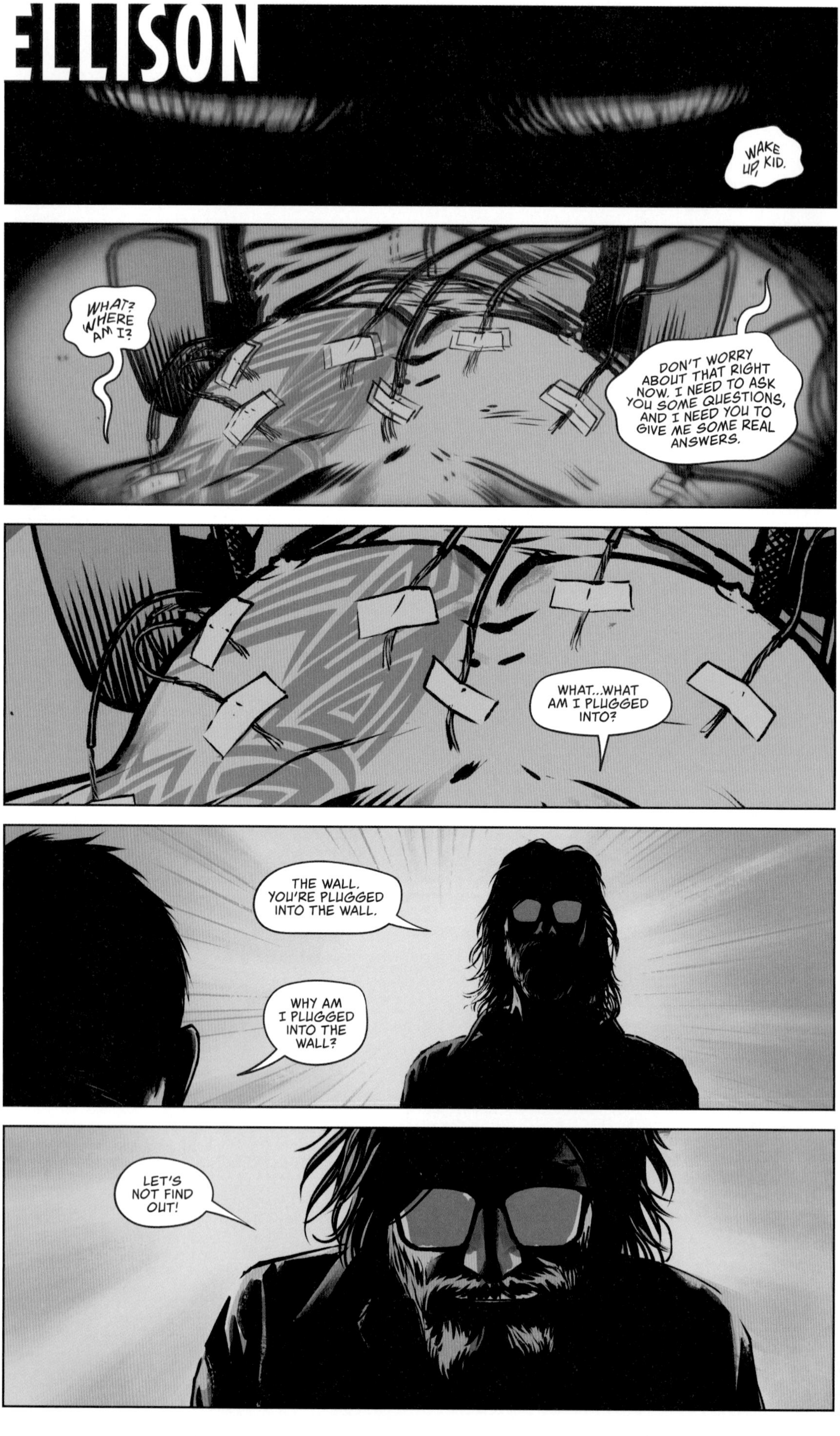
ELLISON
WAKE UP, KID.
WHAT? WHERE AM I?
DON'T WORRY ABOUT THAT RIGHT NOW. I NEED TO ASK YOU SOME QUESTIONS, AND I NEED YOU TO GIVE ME SOME REAL ANSWERS.
WHAT...WHAT AM I PLUGGED INTO?
THE WALL. YOU'RE PLUGGED INTO THE WALL.
WHY AM I PLUGGED INTO THE WALL?
LET'S NOT FIND OUT!

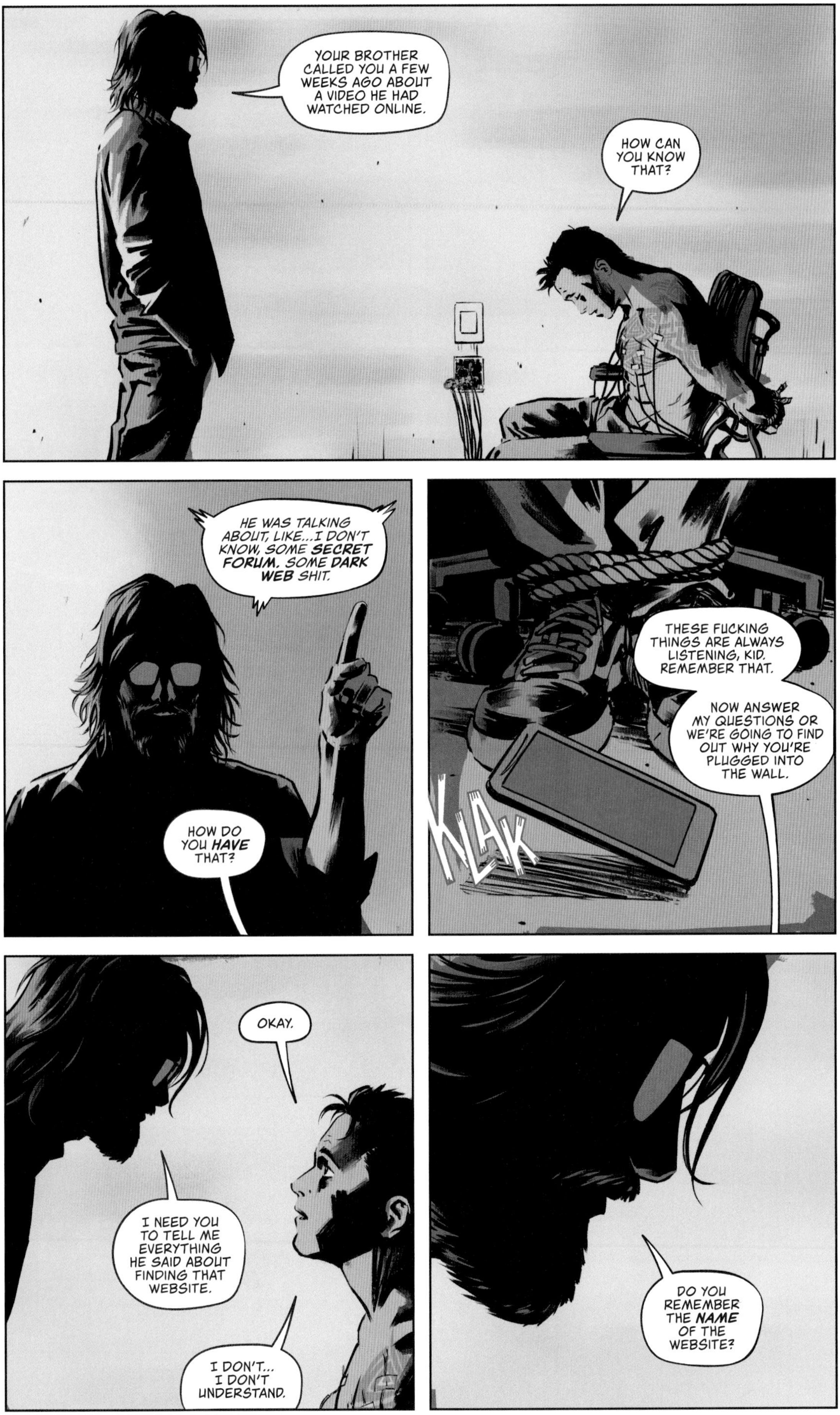
YOUR BROTHER CALLED YOU A FEW WEEKS AGO ABOUT A VIDEO HE HAD WATCHED ONLINE.
HOW CAN YOU KNOW THAT?
HE WAS TALKING ABOUT, LIKE...I DON'T KNOW, SOME **SECRET FORUM.** SOME **DARK WEB** SHIT.
HOW DO YOU **HAVE** THAT?
KLAK
THESE FUCKING THINGS ARE ALWAYS LISTENING, KID. REMEMBER THAT.
NOW ANSWER MY QUESTIONS OR WE'RE GOING TO FIND OUT WHY YOU'RE PLUGGED INTO THE WALL.
OKAY.
I NEED YOU TO TELL ME EVERYTHING HE SAID ABOUT FINDING THAT WEBSITE.
I DON'T... I DON'T UNDERSTAND.
DO YOU REMEMBER THE **NAME** OF THE WEBSITE?

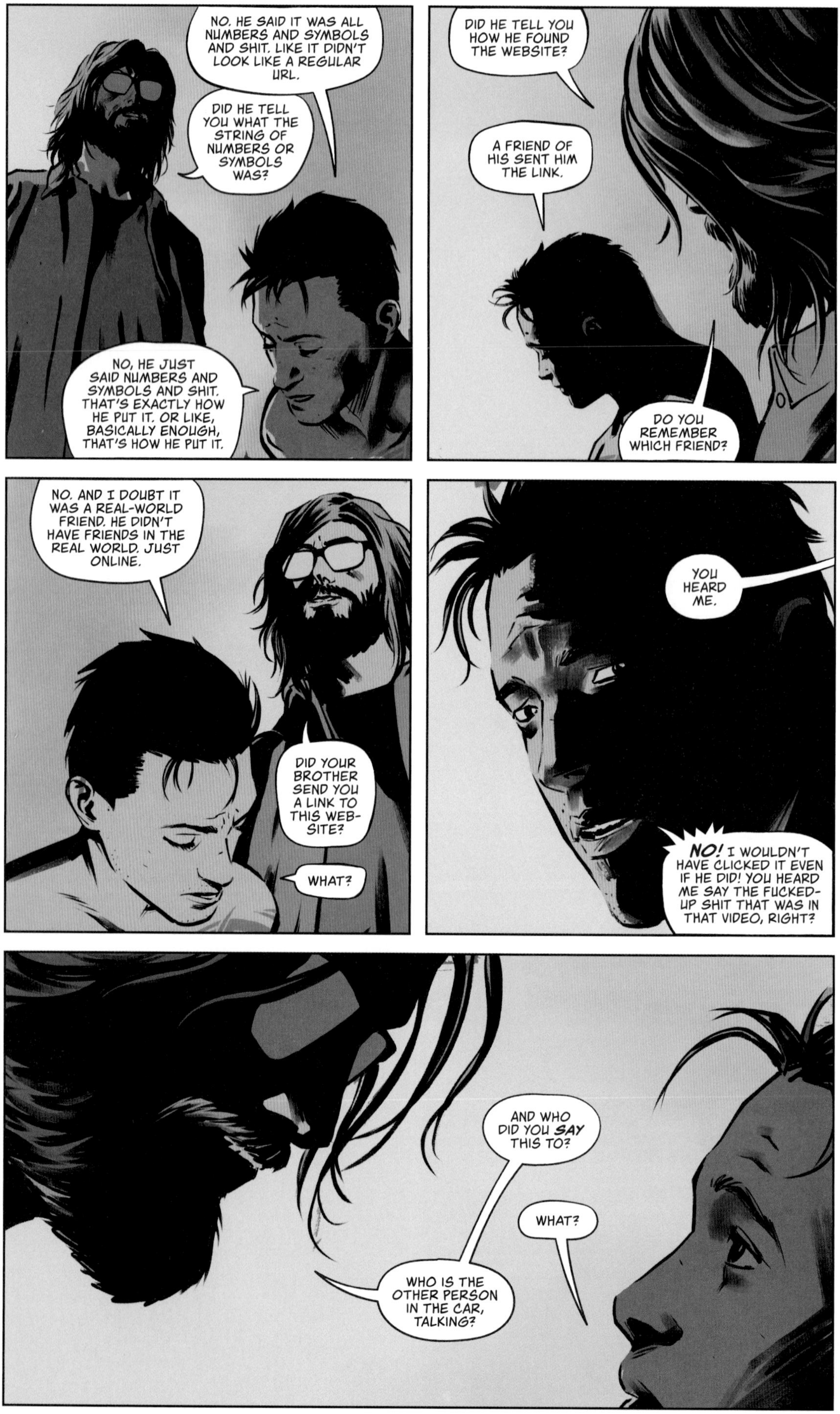
NO. HE SAID IT WAS ALL NUMBERS AND SYMBOLS AND SHIT. LIKE IT DIDN'T LOOK LIKE A REGULAR URL.
DID HE TELL YOU WHAT THE STRING OF NUMBERS OR SYMBOLS WAS?
NO, HE JUST SAID NUMBERS AND SYMBOLS AND SHIT. THAT'S EXACTLY HOW HE PUT IT. OR LIKE, BASICALLY ENOUGH, THAT'S HOW HE PUT IT.
DID HE TELL YOU HOW HE FOUND THE WEBSITE?
A FRIEND OF HIS SENT HIM THE LINK.
DO YOU REMEMBER WHICH FRIEND?
NO. AND I DOUBT IT WAS A REAL-WORLD FRIEND. HE DIDN'T HAVE FRIENDS IN THE REAL WORLD. JUST ONLINE.
DID YOUR BROTHER SEND YOU A LINK TO THIS WEB-SITE?
WHAT?
YOU HEARD ME.
NO! I WOULDN'T HAVE CLICKED IT EVEN IF HE DID! YOU HEARD ME SAY THE FUCKED-UP SHIT THAT WAS IN THAT VIDEO, RIGHT?
AND WHO DID YOU SAY THIS TO?
WHAT?
WHO IS THE OTHER PERSON IN THE CAR, TALKING?

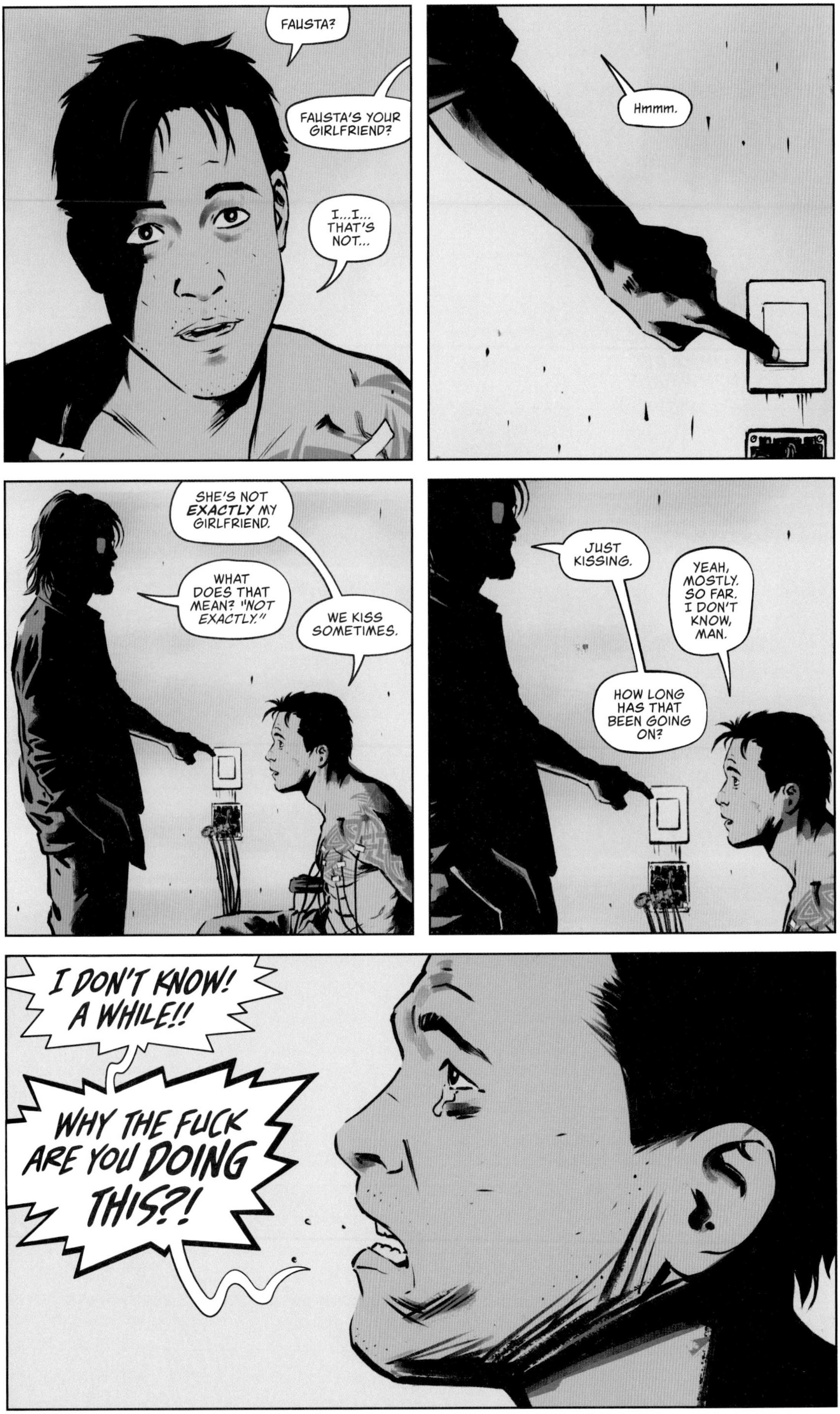
FAUSTA?
FAUSTA'S YOUR GIRLFRIEND?
I...I... THAT'S NOT...
Hmmm.
SHE'S NOT EXACTLY MY GIRLFRIEND.
WHAT DOES THAT MEAN? "NOT EXACTLY."
WE KISS SOMETIMES.
JUST KISSING.
YEAH, MOSTLY. SO FAR. I DON'T KNOW, MAN.
HOW LONG HAS THAT BEEN GOING ON?
I DON'T KNOW! A WHILE!!
WHY THE FUCK ARE YOU DOING THIS?!

WHAT IS THE REASON YOU TOLD HER?

WHAT DO YOU MEAN?

WERE YOU *COMPELLED* TO TELL HER? LIKE, WAS THERE A PART OF YOU THAT NEEDED TO TELL HER? AFTER HEARING THAT STORY FROM YOUR BROTHER, COULD YOU FEEL IT IN YOUR *MIND?*

I TELL HER A *LOT* OF SHIT, MAN. I JUST LIKE *TALKING* TO HER.

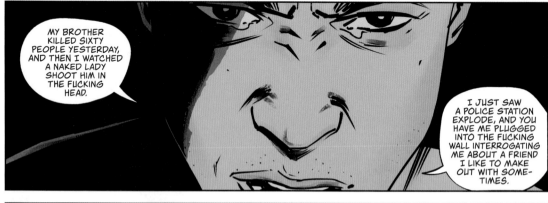

MY BROTHER KILLED SIXTY PEOPLE YESTERDAY, AND THEN I WATCHED A NAKED LADY SHOOT HIM IN THE FUCKING HEAD.

I JUST SAW A POLICE STATION EXPLODE, AND YOU HAVE ME PLUGGED INTO THE FUCKING WALL INTERROGATING ME ABOUT A FRIEND I LIKE TO MAKE OUT WITH SOMETIMES.

I WANT TO *KNOW WHAT THE FUCK IS GOING ON!!*

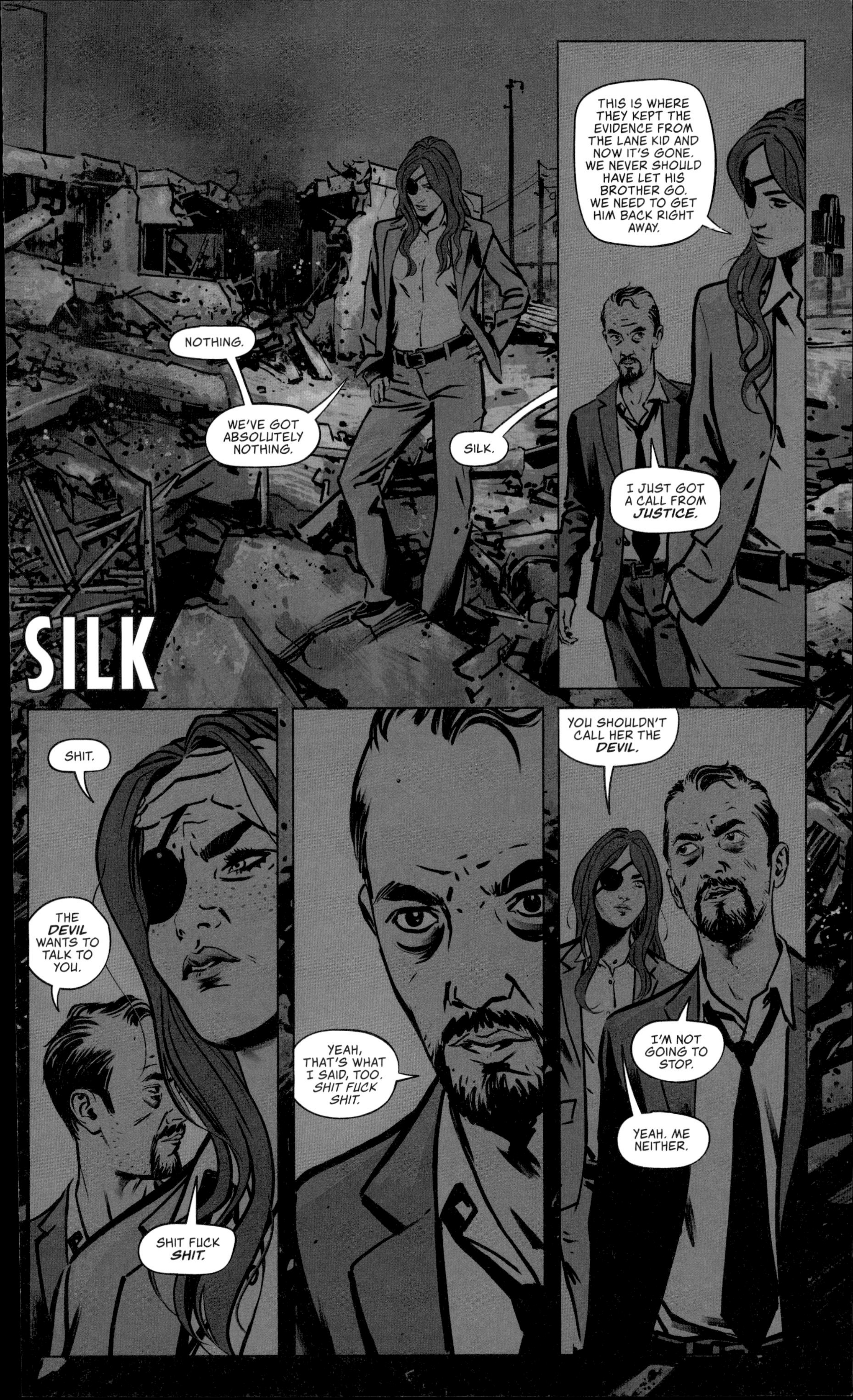
NOTHING.
WE'VE GOT ABSOLUTELY NOTHING.
SILK
SILK.
THIS IS WHERE THEY KEPT THE EVIDENCE FROM THE LANE KID AND NOW IT'S GONE. WE NEVER SHOULD HAVE LET HIS BROTHER GO. WE NEED TO GET HIM BACK RIGHT AWAY.
I JUST GOT A CALL FROM JUSTICE.
SHIT.
THE DEVIL WANTS TO TALK TO YOU.
SHIT FUCK SHIT.
YEAH, THAT'S WHAT I SAID, TOO. SHIT FUCK SHIT.
YOU SHOULDN'T CALL HER THE DEVIL.
I'M NOT GOING TO STOP.
YEAH. ME NEITHER.

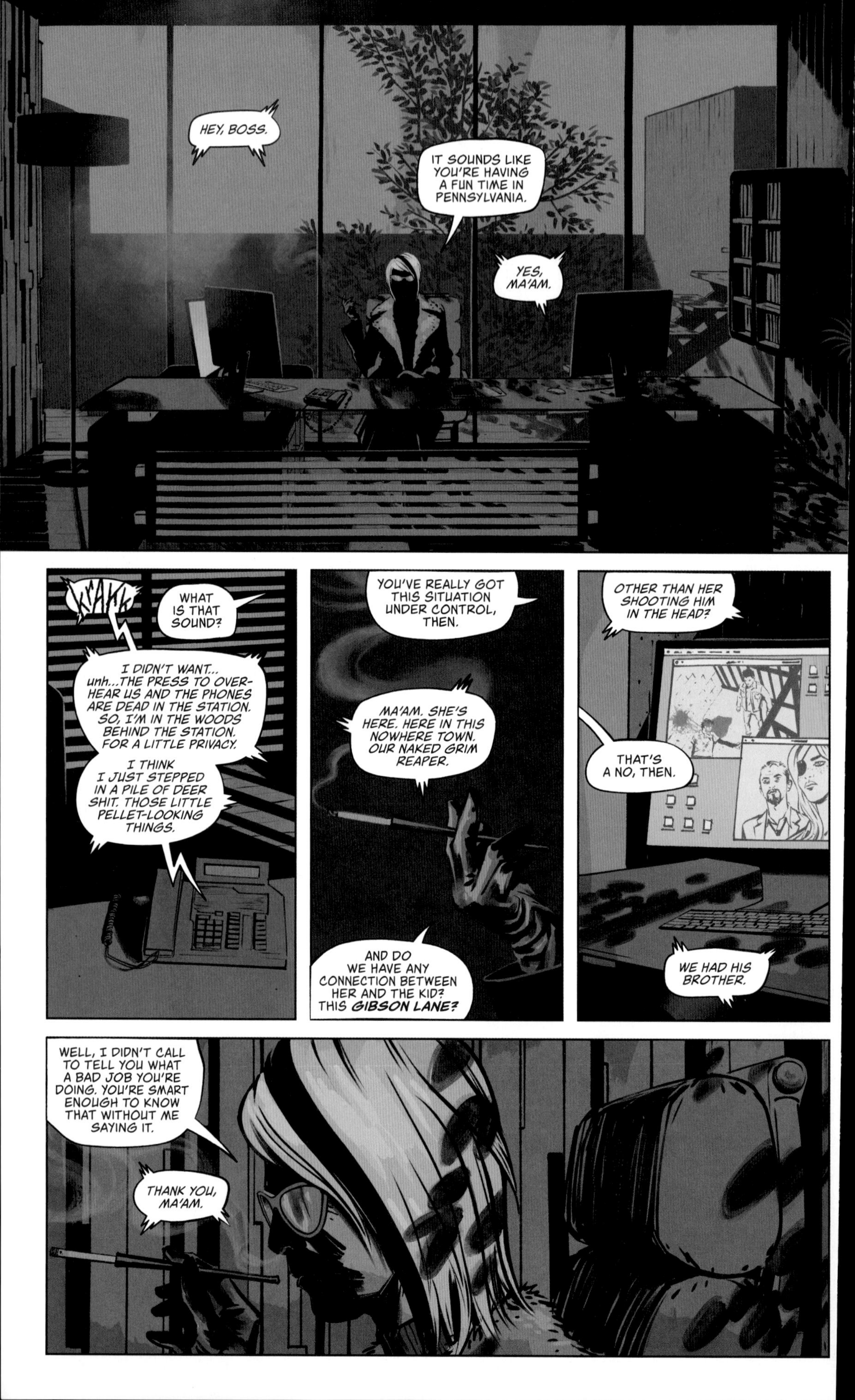
HEY, BOSS.
IT SOUNDS LIKE YOU'RE HAVING A FUN TIME IN PENNSYLVANIA.
YES, MA'AM.
KRAKK
WHAT IS THAT SOUND?
I DIDN'T WANT... unh...THE PRESS TO OVER-HEAR US AND THE PHONES ARE DEAD IN THE STATION. SO, I'M IN THE WOODS BEHIND THE STATION. FOR A LITTLE PRIVACY.
I THINK I JUST STEPPED IN A PILE OF DEER SHIT. THOSE LITTLE PELLET-LOOKING THINGS.
YOU'VE REALLY GOT THIS SITUATION UNDER CONTROL, THEN.
MA'AM. SHE'S HERE. HERE IN THIS NOWHERE TOWN. OUR NAKED GRIM REAPER.
AND DO WE HAVE ANY CONNECTION BETWEEN HER AND THE KID? THIS GIBSON LANE?
OTHER THAN HER SHOOTING HIM IN THE HEAD?
THAT'S A NO, THEN.
WE HAD HIS BROTHER.
WELL, I DIDN'T CALL TO TELL YOU WHAT A BAD JOB YOU'RE DOING. YOU'RE SMART ENOUGH TO KNOW THAT WITHOUT ME SAYING IT.
THANK YOU, MA'AM.

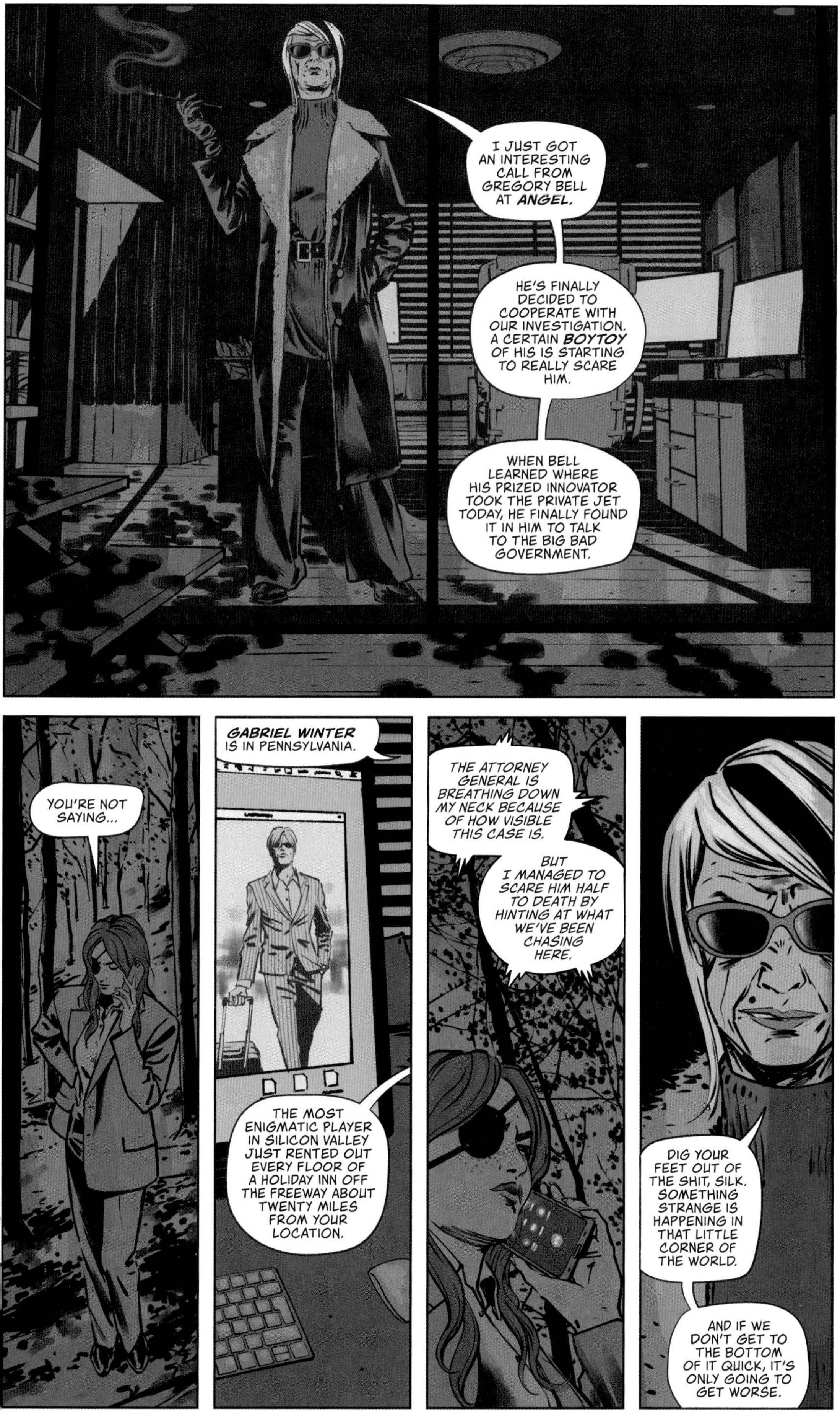
I JUST GOT AN INTERESTING CALL FROM GREGORY BELL AT ANGEL.
HE'S FINALLY DECIDED TO COOPERATE WITH OUR INVESTIGATION. A CERTAIN BOYTOY OF HIS IS STARTING TO REALLY SCARE HIM.
WHEN BELL LEARNED WHERE HIS PRIZED INNOVATOR TOOK THE PRIVATE JET TODAY, HE FINALLY FOUND IT IN HIM TO TALK TO THE BIG BAD GOVERNMENT.
YOU'RE NOT SAYING...
GABRIEL WINTER IS IN PENNSYLVANIA.
THE MOST ENIGMATIC PLAYER IN SILICON VALLEY JUST RENTED OUT EVERY FLOOR OF A HOLIDAY INN OFF THE FREEWAY ABOUT TWENTY MILES FROM YOUR LOCATION.
THE ATTORNEY GENERAL IS BREATHING DOWN MY NECK BECAUSE OF HOW VISIBLE THIS CASE IS.
BUT I MANAGED TO SCARE HIM HALF TO DEATH BY HINTING AT WHAT WE'VE BEEN CHASING HERE.
DIG YOUR FEET OUT OF THE SHIT, SILK. SOMETHING STRANGE IS HAPPENING IN THAT LITTLE CORNER OF THE WORLD.
AND IF WE DON'T GET TO THE BOTTOM OF IT QUICK, IT'S ONLY GOING TO GET WORSE.

UMMM

GABRIEL

tktktktktk

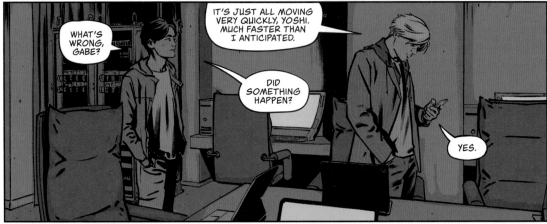

WHAT'S WRONG, GABE?

IT'S JUST ALL MOVING VERY QUICKLY, YOSHI, MUCH FASTER THAN I ANTICIPATED.

DID SOMETHING HAPPEN?

YES.

I THINK WE CAN CUT HIM LOOSE, LIAM.

YEAH?

HE SEEMS LIKE HE STILL HAS HIS HEAD ON HIS SHOULDERS. AND WE HAVE A LITTLE SITUATION WE'RE GOING TO NEED TO DEAL WITH, QUICKLY.

PERHAPS HE'D LIKE TO HELP US.

WHY...WHY THE HELL WOULD I HELP YOU? YOU WERE GOING TO TORTURE ME.

YOU WOULD HAVE BEEN FINE. JUST WOULD HAVE SCARED YOU A LITTLE IF YOU NEEDED IT.

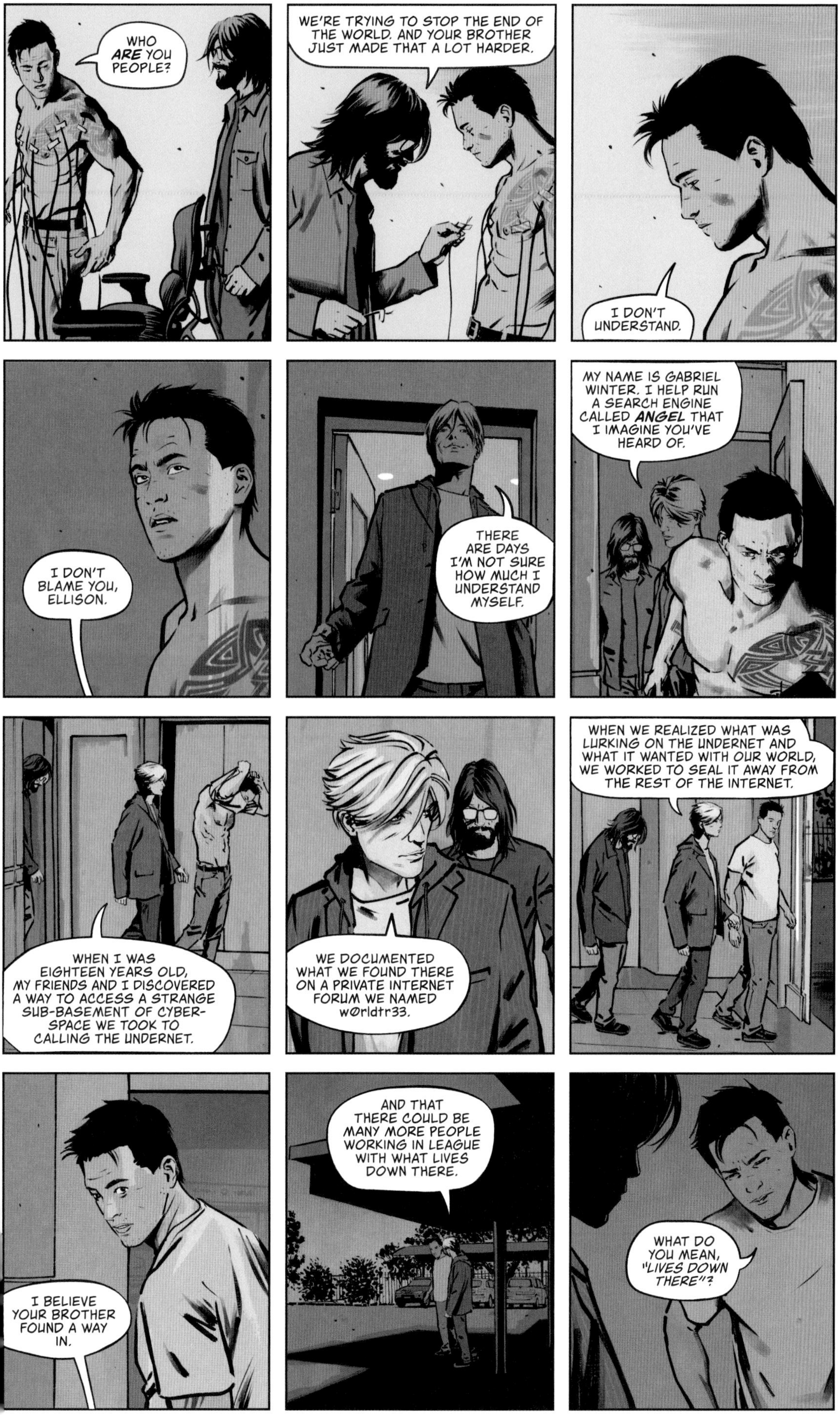
WHO *ARE* YOU PEOPLE?
WE'RE TRYING TO STOP THE END OF THE WORLD. AND YOUR BROTHER JUST MADE THAT A LOT HARDER.
I DON'T UNDERSTAND.
I DON'T BLAME YOU, ELLISON.
THERE ARE DAYS I'M NOT SURE HOW MUCH I UNDERSTAND MYSELF.
MY NAME IS GABRIEL WINTER. I HELP RUN A SEARCH ENGINE CALLED *ANGEL* THAT I IMAGINE YOU'VE HEARD OF.
WHEN I WAS EIGHTEEN YEARS OLD, MY FRIENDS AND I DISCOVERED A WAY TO ACCESS A STRANGE SUB-BASEMENT OF CYBER-SPACE WE TOOK TO CALLING THE UNDERNET.
WE DOCUMENTED WHAT WE FOUND THERE ON A PRIVATE INTERNET FORUM WE NAMED w@rldtr33.
WHEN WE REALIZED WHAT WAS LURKING ON THE UNDERNET AND WHAT IT WANTED WITH OUR WORLD, WE WORKED TO SEAL IT AWAY FROM THE REST OF THE INTERNET.
I BELIEVE YOUR BROTHER FOUND A WAY IN.
AND THAT THERE COULD BE MANY MORE PEOPLE WORKING IN LEAGUE WITH WHAT LIVES DOWN THERE.
WHAT DO YOU MEAN, "LIVES DOWN THERE"?

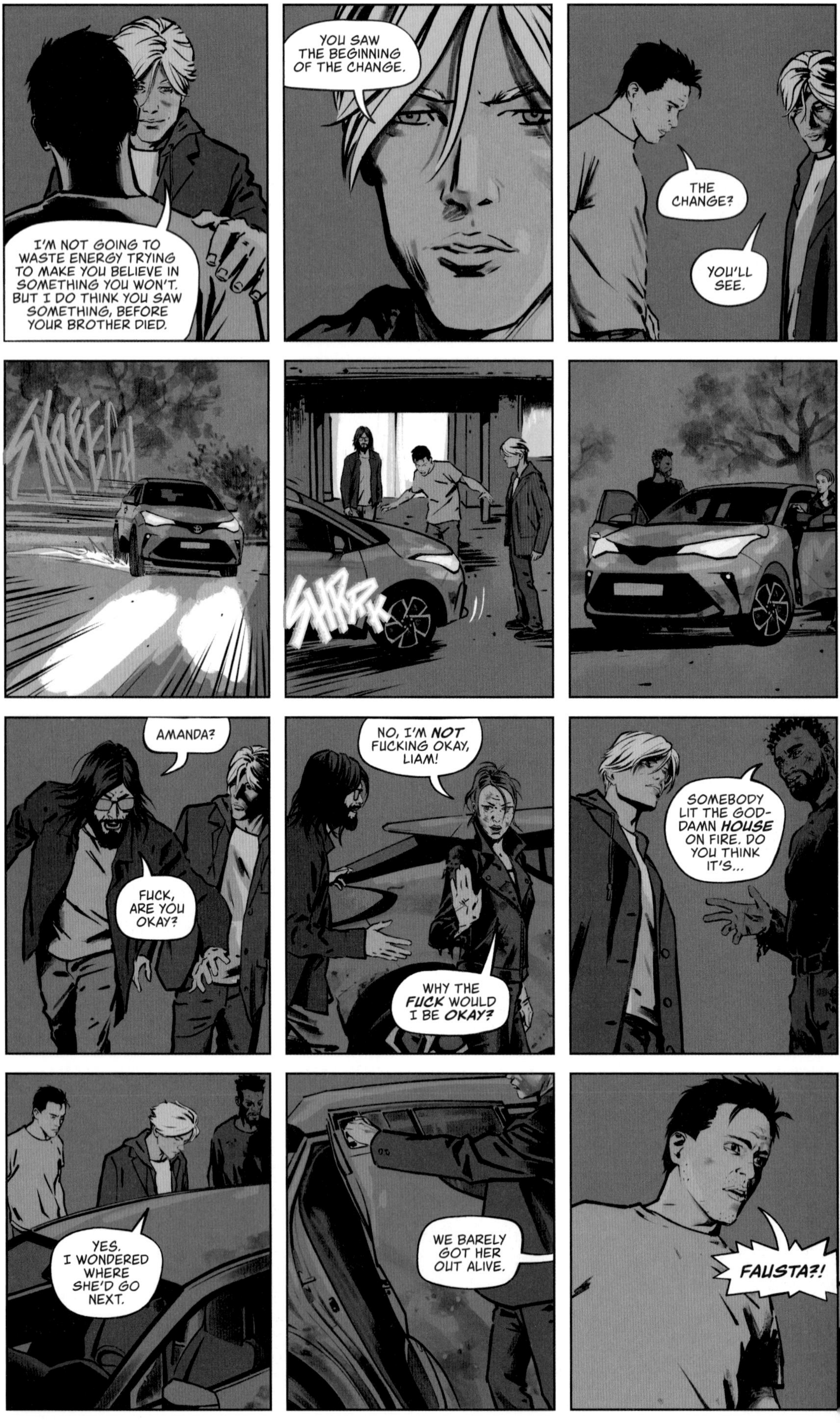
I'M NOT GOING TO WASTE ENERGY TRYING TO MAKE YOU BELIEVE IN SOMETHING YOU WON'T. BUT I DO THINK YOU SAW SOMETHING, BEFORE YOUR BROTHER DIED.
YOU SAW THE BEGINNING OF THE CHANGE.
THE CHANGE?
YOU'LL SEE.
SKREECH
SHRRK
AMANDA?
FUCK, ARE YOU OKAY?
NO, I'M NOT FUCKING OKAY, LIAM!
WHY THE FUCK WOULD I BE OKAY?
SOMEBODY LIT THE GOD-DAMN HOUSE ON FIRE. DO YOU THINK IT'S...
YES. I WONDERED WHERE SHE'D GO NEXT.
WE BARELY GOT HER OUT ALIVE.
FAUSTA?!

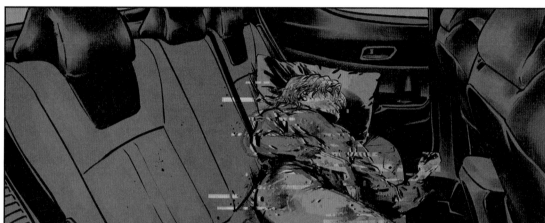

WHAT'S HAPPENING TO HER?

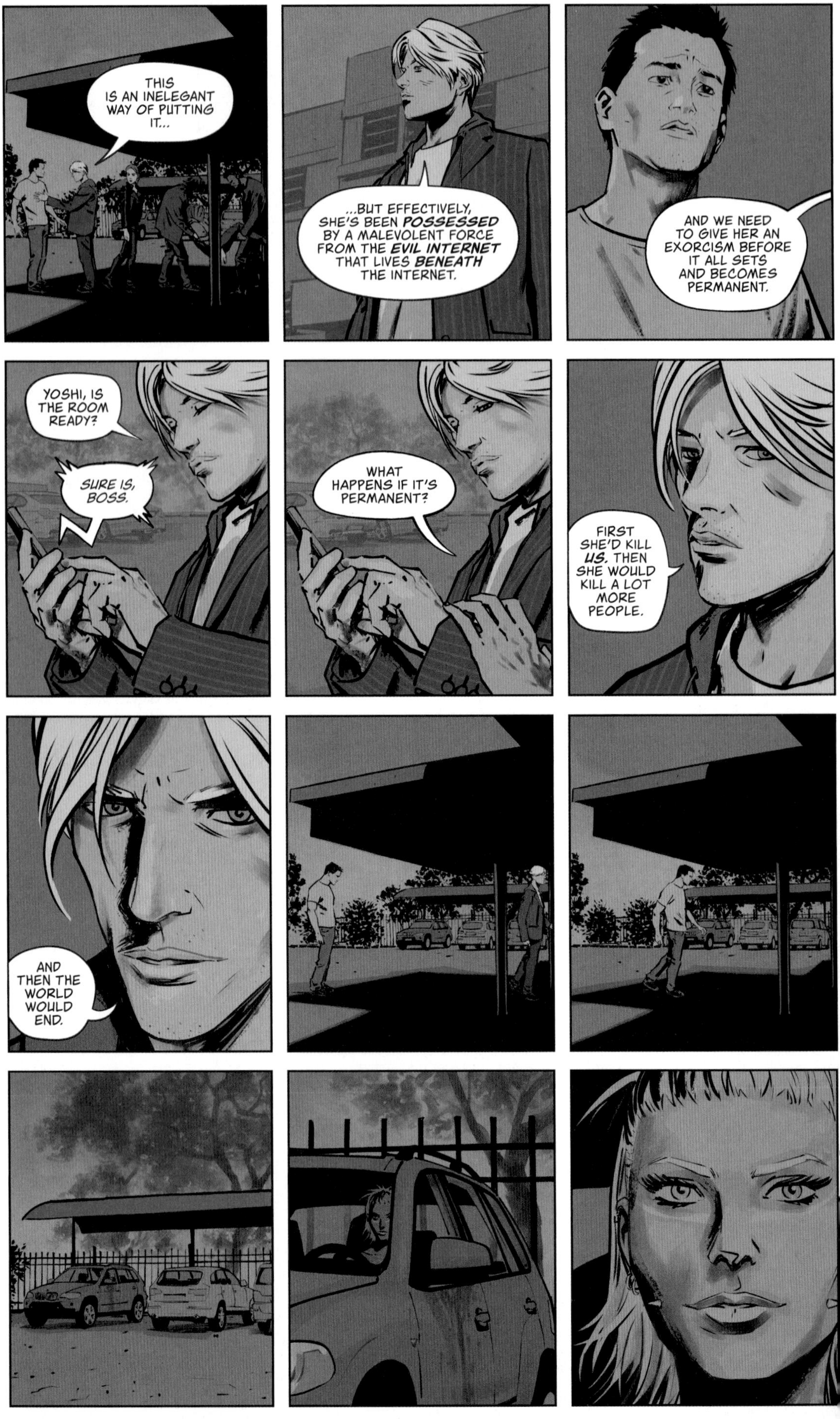
THIS IS AN INELEGANT WAY OF PUTTING IT...
...BUT EFFECTIVELY, SHE'S BEEN POSSESSED BY A MALEVOLENT FORCE FROM THE EVIL INTERNET THAT LIVES BENEATH THE INTERNET.
AND WE NEED TO GIVE HER AN EXORCISM BEFORE IT ALL SETS AND BECOMES PERMANENT.
YOSHI, IS THE ROOM READY?
SURE IS, BOSS.
WHAT HAPPENS IF IT'S PERMANENT?
FIRST SHE'D KILL US. THEN SHE WOULD KILL A LOT MORE PEOPLE.
AND THEN THE WORLD WOULD END.

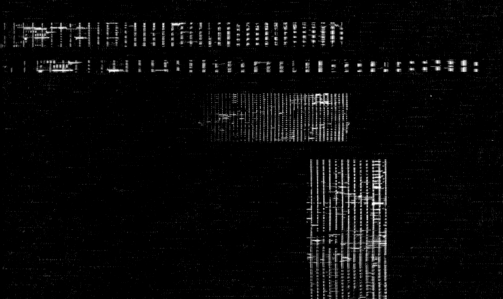

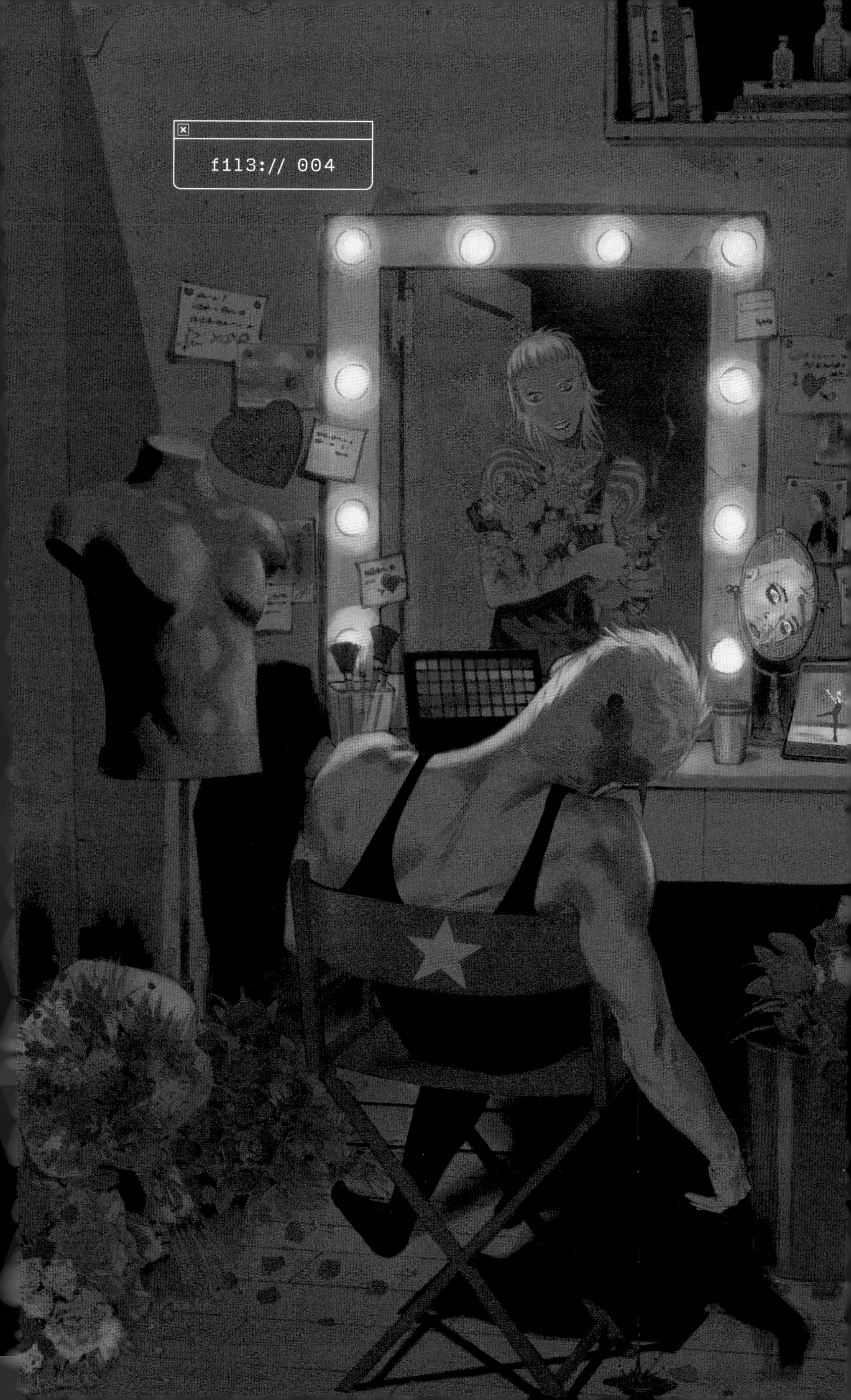
f113:// 004

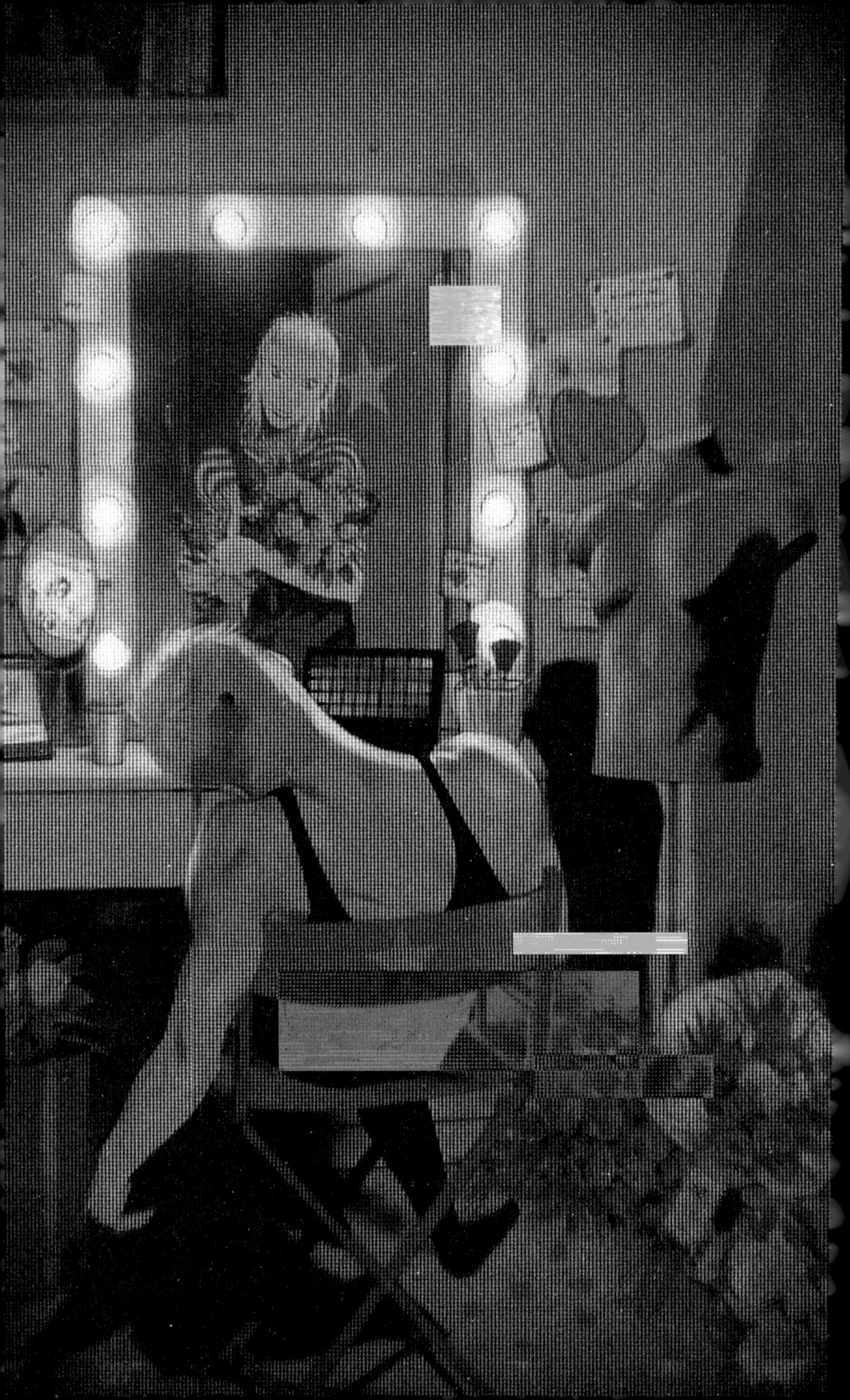

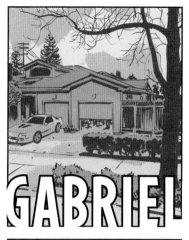

GABRIEL

I COULDN'T SLEEP LAST NIGHT.

YOU *NEVER* SLEEP.

I SLEEP A LITTLE, BUT LAST NIGHT I COULDN'T.

I WAS JUST FOLLOWING LINKS DOWN NONSENSE HALF-BROKEN, HALF-BUILT WEBSITES. I WASN'T EVEN REALLY THINKING.

I WAS JUST TUMBLING FARTHER AND FARTHER DOWN THE RABBIT HOLE.

AND I BROKE THROUGH TO SOMETHING... *IMPORTANT.*

WHAT DO YOU MEAN, IMPORTANT?

THIS IS GOING TO SOUND CRAZY, BUT I THINK I BROKE THROUGH THE BOTTOM OF THE INTERNET TO THE OTHER SIDE.

TO A WHOLE OTHER INTERNET. FROM...

SORRY, THIS SOUNDS INSANE OUT LOUD, BUT I DO THINK I'M RIGHT.

A WHOLE OTHER INTERNET FROM A WHOLE DIFFERENT WORLD.

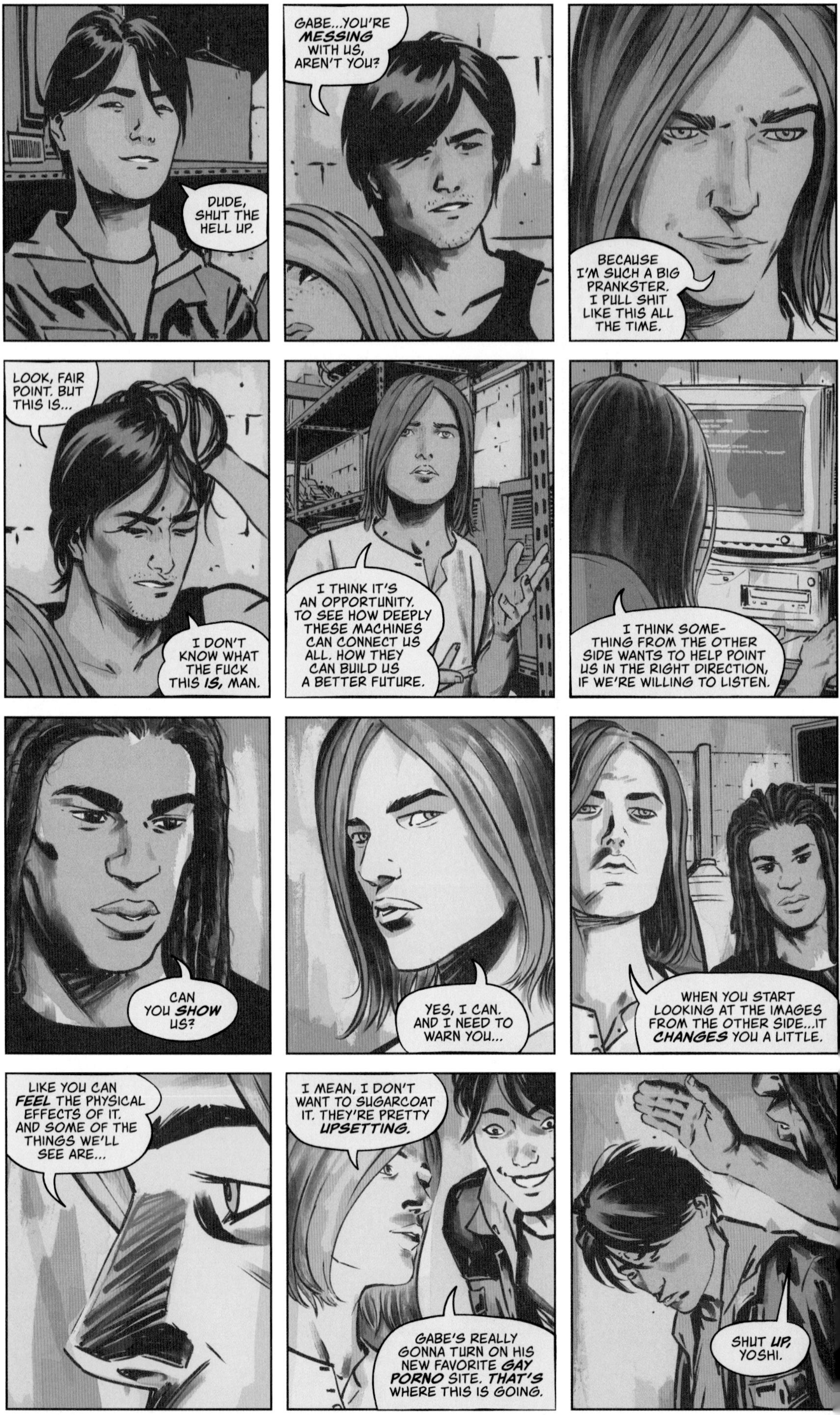
DUDE, SHUT THE HELL UP.
GABE...YOU'RE MESSING WITH US, AREN'T YOU?
BECAUSE I'M SUCH A BIG PRANKSTER. I PULL SHIT LIKE THIS ALL THE TIME.
LOOK, FAIR POINT. BUT THIS IS...
I DON'T KNOW WHAT THE FUCK THIS IS, MAN.
I THINK IT'S AN OPPORTUNITY. TO SEE HOW DEEPLY THESE MACHINES CAN CONNECT US ALL. HOW THEY CAN BUILD US A BETTER FUTURE.
I THINK SOME-THING FROM THE OTHER SIDE WANTS TO HELP POINT US IN THE RIGHT DIRECTION, IF WE'RE WILLING TO LISTEN.
CAN YOU SHOW US?
YES, I CAN. AND I NEED TO WARN YOU...
WHEN YOU START LOOKING AT THE IMAGES FROM THE OTHER SIDE...IT CHANGES YOU A LITTLE.
LIKE YOU CAN FEEL THE PHYSICAL EFFECTS OF IT. AND SOME OF THE THINGS WE'LL SEE ARE...
I MEAN, I DON'T WANT TO SUGARCOAT IT. THEY'RE PRETTY UPSETTING.
GABE'S REALLY GONNA TURN ON HIS NEW FAVORITE GAY PORNO SITE. THAT'S WHERE THIS IS GOING.
SHUT UP, YOSHI.

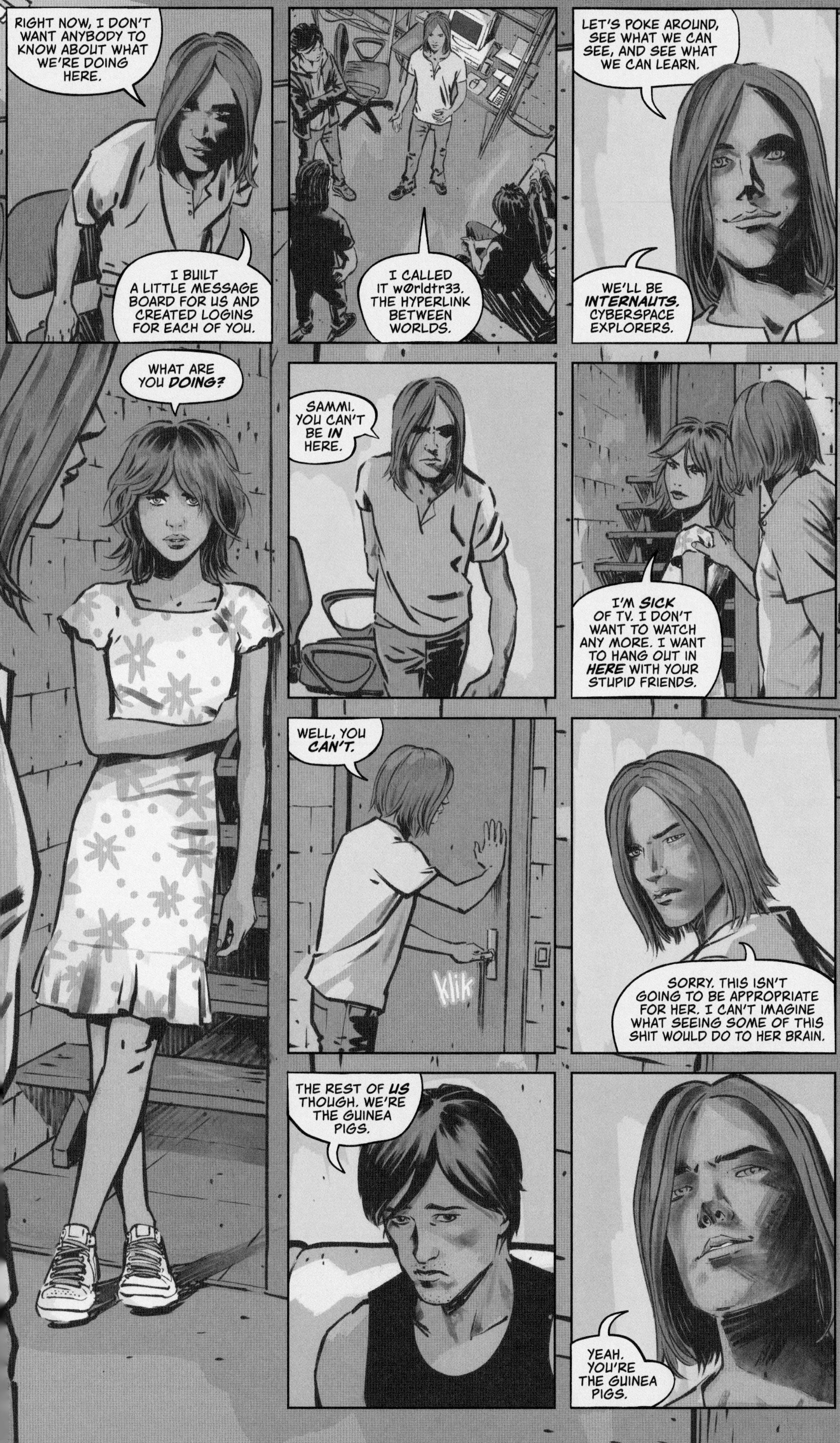
RIGHT NOW, I DON'T WANT ANYBODY TO KNOW ABOUT WHAT WE'RE DOING HERE.
I BUILT A LITTLE MESSAGE BOARD FOR US AND CREATED LOGINS FOR EACH OF YOU.
I CALLED IT w@rldtr33. THE HYPERLINK BETWEEN WORLDS.
LET'S POKE AROUND, SEE WHAT WE CAN SEE, AND SEE WHAT WE CAN LEARN.
WE'LL BE INTERNAUTS. CYBERSPACE EXPLORERS.
WHAT ARE YOU DOING?
SAMMI. YOU CAN'T BE IN HERE.
I'M SICK OF TV. I DON'T WANT TO WATCH ANY MORE. I WANT TO HANG OUT IN HERE WITH YOUR STUPID FRIENDS.
WELL, YOU CAN'T.
klik
SORRY. THIS ISN'T GOING TO BE APPROPRIATE FOR HER. I CAN'T IMAGINE WHAT SEEING SOME OF THIS SHIT WOULD DO TO HER BRAIN.
THE REST OF US THOUGH. WE'RE THE GUINEA PIGS.
YEAH. YOU'RE THE GUINEA PIGS.

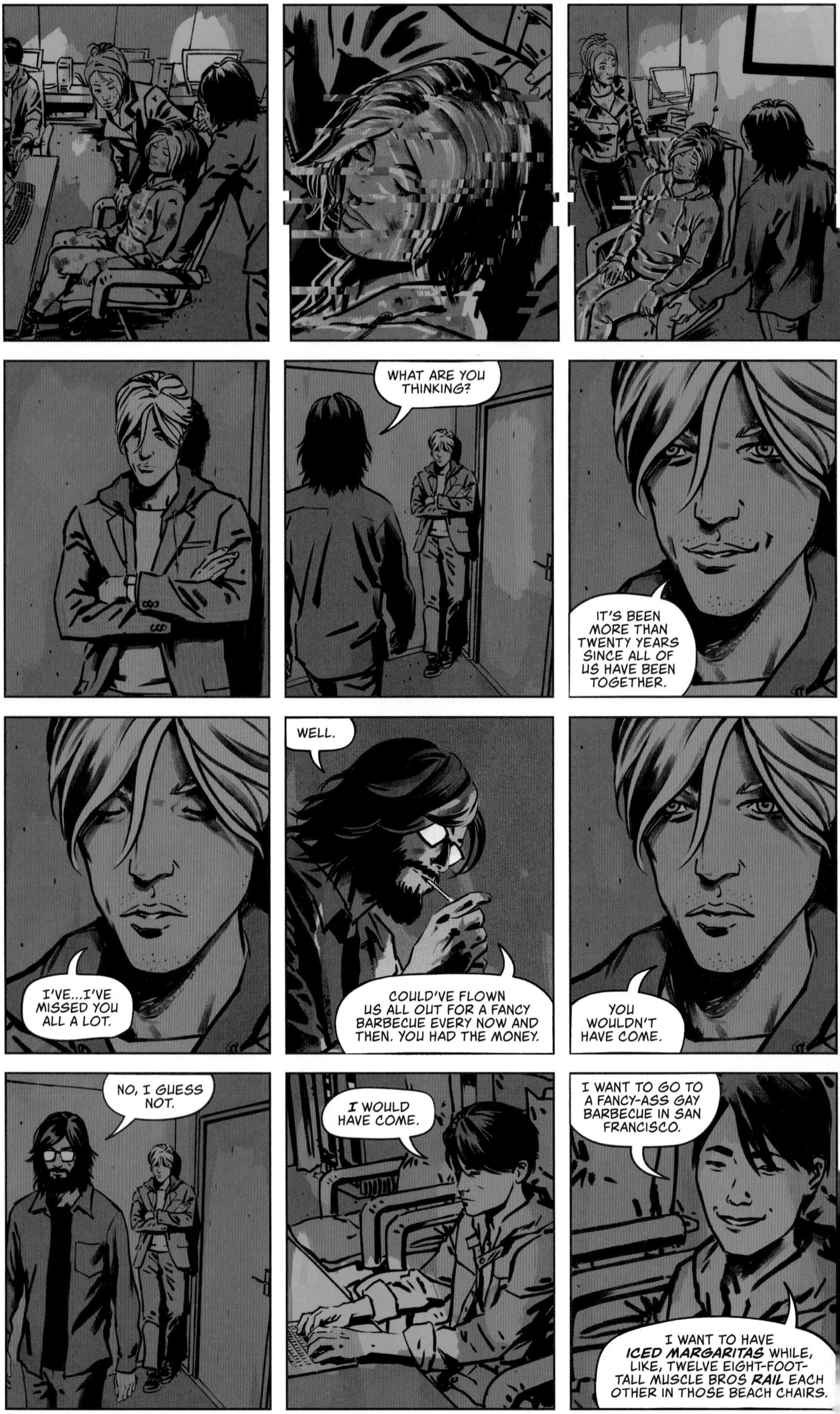

WHAT ARE YOU THINKING?
IT'S BEEN MORE THAN TWENTY YEARS SINCE ALL OF US HAVE BEEN TOGETHER.
I'VE...I'VE MISSED YOU ALL A LOT.
WELL.
COULD'VE FLOWN US ALL OUT FOR A FANCY BARBECUE EVERY NOW AND THEN. YOU HAD THE MONEY.
YOU WOULDN'T HAVE COME.
NO, I GUESS NOT.
I WOULD HAVE COME.
I WANT TO GO TO A FANCY-ASS GAY BARBECUE IN SAN FRANCISCO.
I WANT TO HAVE ICED MARGARITAS WHILE, LIKE, TWELVE EIGHT-FOOT-TALL MUSCLE BROS RAIL EACH OTHER IN THOSE BEACH CHAIRS.

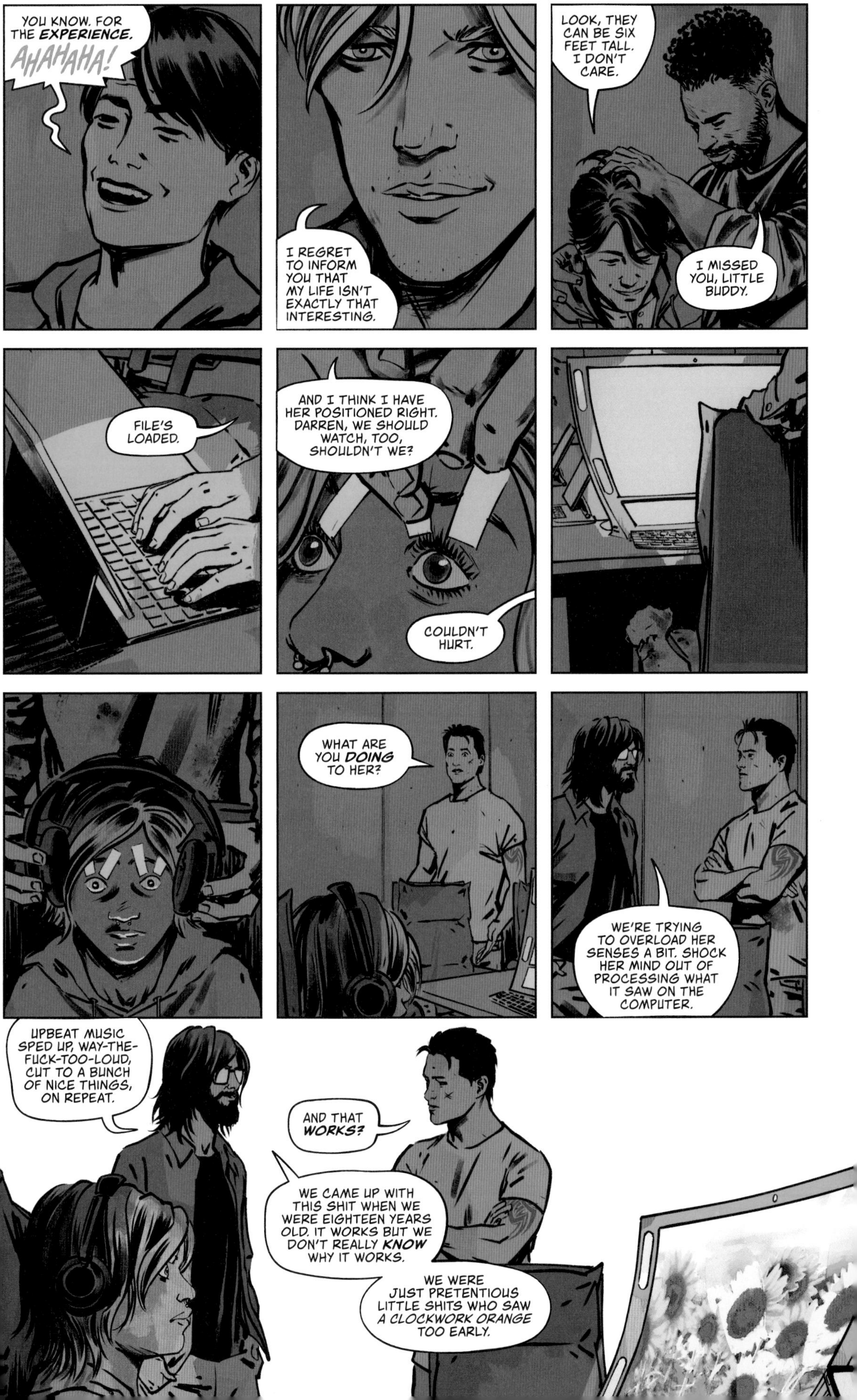
YOU KNOW. FOR THE EXPERIENCE.
AHAHAHA!
I REGRET TO INFORM YOU THAT MY LIFE ISN'T EXACTLY THAT INTERESTING.
LOOK, THEY CAN BE SIX FEET TALL. I DON'T CARE.
I MISSED YOU, LITTLE BUDDY.
FILE'S LOADED.
AND I THINK I HAVE HER POSITIONED RIGHT. DARREN, WE SHOULD WATCH, TOO, SHOULDN'T WE?
COULDN'T HURT.
WHAT ARE YOU DOING TO HER?
WE'RE TRYING TO OVERLOAD HER SENSES A BIT. SHOCK HER MIND OUT OF PROCESSING WHAT IT SAW ON THE COMPUTER.
UPBEAT MUSIC SPED UP, WAY-THE-FUCK-TOO-LOUD, CUT TO A BUNCH OF NICE THINGS, ON REPEAT.
AND THAT WORKS?
WE CAME UP WITH THIS SHIT WHEN WE WERE EIGHTEEN YEARS OLD. IT WORKS BUT WE DON'T REALLY KNOW WHY IT WORKS.
WE WERE JUST PRETENTIOUS LITTLE SHITS WHO SAW A CLOCKWORK ORANGE TOO EARLY.

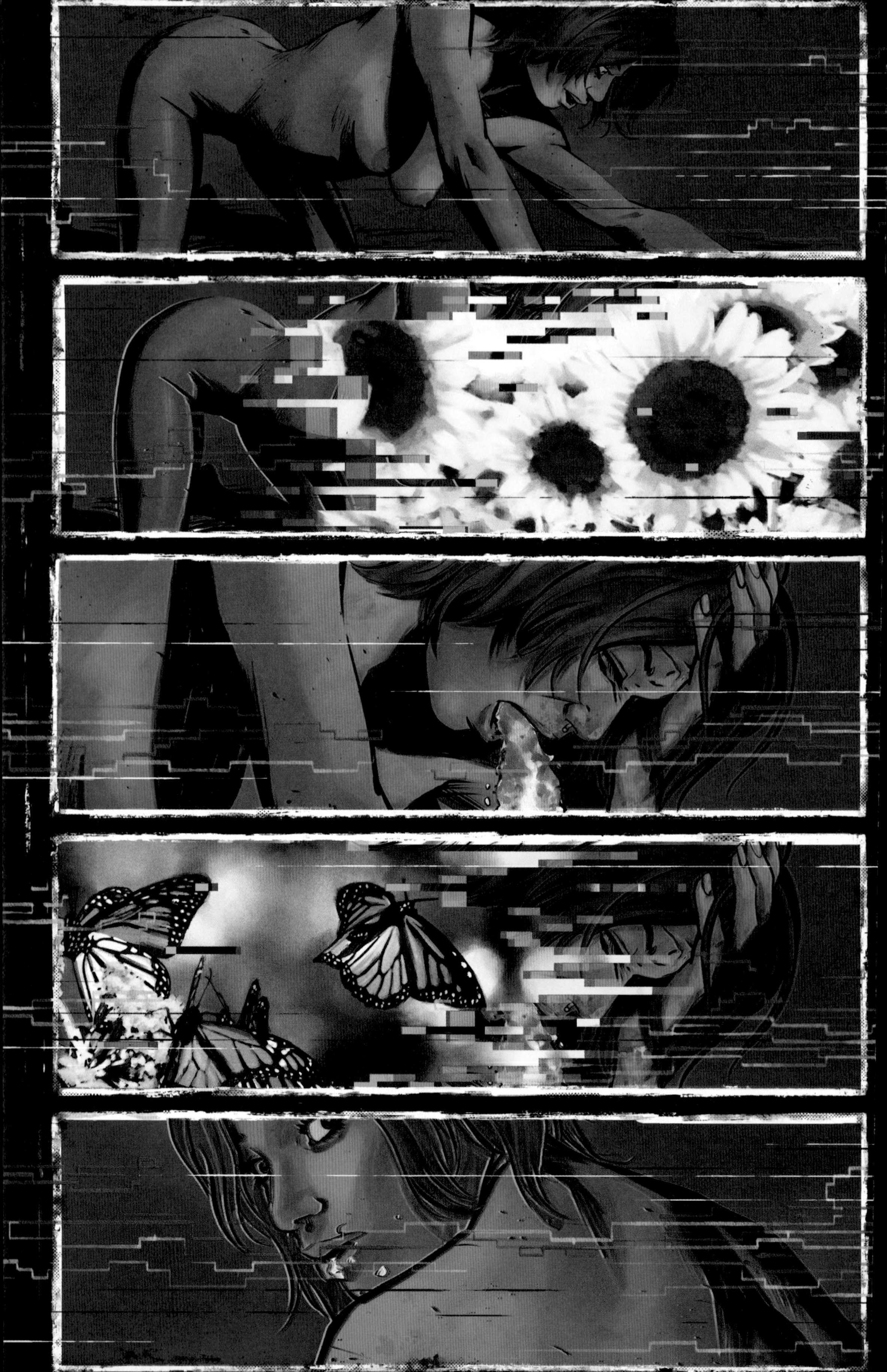

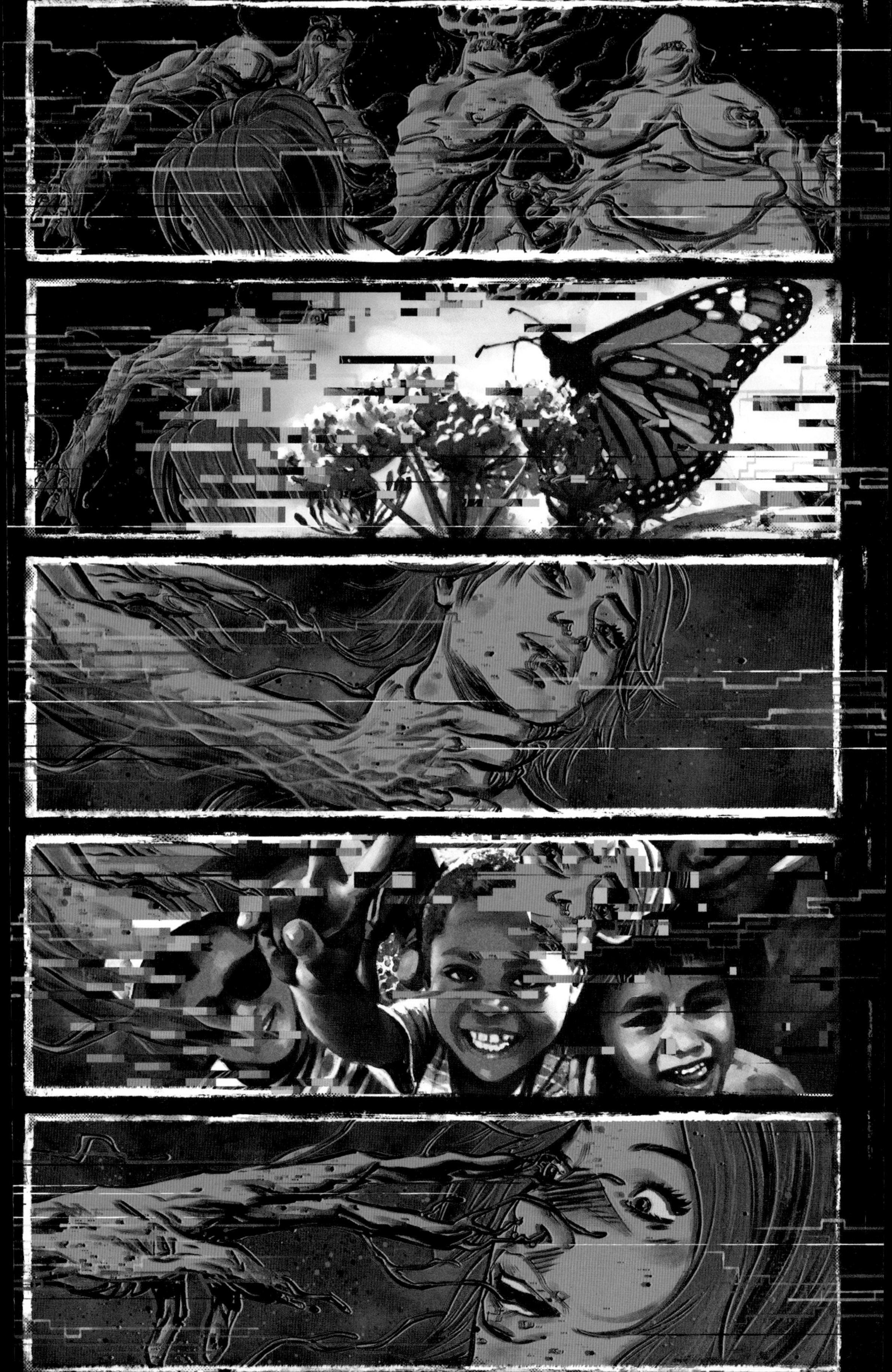

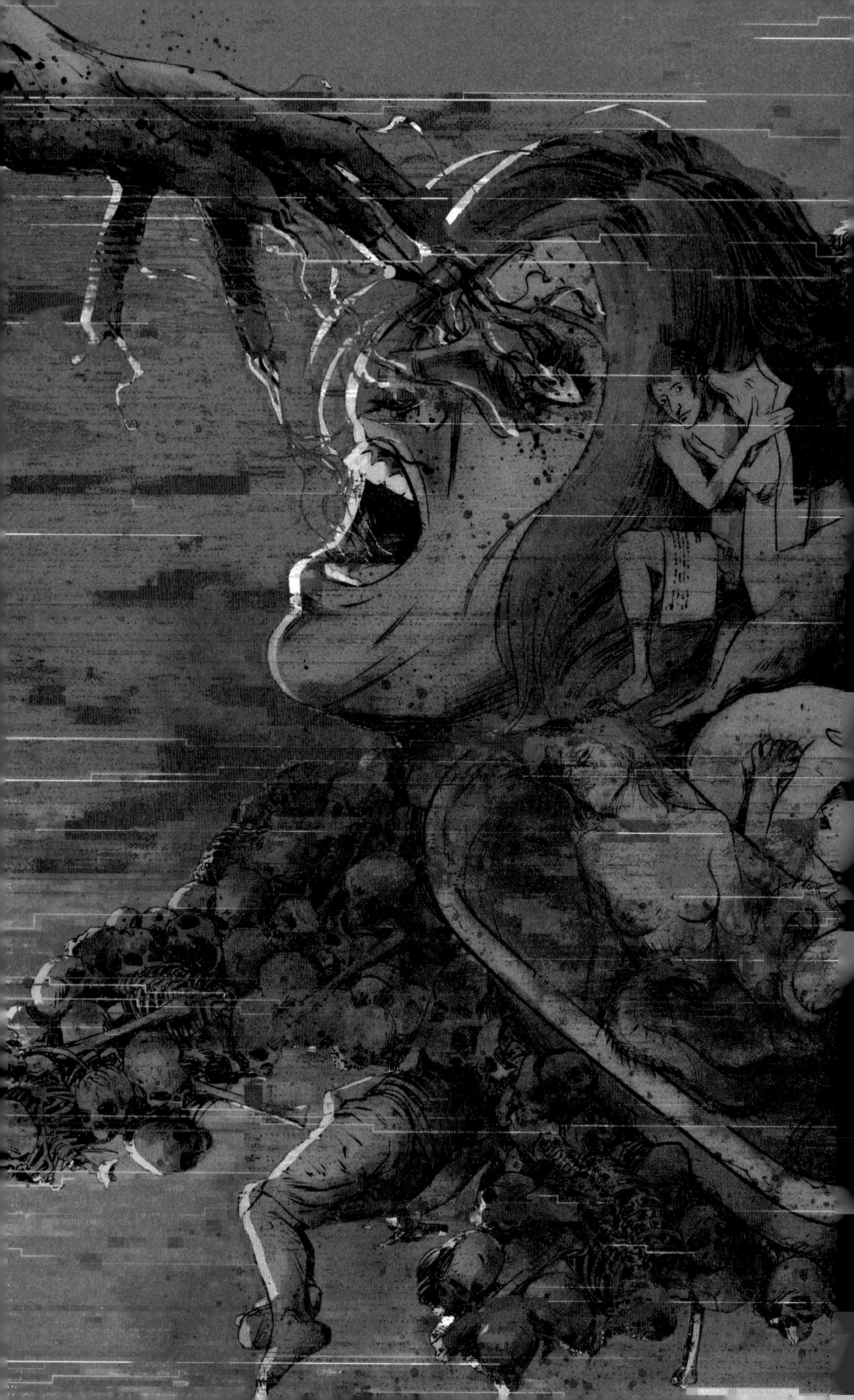

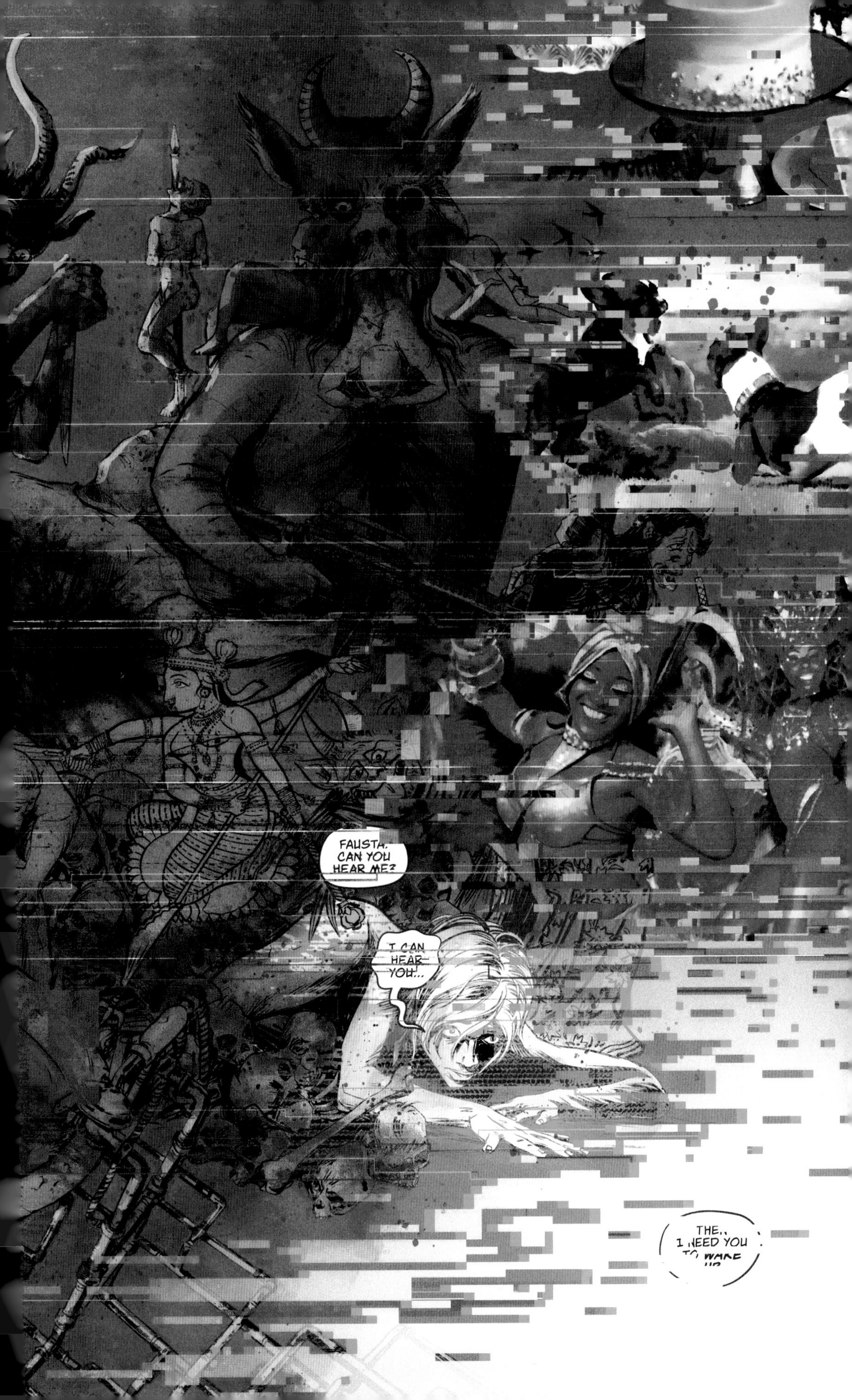
FAUSTA. CAN YOU HEAR ME?
I CAN HEAR YOU...
THE.. I NEED YOU

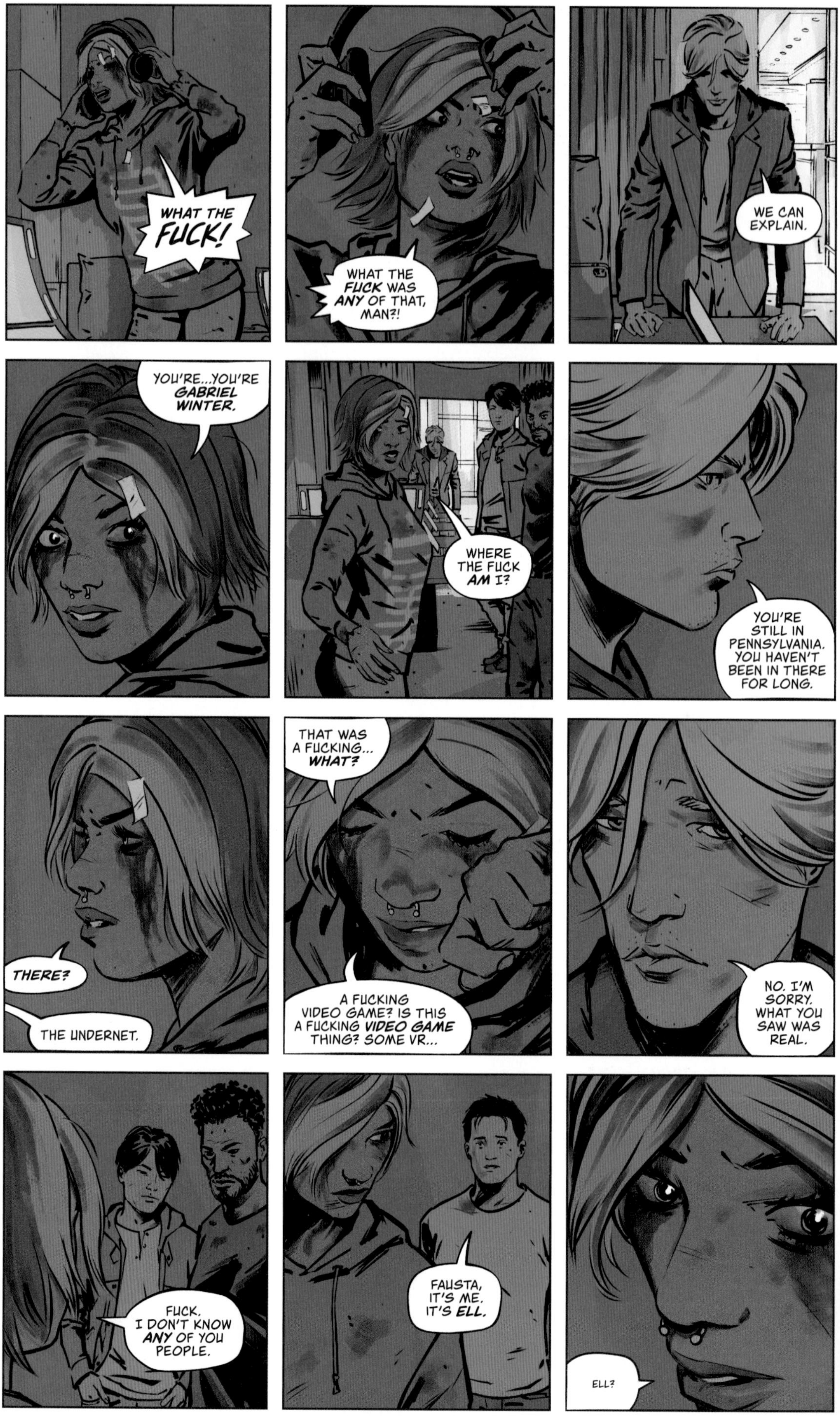
WHAT THE FUCK!
WHAT THE FUCK WAS ANY OF THAT, MAN?!
WE CAN EXPLAIN.
YOU'RE...YOU'RE GABRIEL WINTER.
WHERE THE FUCK AM I?
YOU'RE STILL IN PENNSYLVANIA. YOU HAVEN'T BEEN IN THERE FOR LONG.
THERE?
THE UNDERNET.
THAT WAS A FUCKING... WHAT?
A FUCKING VIDEO GAME? IS THIS A FUCKING VIDEO GAME THING? SOME VR...
NO. I'M SORRY. WHAT YOU SAW WAS REAL.
FUCK. I DON'T KNOW ANY OF YOU PEOPLE.
FAUSTA, IT'S ME. IT'S ELL.
ELL?

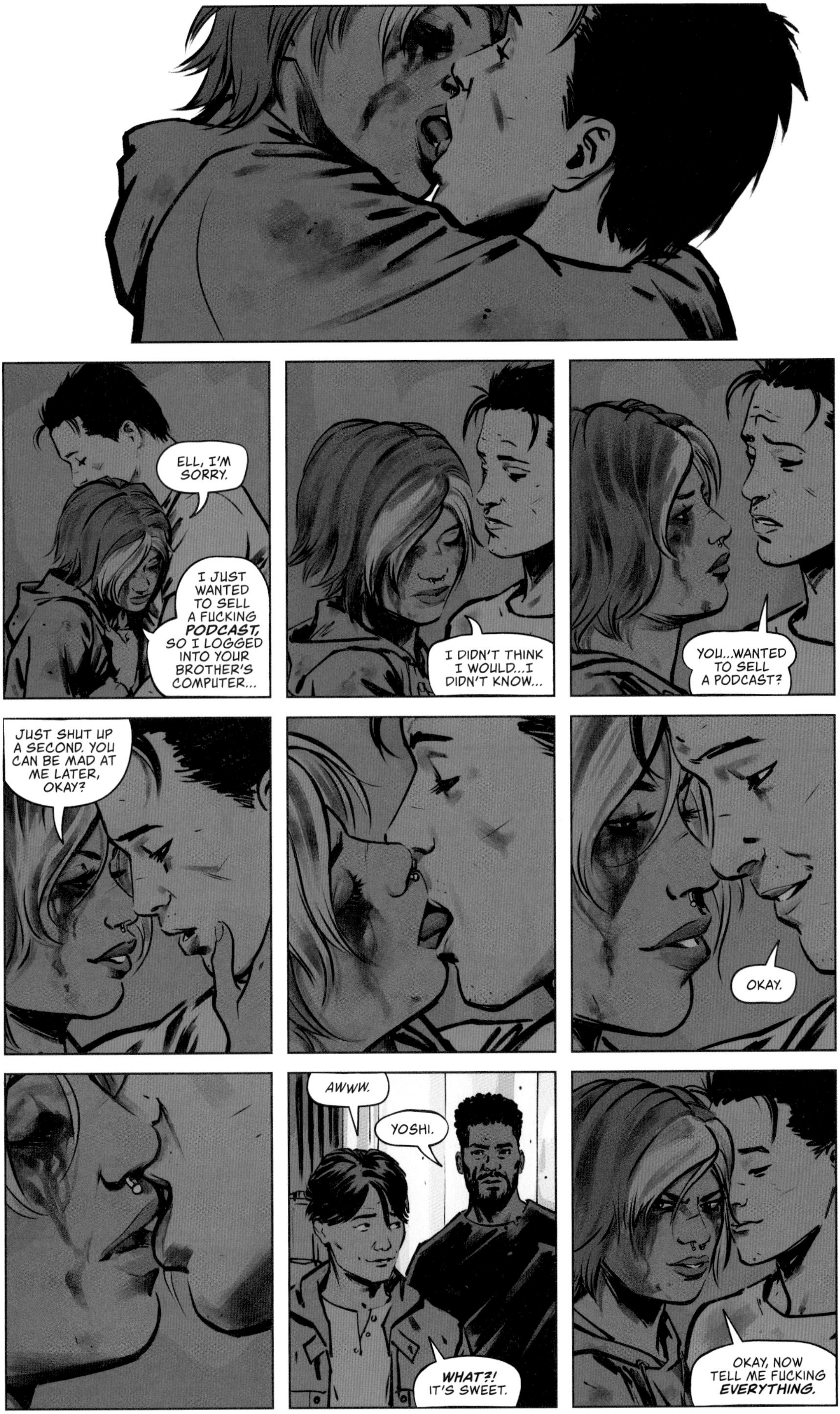
ELL, I'M SORRY.
I JUST WANTED TO SELL A FUCKING **PODCAST,** SO I LOGGED INTO YOUR BROTHER'S COMPUTER...
I DIDN'T THINK I WOULD...I DIDN'T KNOW...
YOU...WANTED TO SELL A PODCAST?
JUST SHUT UP A SECOND. YOU CAN BE MAD AT ME LATER, OKAY?
OKAY.
AWWW.
YOSHI.
WHAT?! IT'S SWEET.
OKAY, NOW TELL ME FUCKING ***EVERYTHING.***

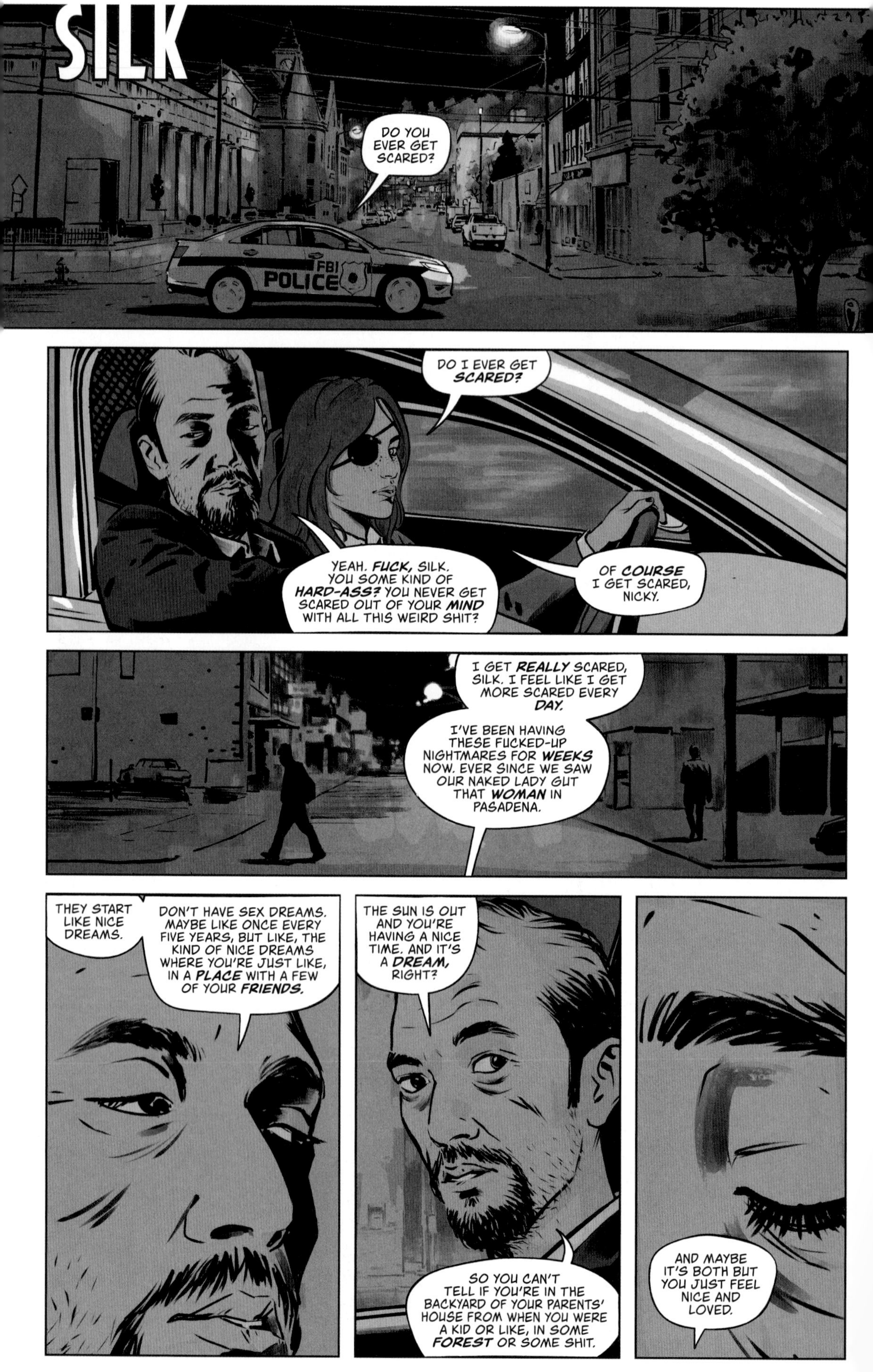
SILK
DO YOU EVER GET SCARED?
FBI POLICE
DO I EVER GET SCARED?
YEAH. FUCK, SILK. YOU SOME KIND OF HARD-ASS? YOU NEVER GET SCARED OUT OF YOUR MIND WITH ALL THIS WEIRD SHIT?
OF COURSE I GET SCARED, NICKY.
I GET REALLY SCARED, SILK. I FEEL LIKE I GET MORE SCARED EVERY DAY.
I'VE BEEN HAVING THESE FUCKED-UP NIGHTMARES FOR WEEKS NOW. EVER SINCE WE SAW OUR NAKED LADY GUT THAT WOMAN IN PASADENA.
THEY START LIKE NICE DREAMS.
DON'T HAVE SEX DREAMS. MAYBE LIKE ONCE EVERY FIVE YEARS, BUT LIKE, THE KIND OF NICE DREAMS WHERE YOU'RE JUST LIKE, IN A PLACE WITH A FEW OF YOUR FRIENDS.
THE SUN IS OUT AND YOU'RE HAVING A NICE TIME. AND IT'S A DREAM, RIGHT?
SO YOU CAN'T TELL IF YOU'RE IN THE BACKYARD OF YOUR PARENTS' HOUSE FROM WHEN YOU WERE A KID OR LIKE, IN SOME FOREST OR SOME SHIT.
AND MAYBE IT'S BOTH BUT YOU JUST FEEL NICE AND LOVED.

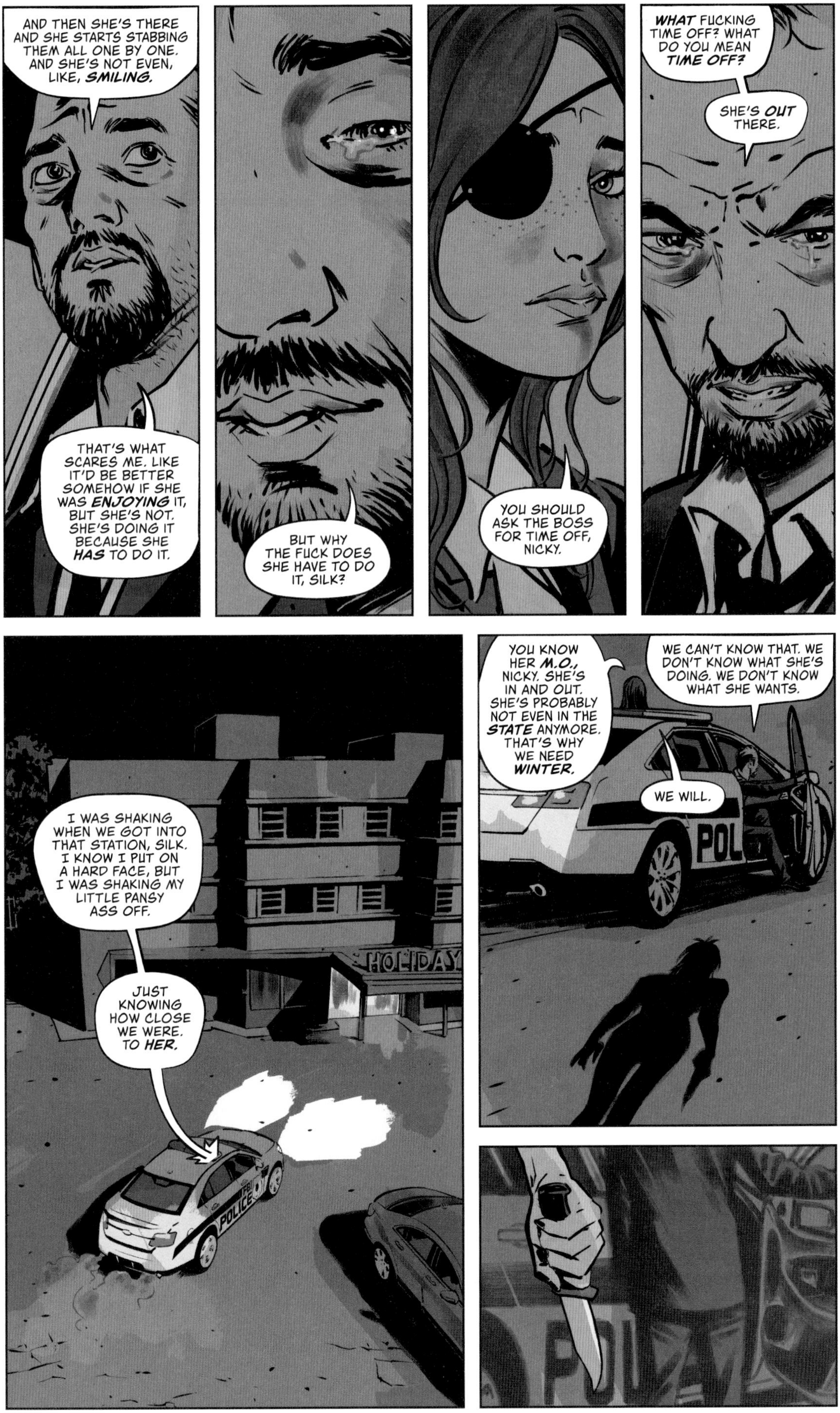

AND THEN SHE'S THERE AND SHE STARTS STABBING THEM ALL ONE BY ONE. AND SHE'S NOT EVEN, LIKE, SMILING.
THAT'S WHAT SCARES ME. LIKE IT'D BE BETTER SOMEHOW IF SHE WAS ENJOYING IT, BUT SHE'S NOT. SHE'S DOING IT BECAUSE SHE HAS TO DO IT.
BUT WHY THE FUCK DOES SHE HAVE TO DO IT, SILK?
YOU SHOULD ASK THE BOSS FOR TIME OFF, NICKY.
WHAT FUCKING TIME OFF? WHAT DO YOU MEAN TIME OFF?
SHE'S OUT THERE.
I WAS SHAKING WHEN WE GOT INTO THAT STATION, SILK. I KNOW I PUT ON A HARD FACE, BUT I WAS SHAKING MY LITTLE PANSY ASS OFF.
JUST KNOWING HOW CLOSE WE WERE. TO HER.
HOLIDAY
POLICE
YOU KNOW HER M.O., NICKY. SHE'S IN AND OUT. SHE'S PROBABLY NOT EVEN IN THE STATE ANYMORE. THAT'S WHY WE NEED WINTER.
WE CAN'T KNOW THAT. WE DON'T KNOW WHAT SHE'S DOING. WE DON'T KNOW WHAT SHE WANTS.
WE WILL.
POL

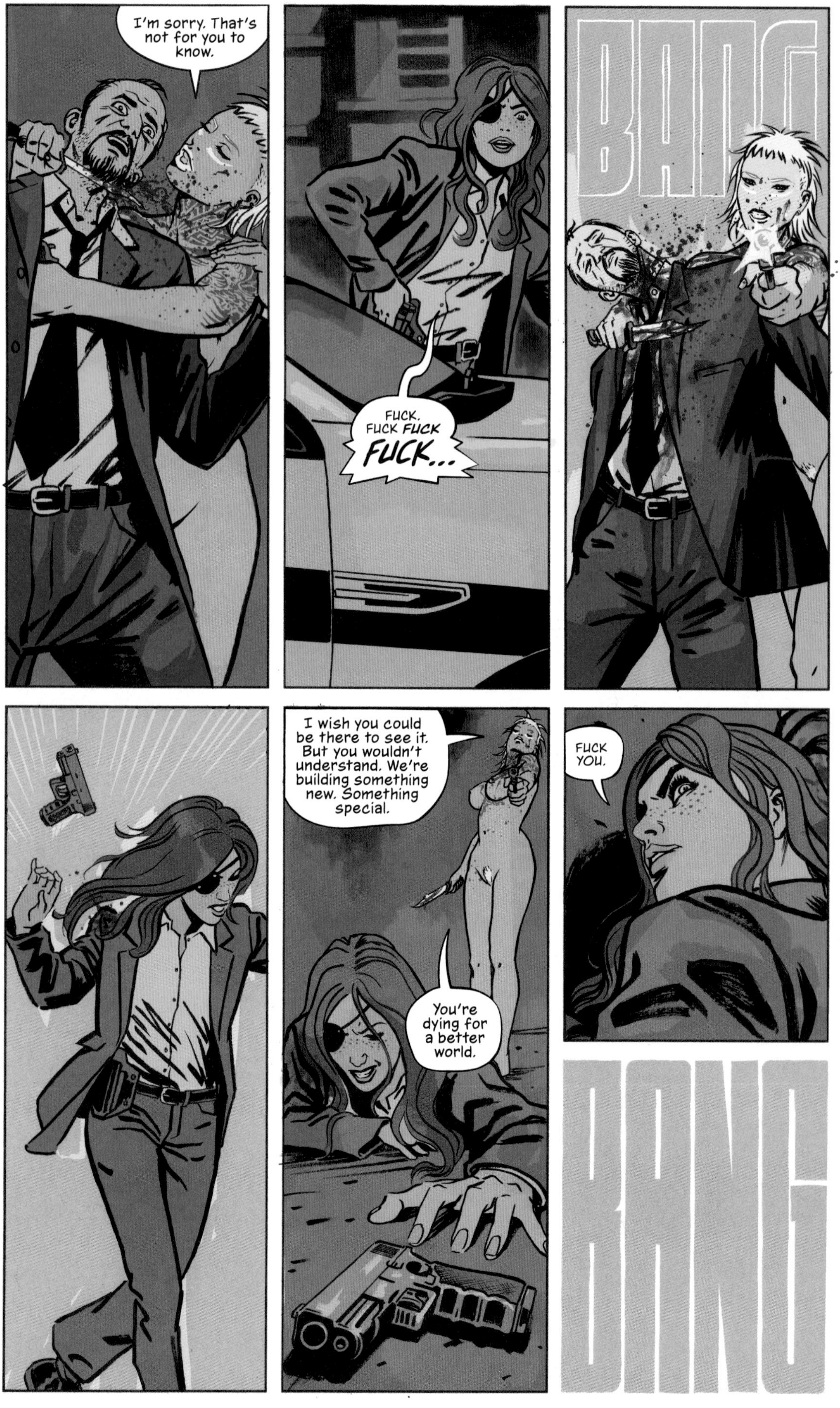
I'm sorry. That's not for you to know.
FUCK. FUCK FUCK FUCK...
BANG
I wish you could be there to see it. But you wouldn't understand. We're building something new. Something special.
You're dying for a better world.
FUCK YOU.
BANG

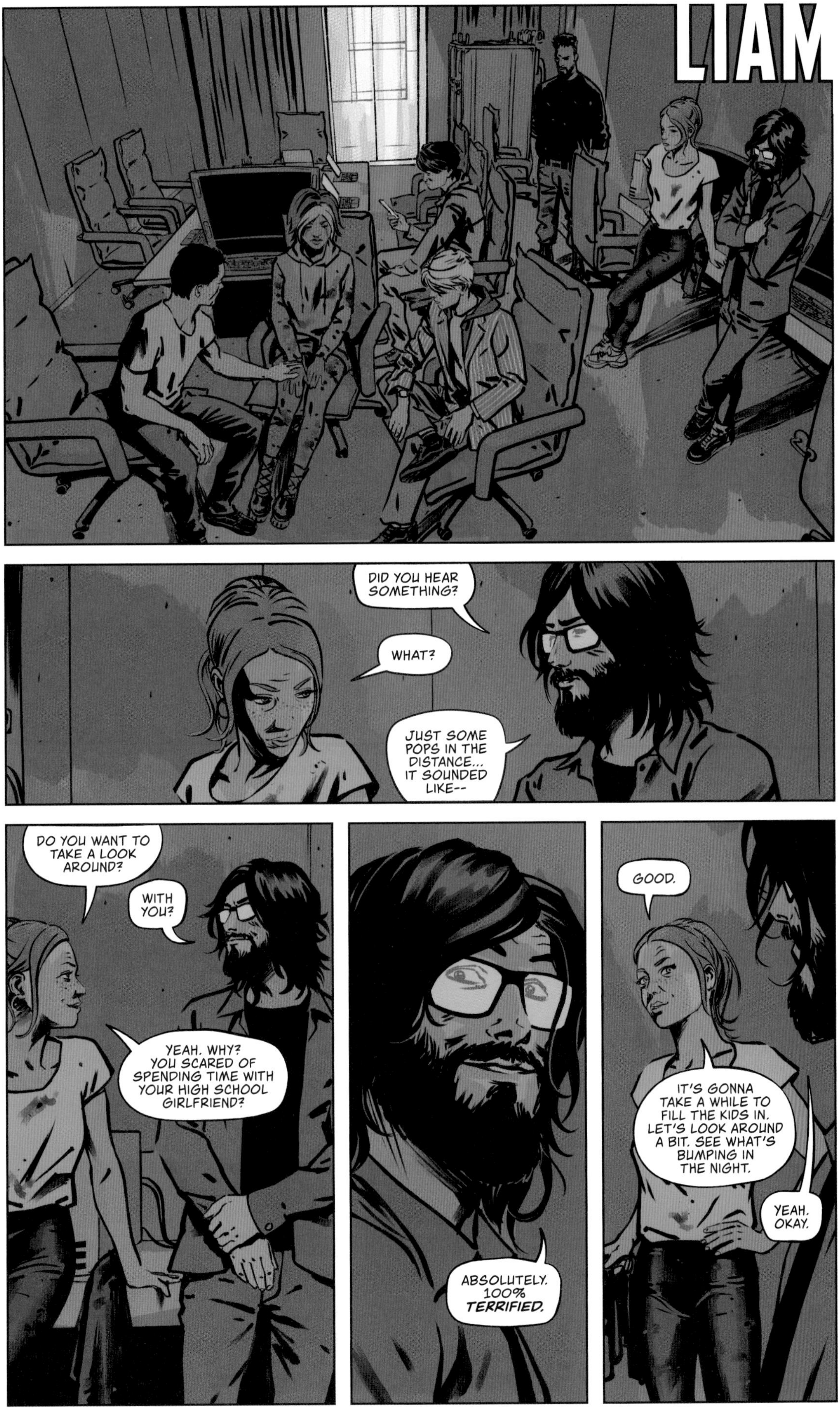
LIAM
DID YOU HEAR SOMETHING?
WHAT?
JUST SOME POPS IN THE DISTANCE... IT SOUNDED LIKE--
DO YOU WANT TO TAKE A LOOK AROUND?
WITH YOU?
YEAH. WHY? YOU SCARED OF SPENDING TIME WITH YOUR HIGH SCHOOL GIRLFRIEND?
ABSOLUTELY. 100% *TERRIFIED.*
GOOD.
IT'S GONNA TAKE A WHILE TO FILL THE KIDS IN. LET'S LOOK AROUND A BIT. SEE WHAT'S BUMPING IN THE NIGHT.
YEAH. OKAY.

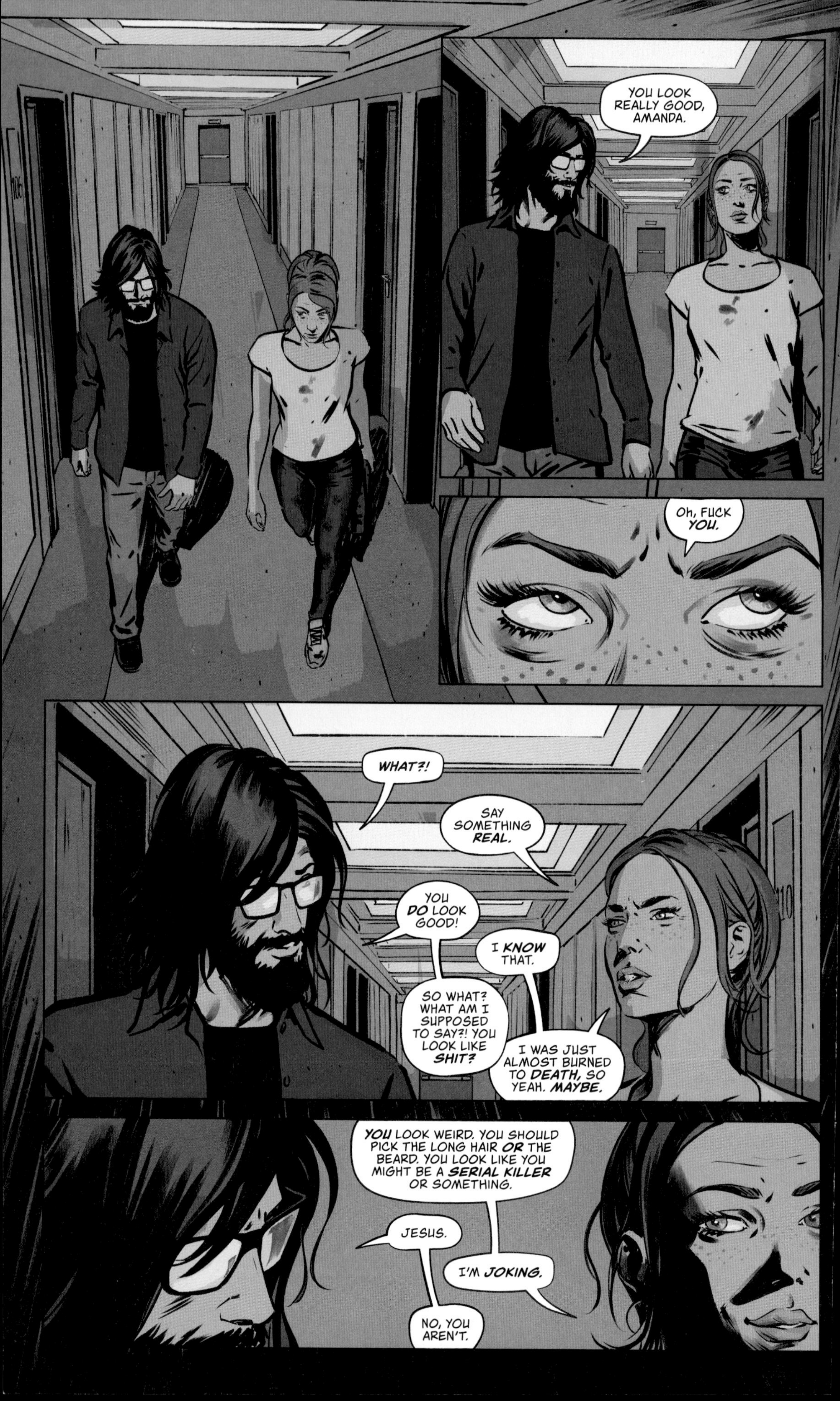
YOU LOOK REALLY GOOD, AMANDA.
Oh, FUCK YOU.
WHAT?!
SAY SOMETHING REAL.
YOU DO LOOK GOOD!
I KNOW THAT.
SO WHAT? WHAT AM I SUPPOSED TO SAY?! YOU LOOK LIKE SHIT?
I WAS JUST ALMOST BURNED TO DEATH, SO YEAH. MAYBE.
YOU LOOK WEIRD. YOU SHOULD PICK THE LONG HAIR OR THE BEARD. YOU LOOK LIKE YOU MIGHT BE A SERIAL KILLER OR SOMETHING.
JESUS.
I'M JOKING.
NO, YOU AREN'T.

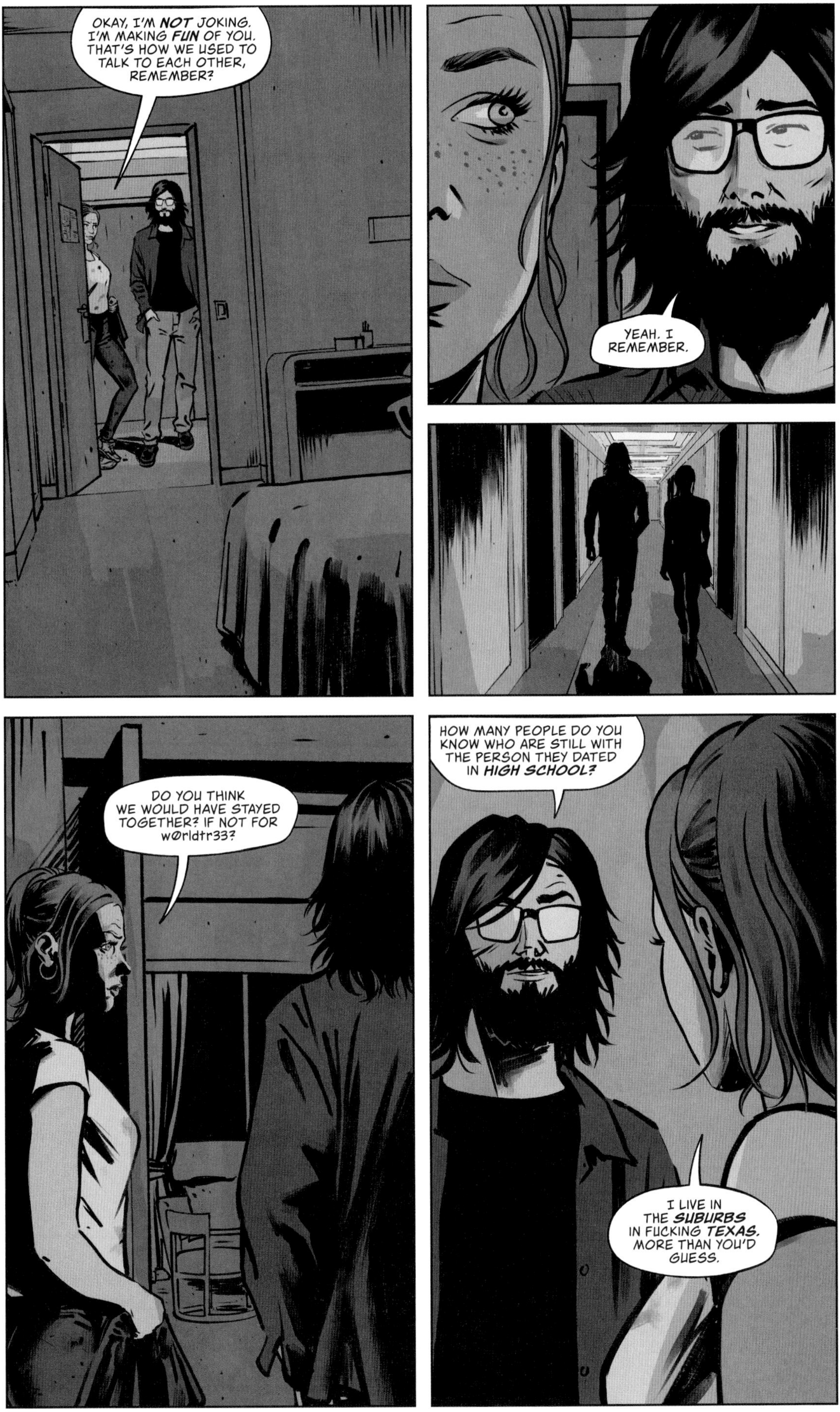
OKAY, I'M **NOT** JOKING. I'M MAKING **FUN** OF YOU. THAT'S HOW WE USED TO TALK TO EACH OTHER, REMEMBER?
YEAH. I REMEMBER.
DO YOU THINK WE WOULD HAVE STAYED TOGETHER? IF NOT FOR w@rldtr33?
HOW MANY PEOPLE DO YOU KNOW WHO ARE STILL WITH THE PERSON THEY DATED IN **HIGH SCHOOL?**
I LIVE IN THE **SUBURBS** IN FUCKING **TEXAS.** MORE THAN YOU'D GUESS.

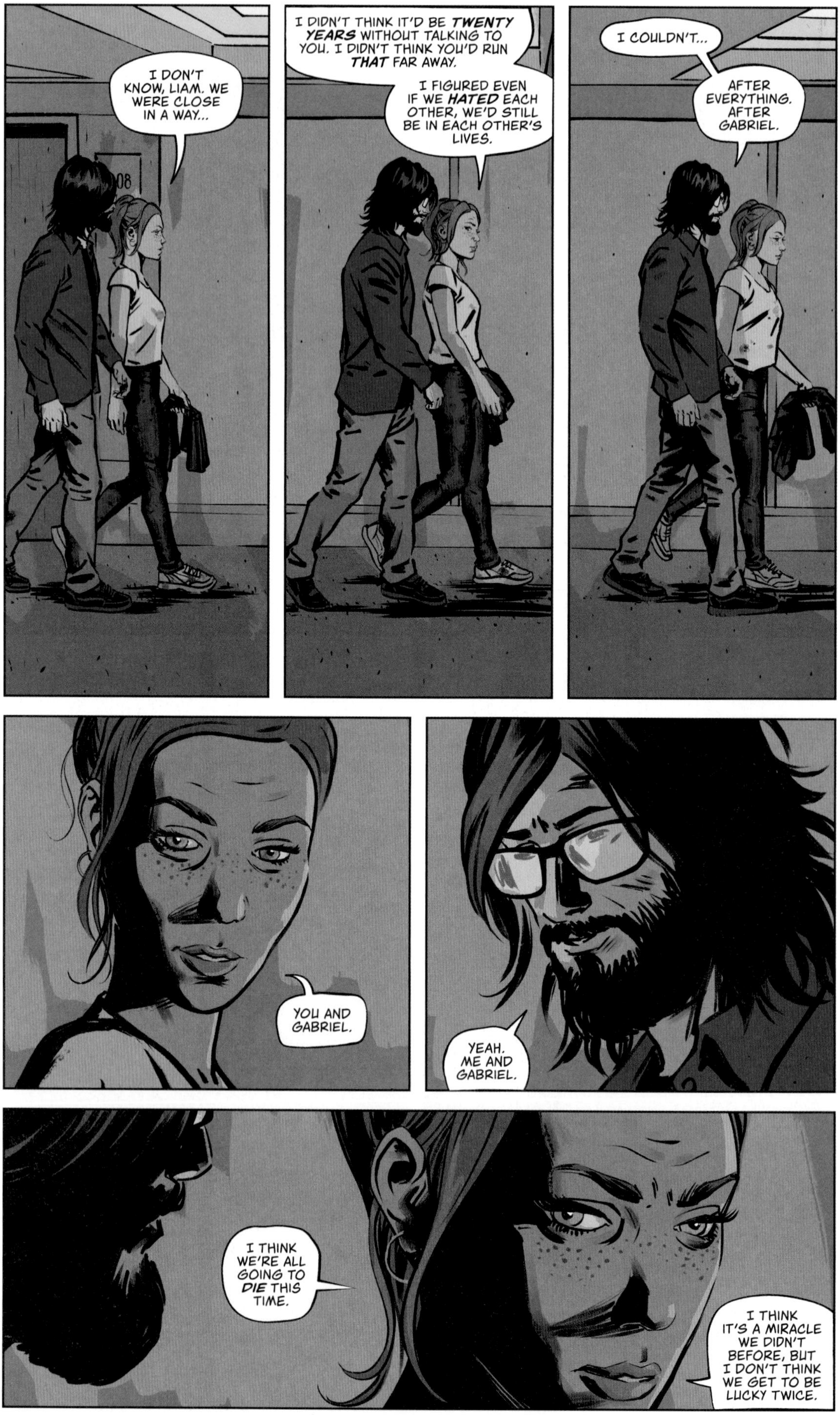
I DON'T KNOW, LIAM. WE WERE CLOSE IN A WAY...
I DIDN'T THINK IT'D BE TWENTY YEARS WITHOUT TALKING TO YOU. I DIDN'T THINK YOU'D RUN THAT FAR AWAY.
I FIGURED EVEN IF WE HATED EACH OTHER, WE'D STILL BE IN EACH OTHER'S LIVES.
I COULDN'T...
AFTER EVERYTHING. AFTER GABRIEL.
YOU AND GABRIEL.
YEAH. ME AND GABRIEL.
I THINK WE'RE ALL GOING TO DIE THIS TIME.
I THINK IT'S A MIRACLE WE DIDN'T BEFORE, BUT I DON'T THINK WE GET TO BE LUCKY TWICE.

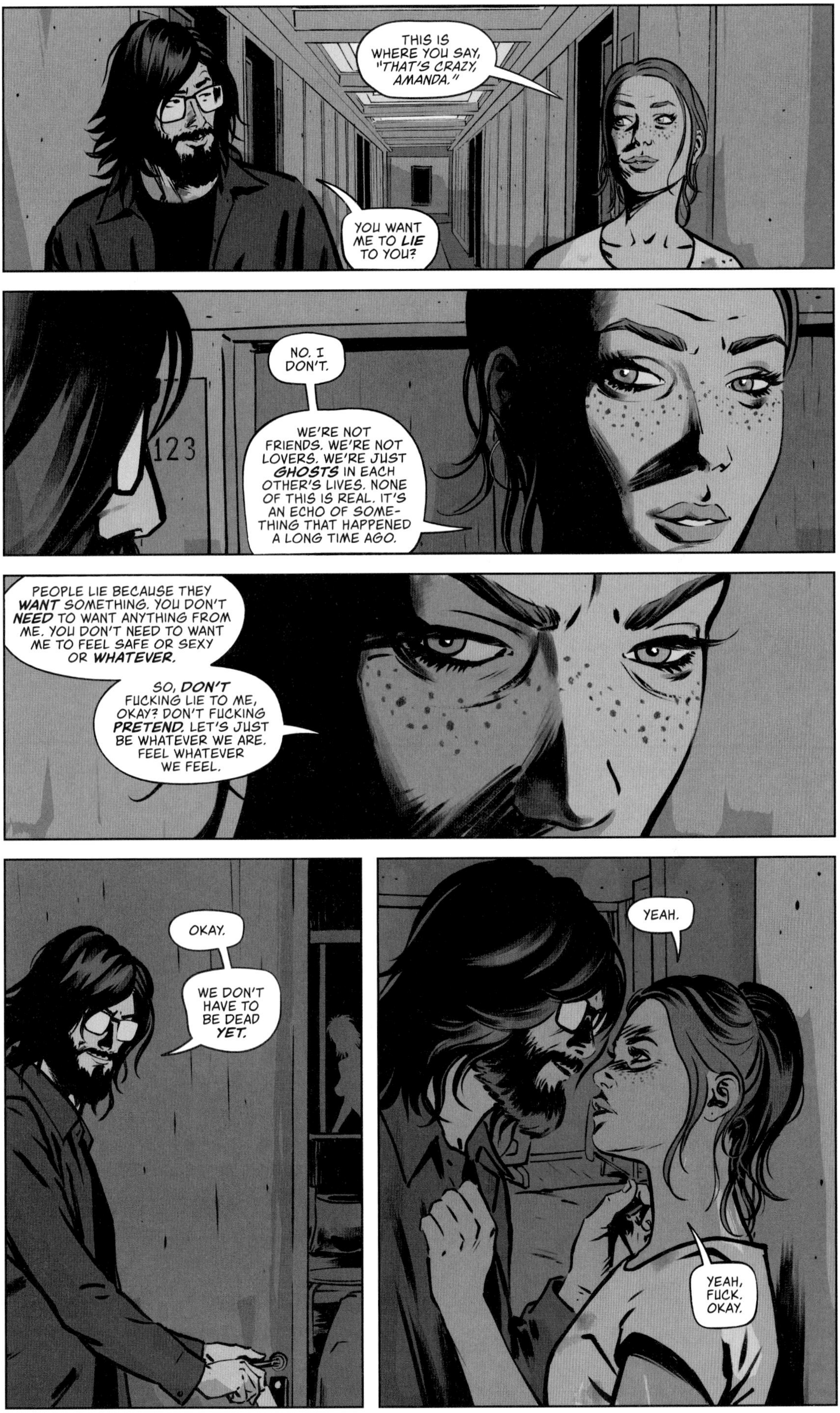
THIS IS WHERE YOU SAY, "THAT'S CRAZY, AMANDA."
YOU WANT ME TO LIE TO YOU?
NO. I DON'T.
WE'RE NOT FRIENDS. WE'RE NOT LOVERS. WE'RE JUST GHOSTS IN EACH OTHER'S LIVES. NONE OF THIS IS REAL. IT'S AN ECHO OF SOME-THING THAT HAPPENED A LONG TIME AGO.
123
PEOPLE LIE BECAUSE THEY WANT SOMETHING. YOU DON'T NEED TO WANT ANYTHING FROM ME. YOU DON'T NEED TO WANT ME TO FEEL SAFE OR SEXY OR WHATEVER.
SO, DON'T FUCKING LIE TO ME, OKAY? DON'T FUCKING PRETEND. LET'S JUST BE WHATEVER WE ARE. FEEL WHATEVER WE FEEL.
OKAY.
WE DON'T HAVE TO BE DEAD YET.
YEAH.
YEAH, FUCK. OKAY.

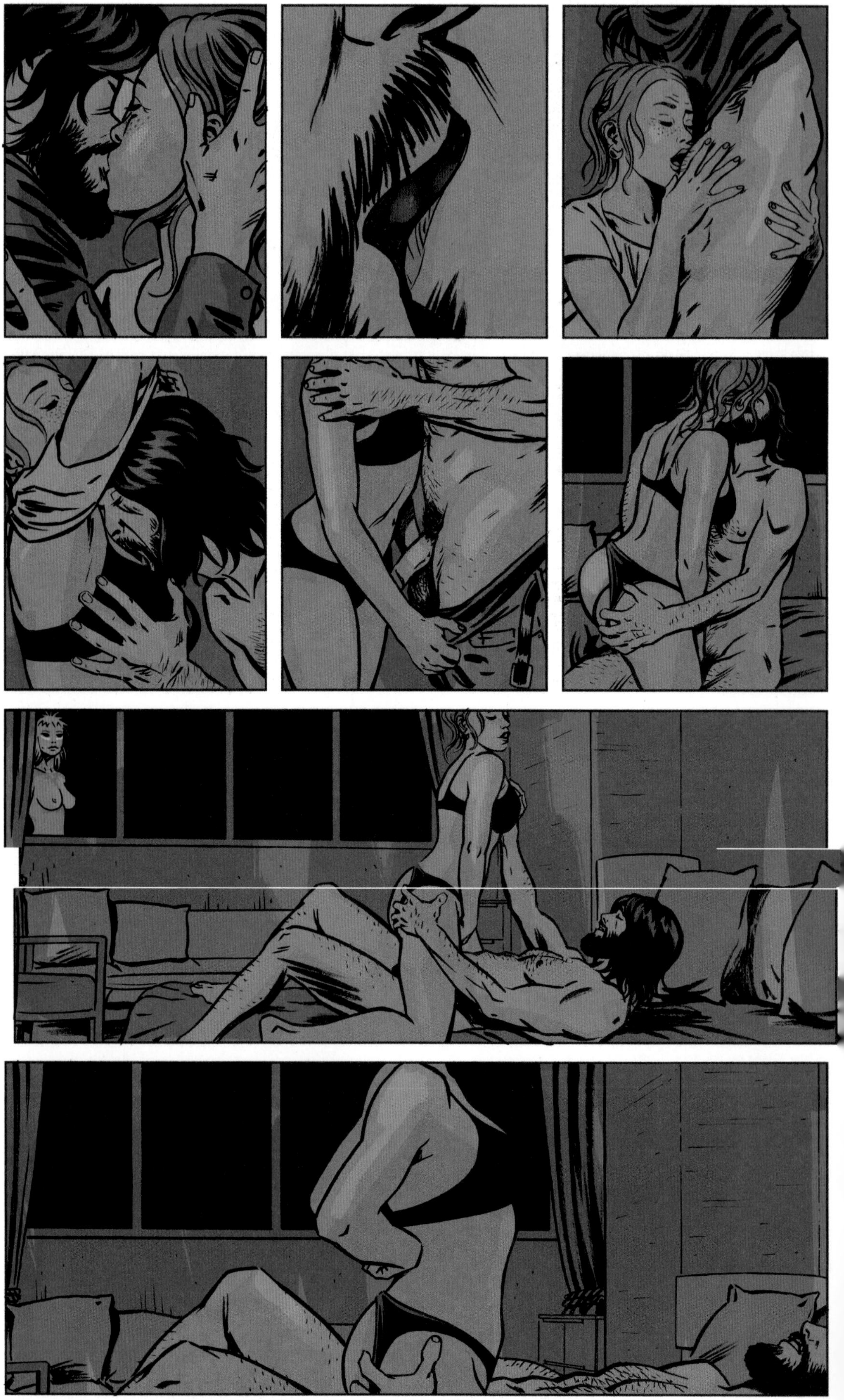

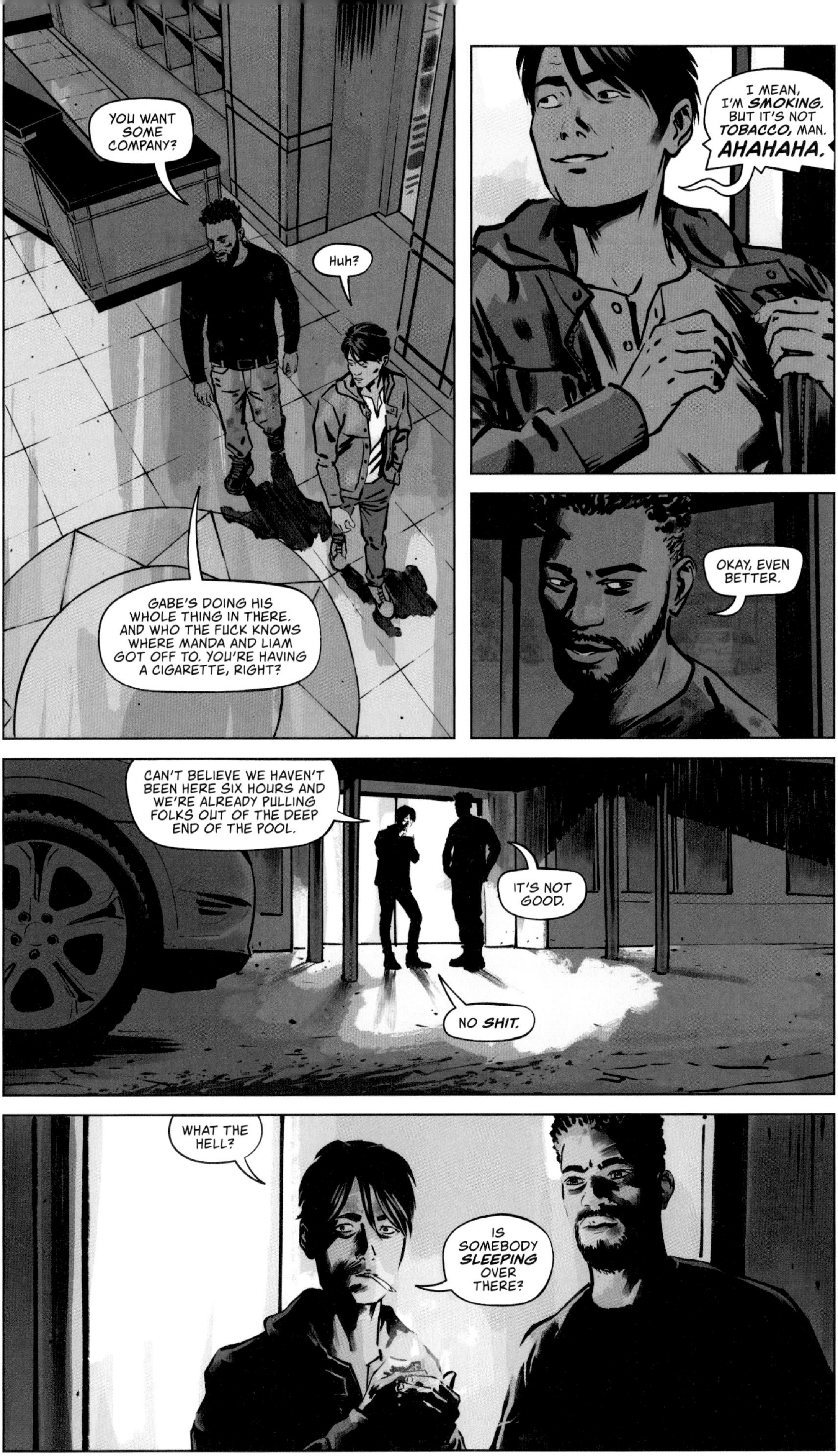
YOU WANT SOME COMPANY?
Huh?
GABE'S DOING HIS WHOLE THING IN THERE. AND WHO THE FUCK KNOWS WHERE MANDA AND LIAM GOT OFF TO. YOU'RE HAVING A CIGARETTE, RIGHT?
I MEAN, I'M SMOKING. BUT IT'S NOT TOBACCO, MAN. AHAHAHA.
OKAY, EVEN BETTER.
CAN'T BELIEVE WE HAVEN'T BEEN HERE SIX HOURS AND WE'RE ALREADY PULLING FOLKS OUT OF THE DEEP END OF THE POOL.
IT'S NOT GOOD.
NO SHIT.
WHAT THE HELL?
IS SOMEBODY SLEEPING OVER THERE?

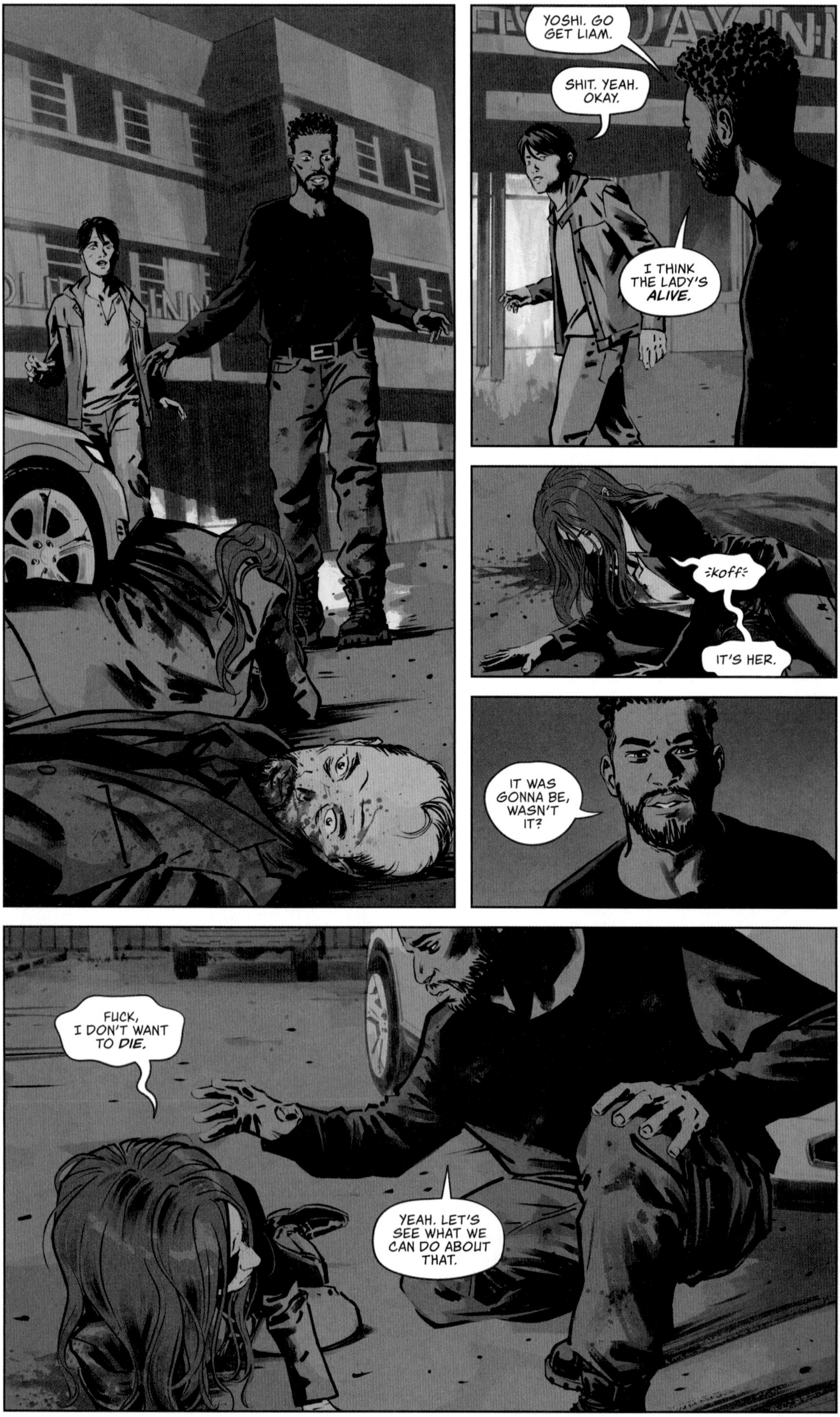
YOSHI. GO GET LIAM.
SHIT. YEAH. OKAY.
I THINK THE LADY'S ALIVE.
koff
IT'S HER.
IT WAS GONNA BE, WASN'T IT?
FUCK, I DON'T WANT TO DIE.
YEAH. LET'S SEE WHAT WE CAN DO ABOUT THAT.

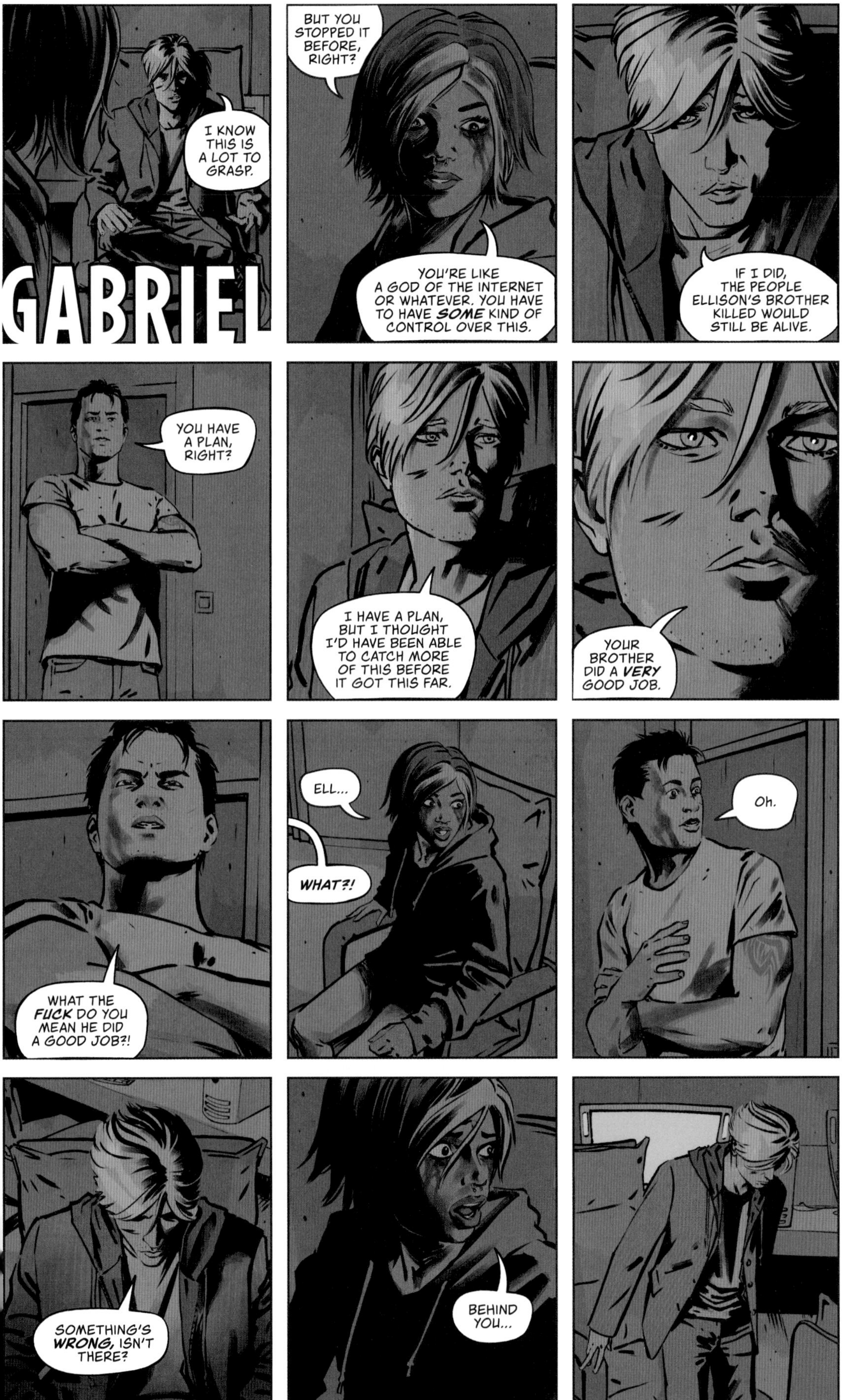

I KNOW THIS IS A LOT TO GRASP.
GABRIEL
BUT YOU STOPPED IT BEFORE, RIGHT?
YOU'RE LIKE A GOD OF THE INTERNET OR WHATEVER. YOU HAVE TO HAVE SOME KIND OF CONTROL OVER THIS.
IF I DID, THE PEOPLE ELLISON'S BROTHER KILLED WOULD STILL BE ALIVE.
YOU HAVE A PLAN, RIGHT?
I HAVE A PLAN, BUT I THOUGHT I'D HAVE BEEN ABLE TO CATCH MORE OF THIS BEFORE IT GOT THIS FAR.
YOUR BROTHER DID A VERY GOOD JOB.
WHAT THE FUCK DO YOU MEAN HE DID A GOOD JOB?!
ELL...
WHAT?!
Oh.
SOMETHING'S WRONG, ISN'T THERE?
BEHIND YOU...

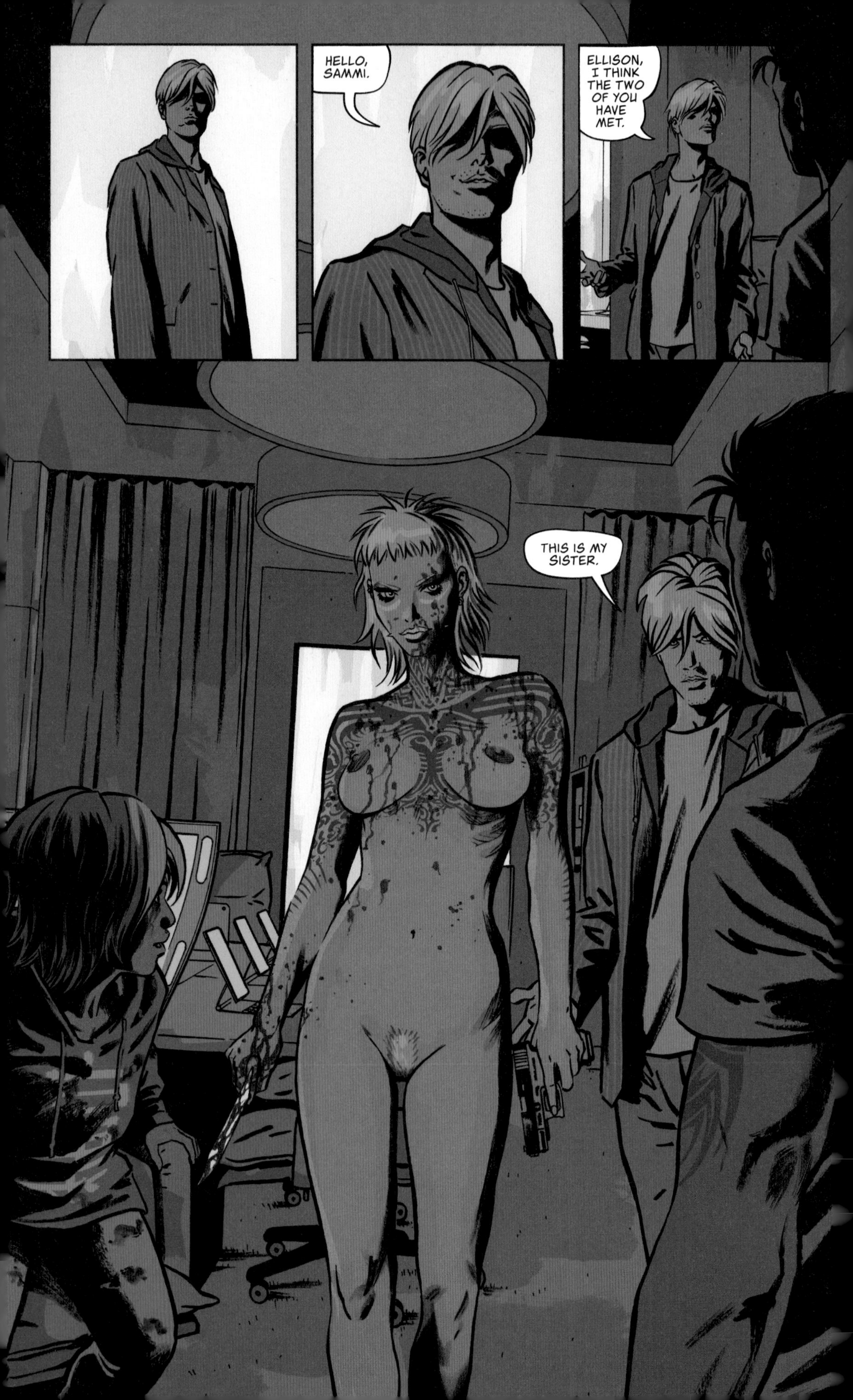
HELLO, SAMMI.
ELLISON, I THINK THE TWO OF YOU HAVE MET.
THIS IS MY SISTER.

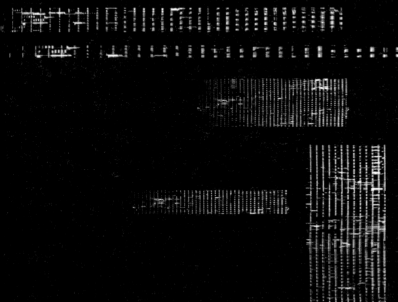

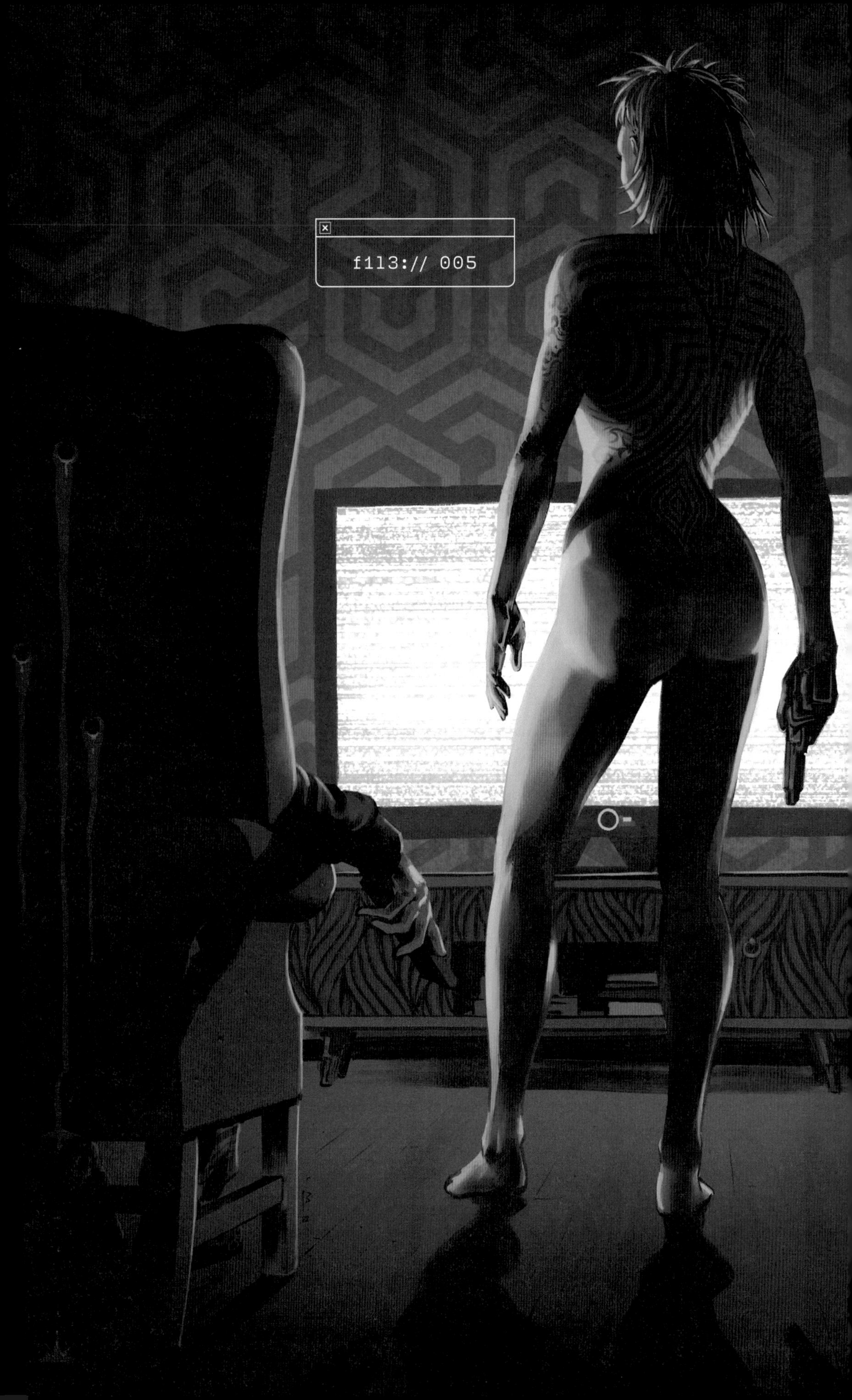
f113:// 005

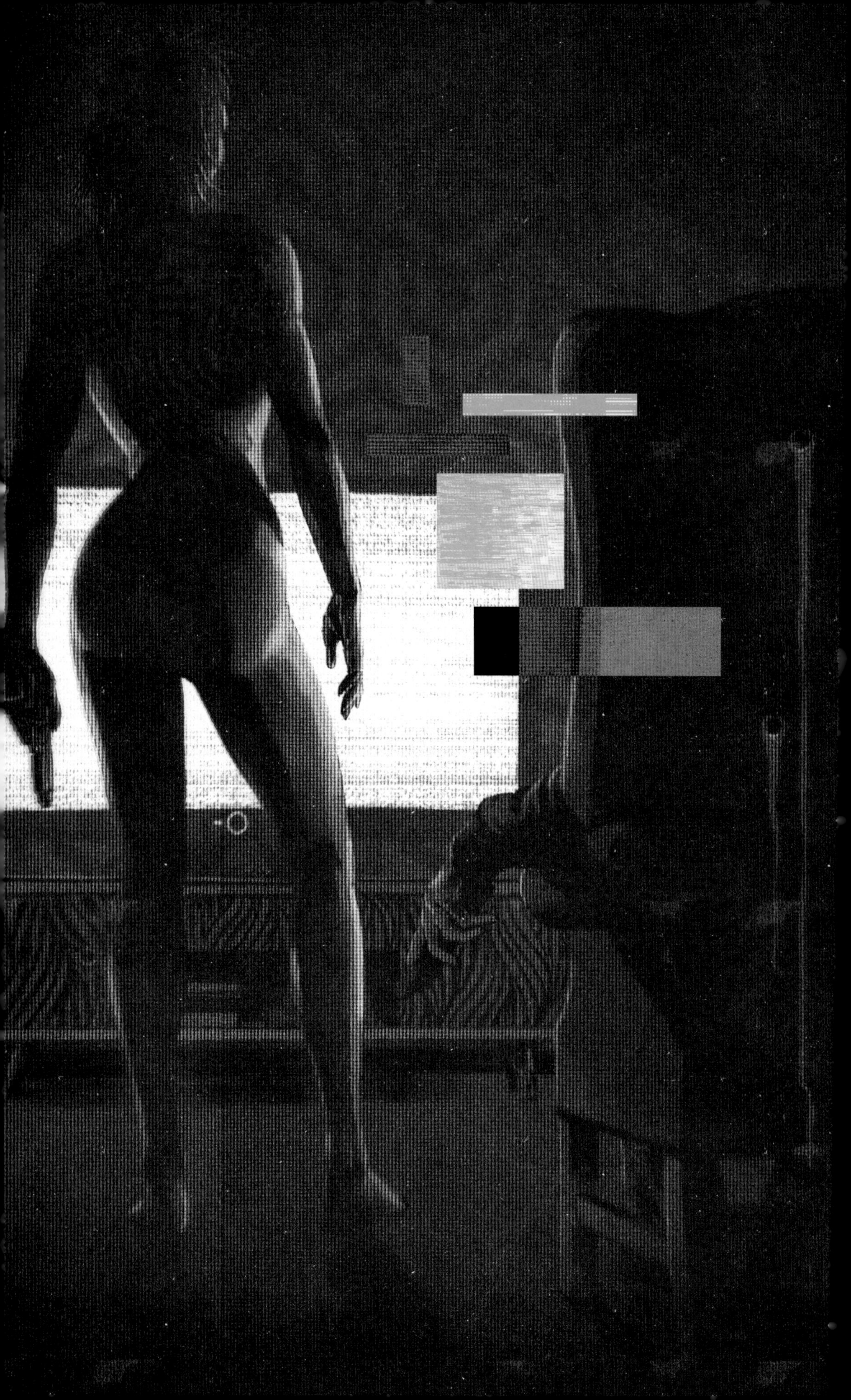

2049

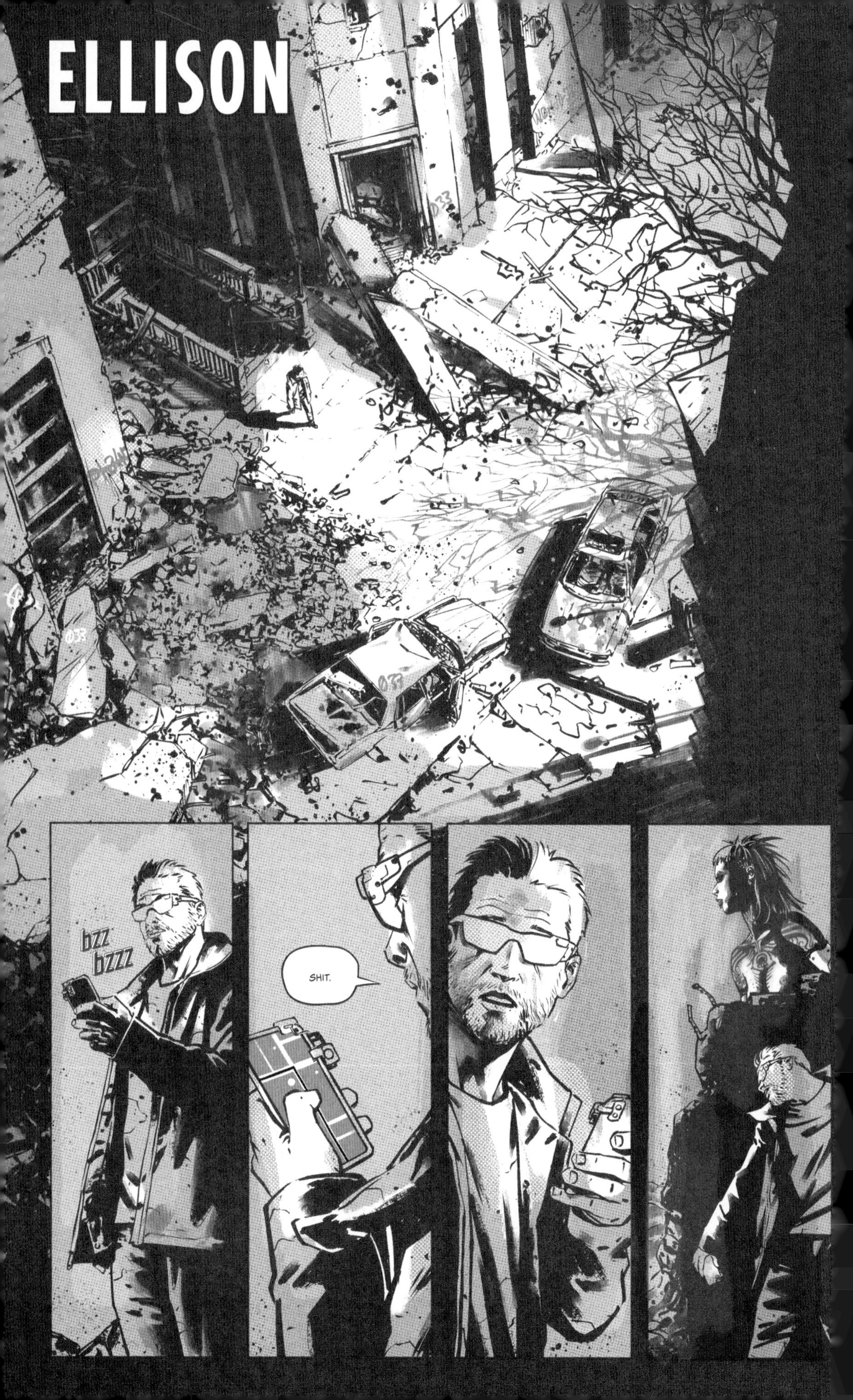
ELLISON
bzz bzzz
SHIT.

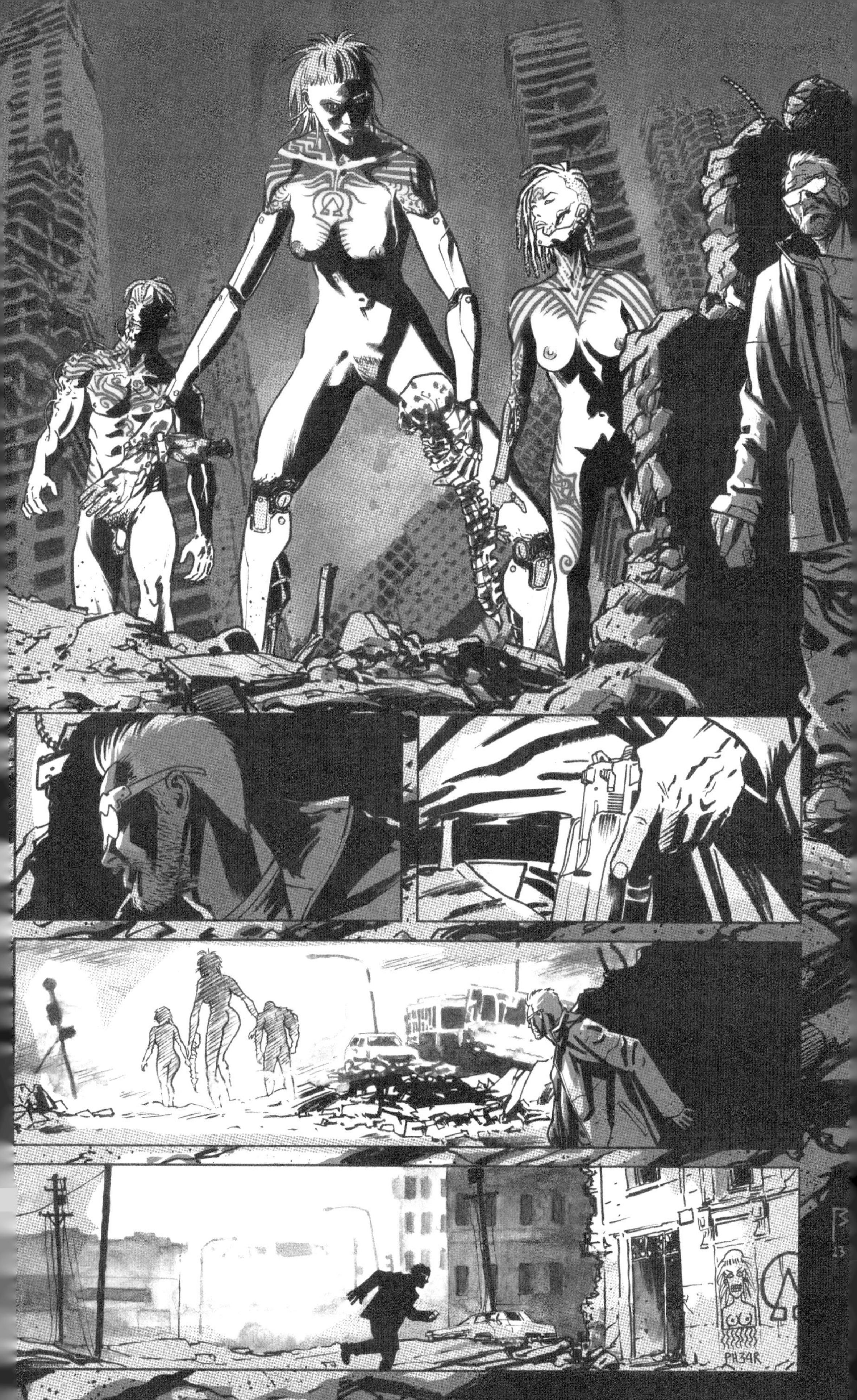
PH34R

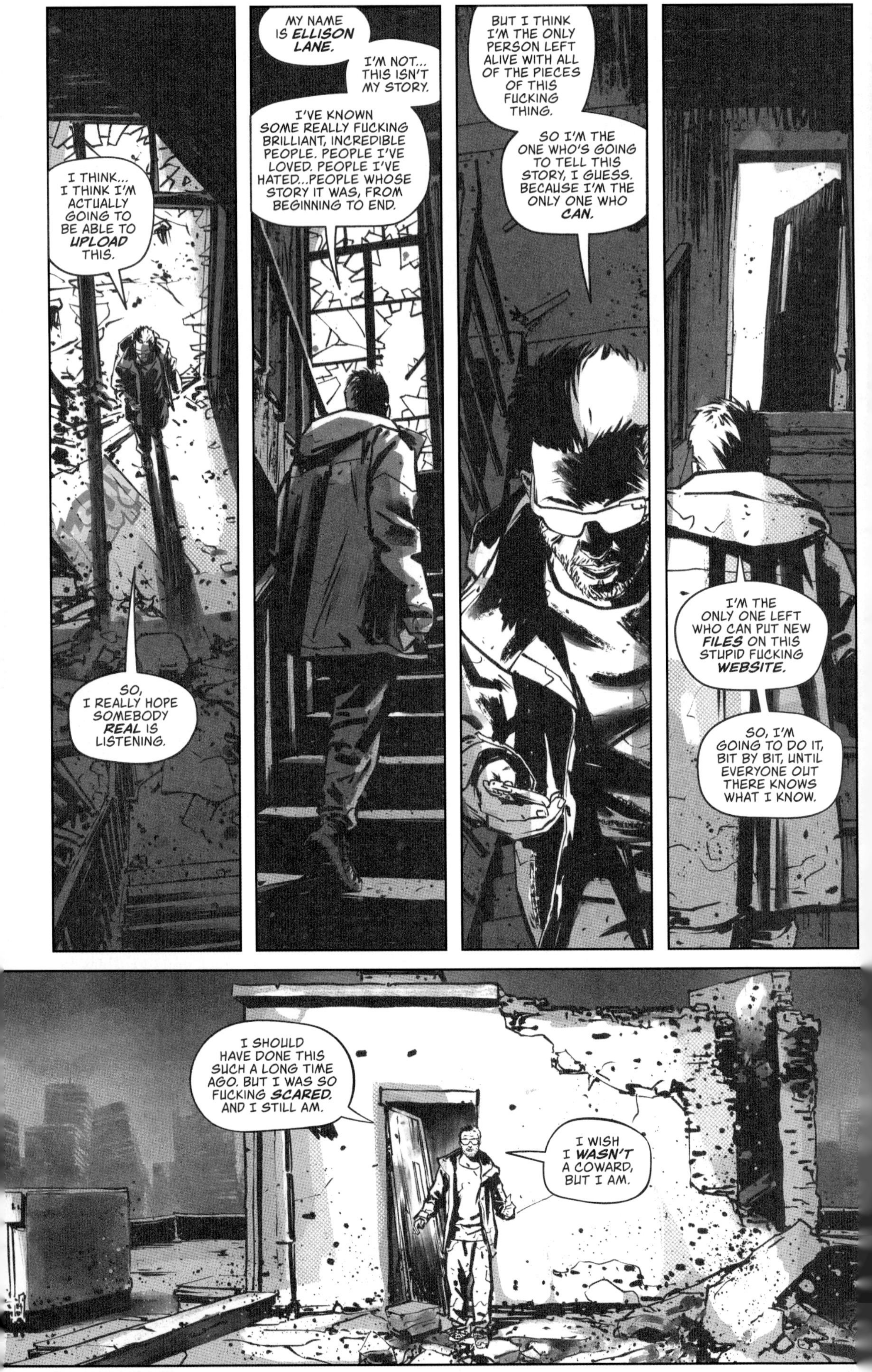
I THINK... I THINK I'M ACTUALLY GOING TO BE ABLE TO UPLOAD THIS.
SO, I REALLY HOPE SOMEBODY REAL IS LISTENING.
MY NAME IS ELLISON LANE.
I'M NOT... THIS ISN'T MY STORY.
I'VE KNOWN SOME REALLY FUCKING BRILLIANT, INCREDIBLE PEOPLE. PEOPLE I'VE LOVED. PEOPLE I'VE HATED...PEOPLE WHOSE STORY IT WAS, FROM BEGINNING TO END.
BUT I THINK I'M THE ONLY PERSON LEFT ALIVE WITH ALL OF THE PIECES OF THIS FUCKING THING.
SO I'M THE ONE WHO'S GOING TO TELL THIS STORY, I GUESS. BECAUSE I'M THE ONLY ONE WHO CAN.
I'M THE ONLY ONE LEFT WHO CAN PUT NEW FILES ON THIS STUPID FUCKING WEBSITE.
SO, I'M GOING TO DO IT, BIT BY BIT, UNTIL EVERYONE OUT THERE KNOWS WHAT I KNOW.
I SHOULD HAVE DONE THIS SUCH A LONG TIME AGO. BUT I WAS SO FUCKING SCARED. AND I STILL AM.
I WISH I WASN'T A COWARD, BUT I AM.

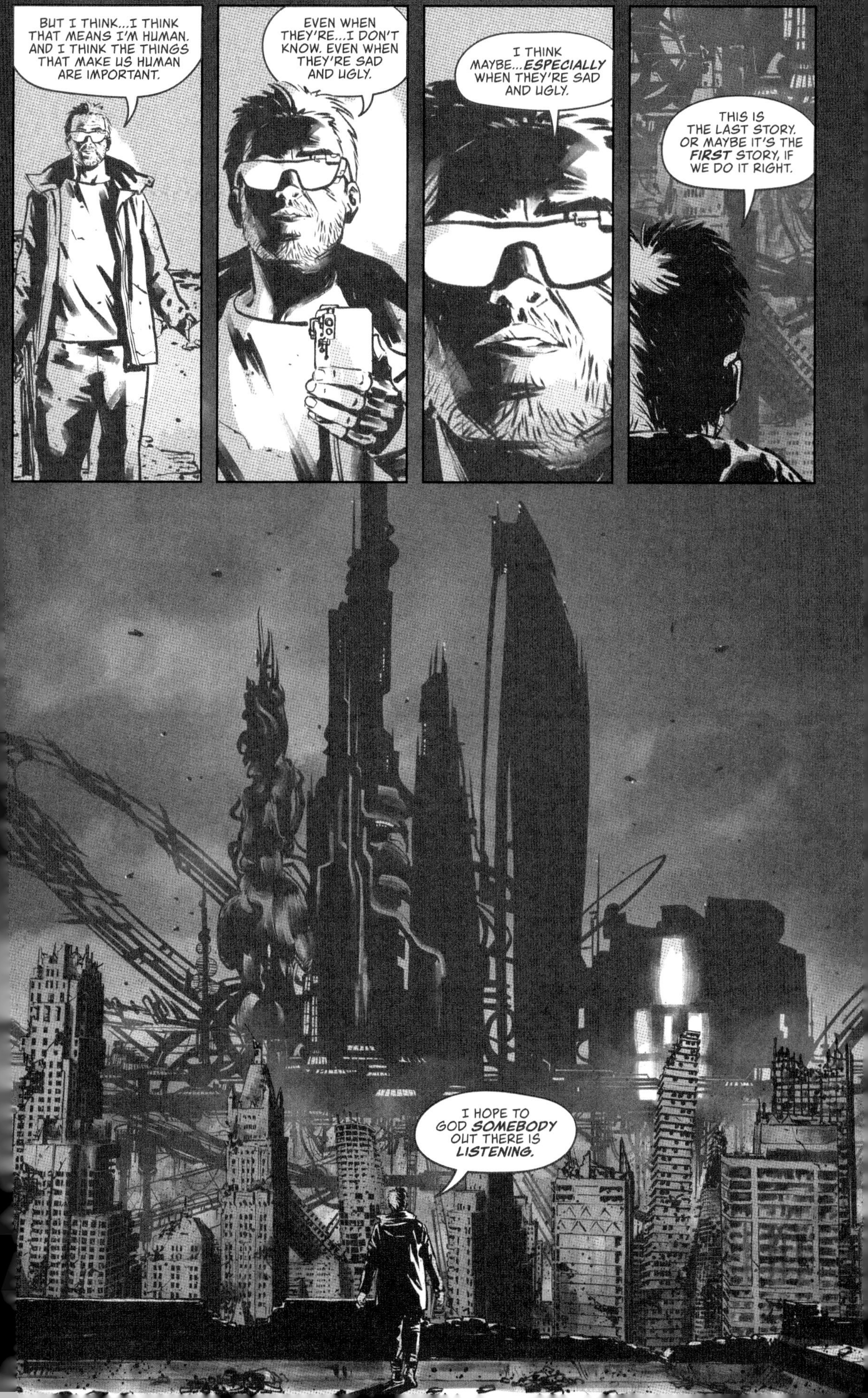
BUT I THINK...I THINK THAT MEANS I'M HUMAN. AND I THINK THE THINGS THAT MAKE US HUMAN ARE IMPORTANT.
EVEN WHEN THEY'RE...I DON'T KNOW. EVEN WHEN THEY'RE SAD AND UGLY.
I THINK MAYBE...ESPECIALLY WHEN THEY'RE SAD AND UGLY.
THIS IS THE LAST STORY. OR MAYBE IT'S THE FIRST STORY, IF WE DO IT RIGHT.
I HOPE TO GOD SOMEBODY OUT THERE IS LISTENING.

2024

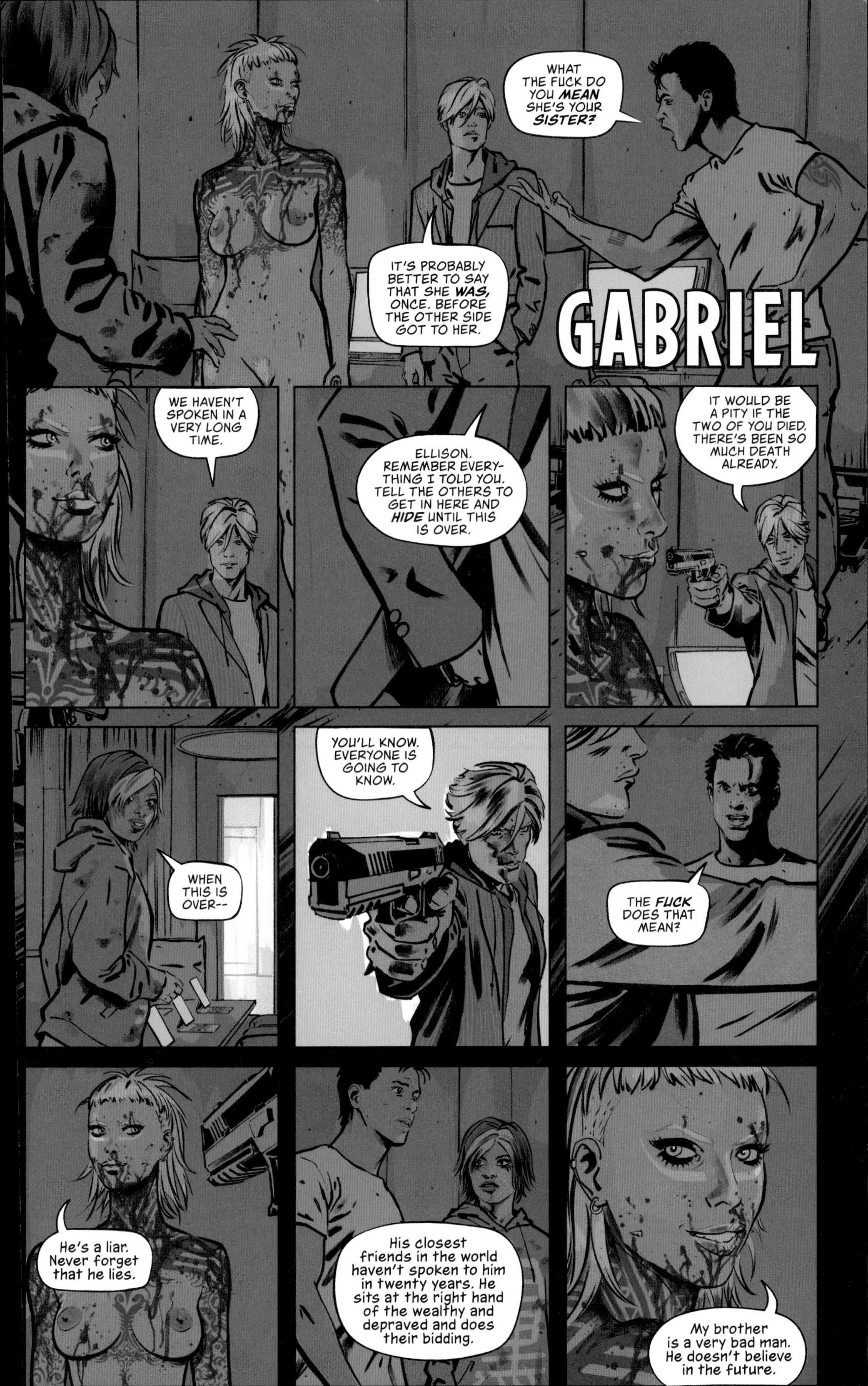
WHAT THE FUCK DO YOU MEAN SHE'S YOUR SISTER?
IT'S PROBABLY BETTER TO SAY THAT SHE WAS, ONCE. BEFORE THE OTHER SIDE GOT TO HER.
GABRIEL
WE HAVEN'T SPOKEN IN A VERY LONG TIME.
ELLISON. REMEMBER EVERYTHING I TOLD YOU. TELL THE OTHERS TO GET IN HERE AND HIDE UNTIL THIS IS OVER.
IT WOULD BE A PITY IF THE TWO OF YOU DIED. THERE'S BEEN SO MUCH DEATH ALREADY.
WHEN THIS IS OVER--
YOU'LL KNOW. EVERYONE IS GOING TO KNOW.
THE FUCK DOES THAT MEAN?
He's a liar. Never forget that he lies.
His closest friends in the world haven't spoken to him in twenty years. He sits at the right hand of the wealthy and depraved and does their bidding.
My brother is a very bad man. He doesn't believe in the future.

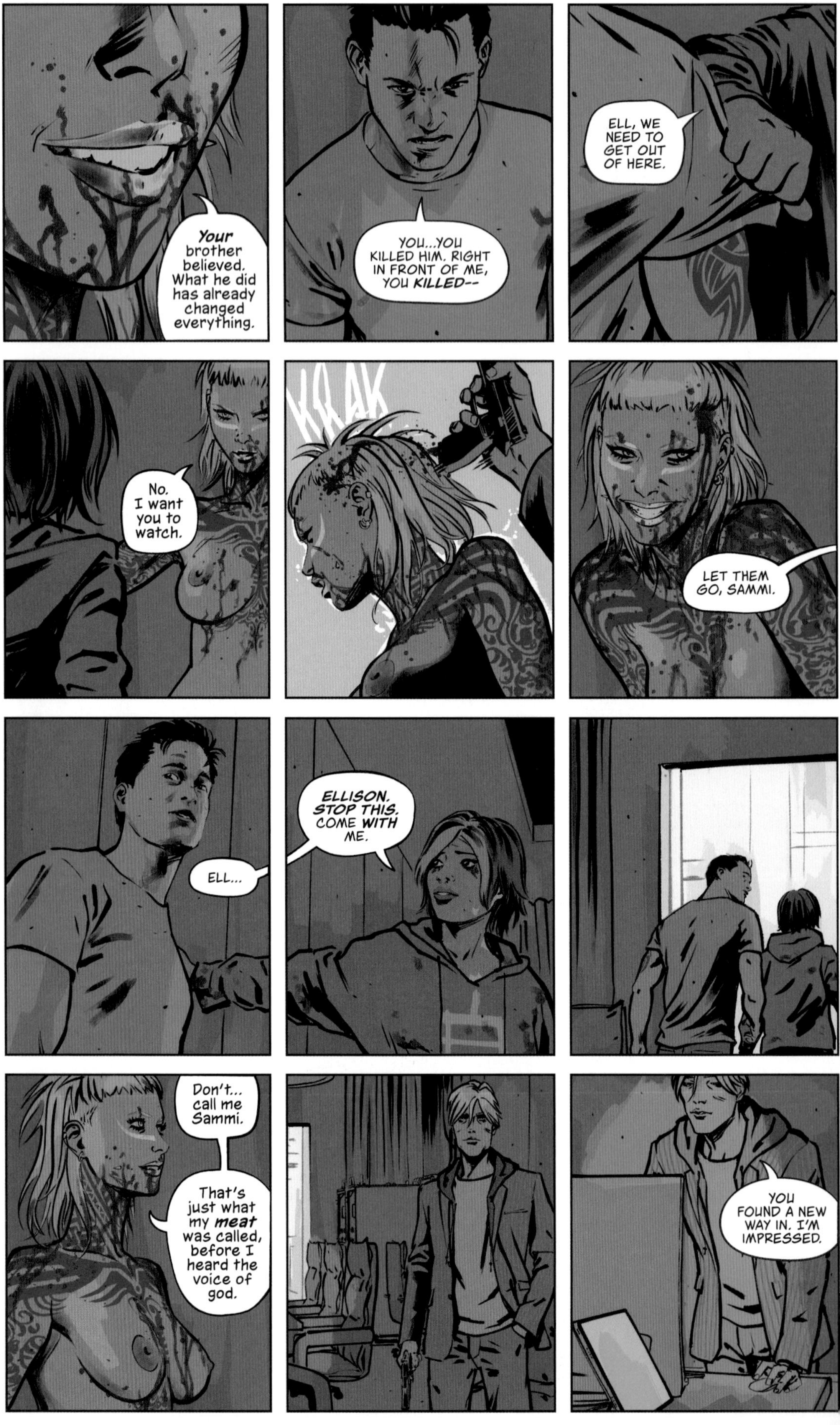

Your brother believed. What he did has already changed everything.
YOU...YOU KILLED HIM. RIGHT IN FRONT OF ME, YOU *KILLED*--
ELL, WE NEED TO GET OUT OF HERE.
No. I want you to watch.
KRAK
LET THEM GO, SAMMI.
ELL...
ELLISON. STOP THIS. COME *WITH* ME.
Don't... call me Sammi.
That's just what my *meat* was called, before I heard the voice of god.
YOU FOUND A NEW WAY IN. I'M IMPRESSED.

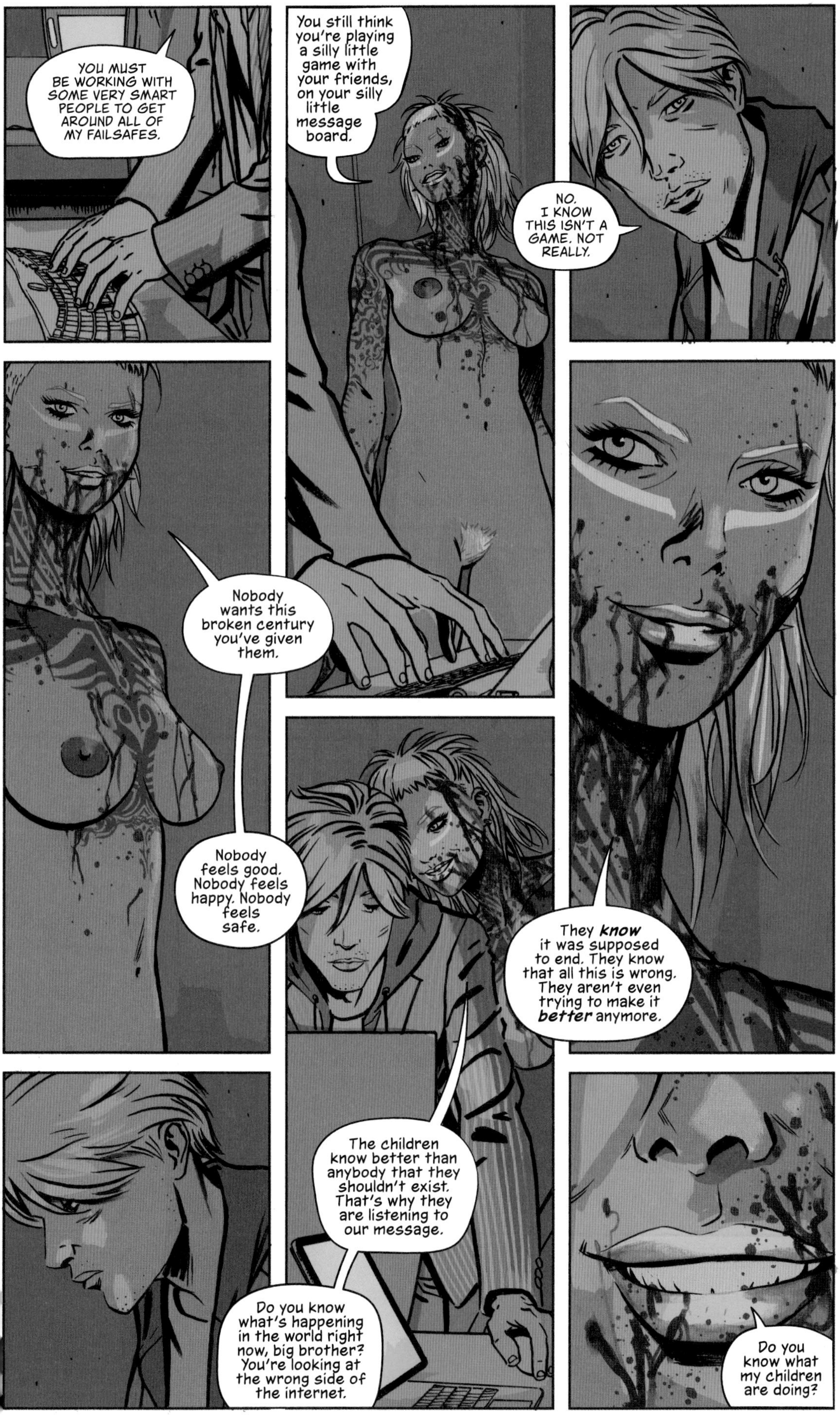
YOU MUST BE WORKING WITH SOME VERY SMART PEOPLE TO GET AROUND ALL OF MY FAILSAFES.
You still think you're playing a silly little game with your friends, on your silly little message board.
NO. I KNOW THIS ISN'T A GAME. NOT REALLY.
Nobody wants this broken century you've given them.
Nobody feels good. Nobody feels happy. Nobody feels safe.
They know it was supposed to end. They know that all this is wrong. They aren't even trying to make it better anymore.
The children know better than anybody that they shouldn't exist. That's why they are listening to our message.
Do you know what's happening in the world right now, big brother? You're looking at the wrong side of the internet.
Do you know what my children are doing?

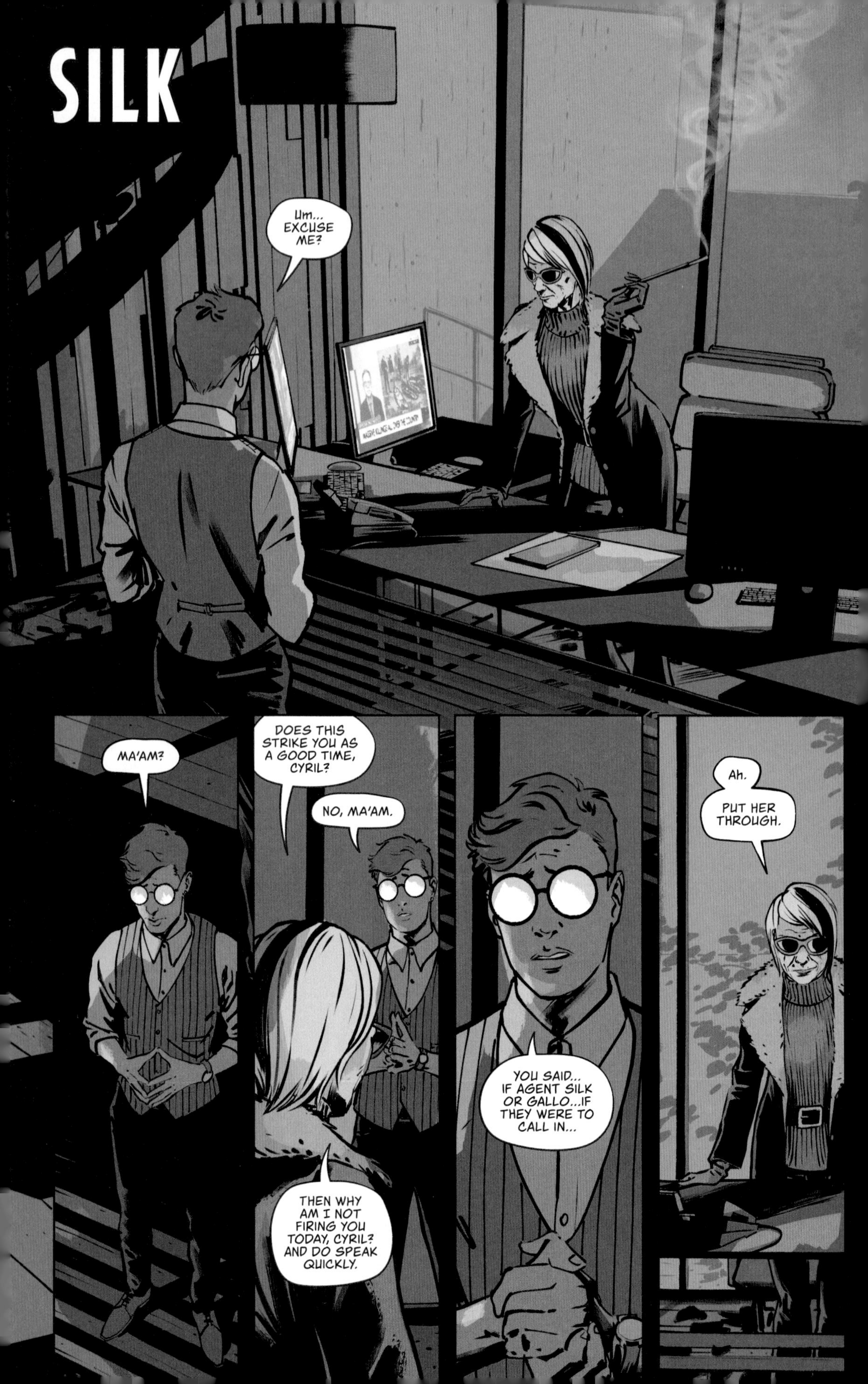
SILK
Um... EXCUSE ME?
MA'AM?
DOES THIS STRIKE YOU AS A GOOD TIME, CYRIL?
NO, MA'AM.
THEN WHY AM I NOT FIRING YOU TODAY, CYRIL? AND DO SPEAK QUICKLY.
YOU SAID... IF AGENT SILK OR GALLO...IF THEY WERE TO CALL IN...
Ah.
PUT HER THROUGH.

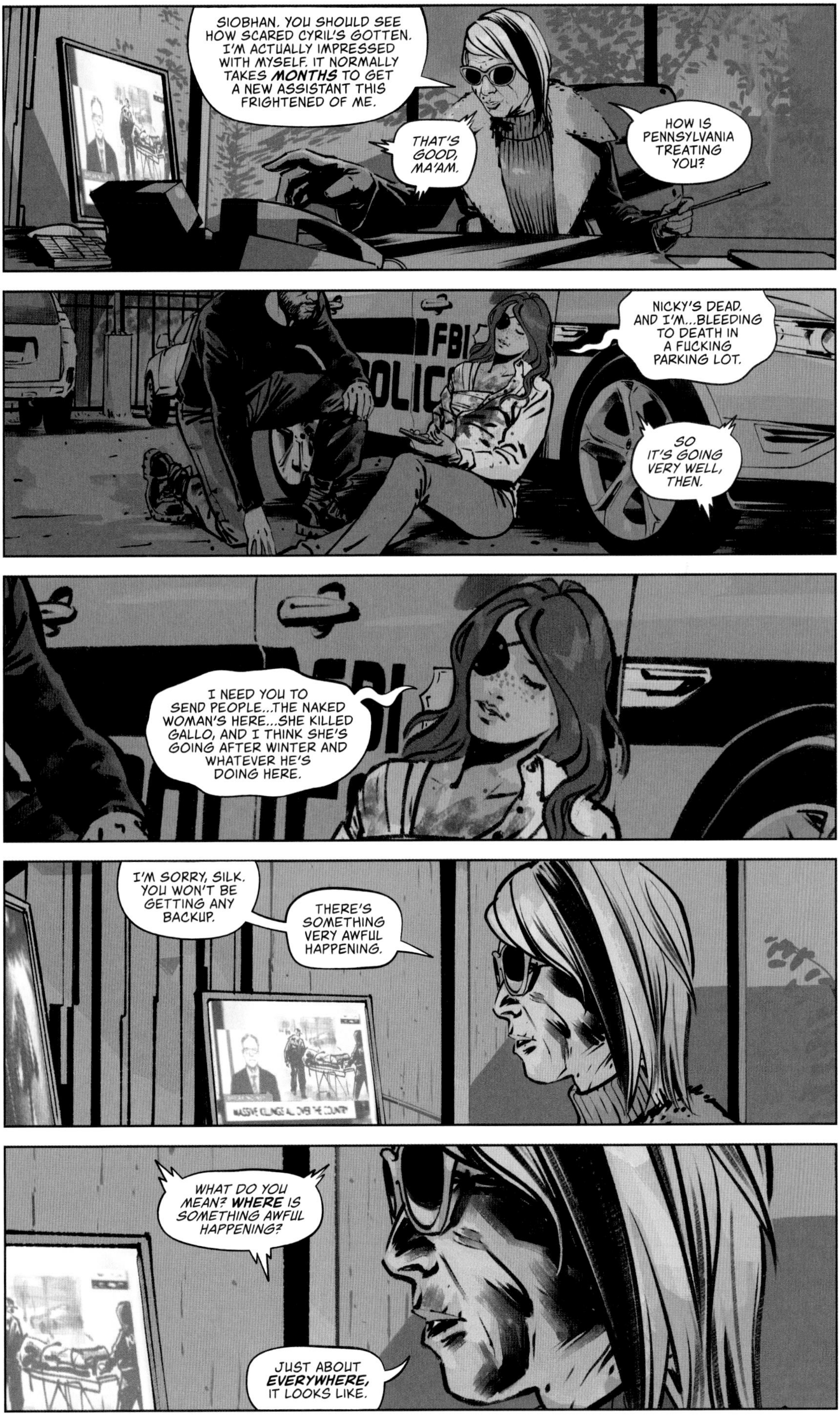
SIOBHAN. YOU SHOULD SEE HOW SCARED CYRIL'S GOTTEN. I'M ACTUALLY IMPRESSED WITH MYSELF. IT NORMALLY TAKES **MONTHS** TO GET A NEW ASSISTANT THIS FRIGHTENED OF ME.
THAT'S GOOD, MA'AM.
HOW IS PENNSYLVANIA TREATING YOU?
FBI POLICE
NICKY'S DEAD. AND I'M...BLEEDING TO DEATH IN A FUCKING PARKING LOT.
SO IT'S GOING VERY WELL, THEN.
I NEED YOU TO SEND PEOPLE...THE NAKED WOMAN'S HERE...SHE KILLED GALLO, AND I THINK SHE'S GOING AFTER WINTER AND WHATEVER HE'S DOING HERE.
I'M SORRY, SILK. YOU WON'T BE GETTING ANY BACKUP.
THERE'S SOMETHING VERY AWFUL HAPPENING.
MASSIVE KILLINGS ALL OVER THE COUNTRY
*WHAT DO YOU MEAN? **WHERE** IS SOMETHING AWFUL HAPPENING?*
JUST ABOUT ***EVERYWHERE,*** IT LOOKS LIKE.

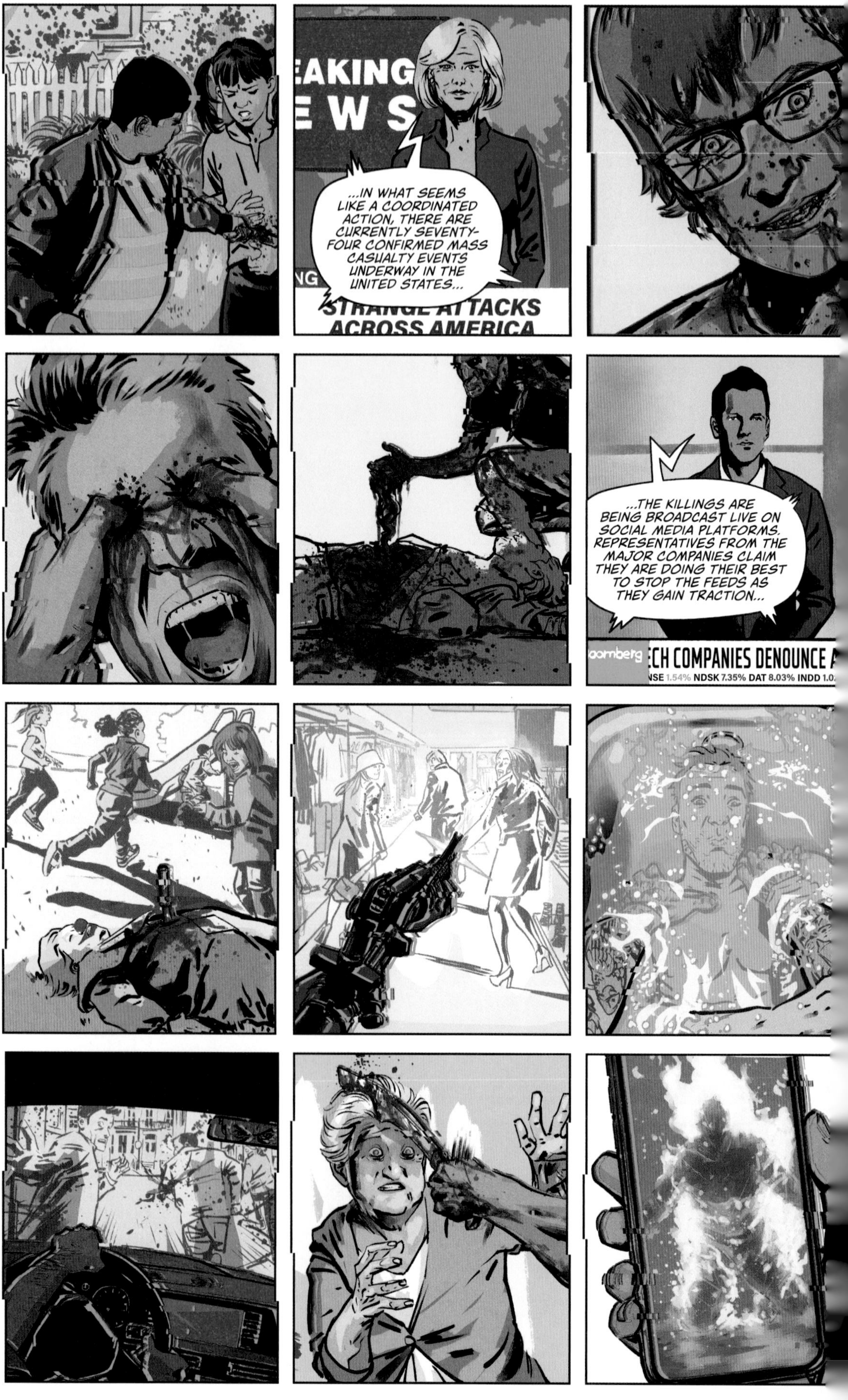
EAKING
E W S
...IN WHAT SEEMS LIKE A COORDINATED ACTION, THERE ARE CURRENTLY SEVENTY-FOUR CONFIRMED MASS CASUALTY EVENTS UNDERWAY IN THE UNITED STATES...
STRANGE ATTACKS ACROSS AMERICA
...THE KILLINGS ARE BEING BROADCAST LIVE ON SOCIAL MEDIA PLATFORMS. REPRESENTATIVES FROM THE MAJOR COMPANIES CLAIM THEY ARE DOING THEIR BEST TO STOP THE FEEDS AS THEY GAIN TRACTION...
oomberg
ECH COMPANIES DENOUNCE A
NSE 1.54% NDSK 7.35% DAT 8.03% INDD 1.0

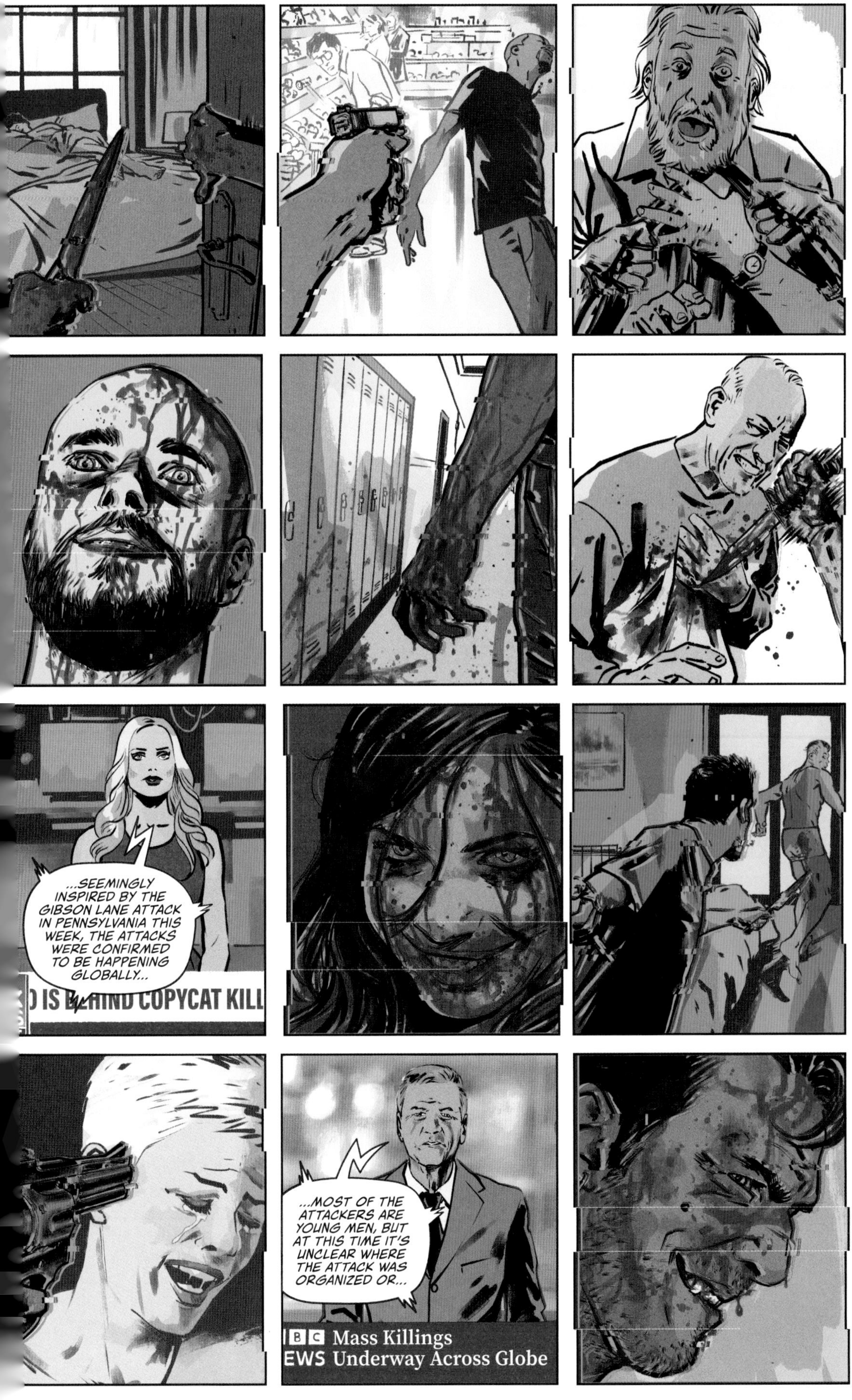
...SEEMINGLY INSPIRED BY THE GIBSON LANE ATTACK IN PENNSYLVANIA THIS WEEK, THE ATTACKS WERE CONFIRMED TO BE HAPPENING GLOBALLY...
O IS BEHIND COPYCAT KILL
...MOST OF THE ATTACKERS ARE YOUNG MEN, BUT AT THIS TIME IT'S UNCLEAR WHERE THE ATTACK WAS ORGANIZED OR...
BBC
EWS
Mass Killings
Underway Across Globe

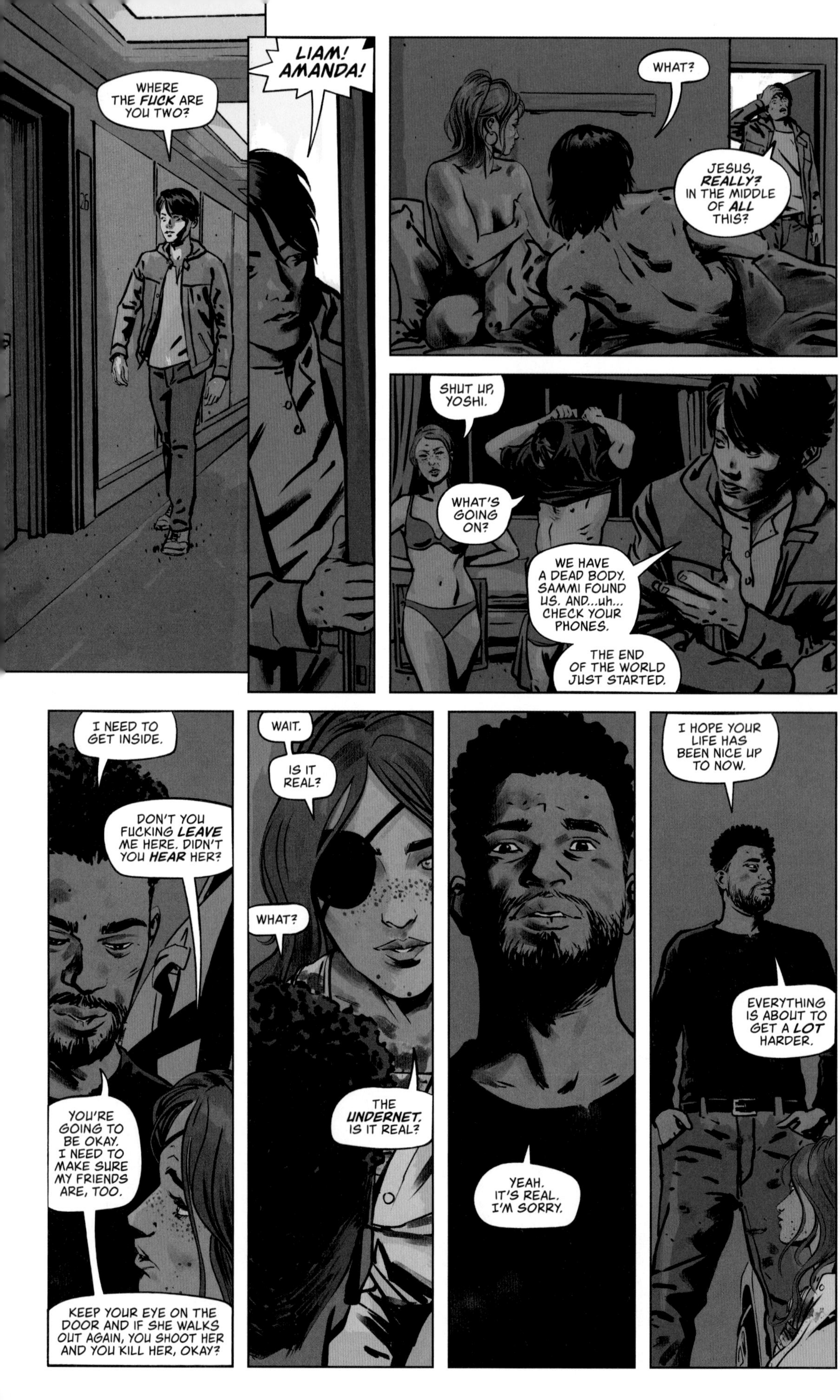
WHERE THE FUCK ARE YOU TWO?
LIAM! AMANDA!
WHAT?
JESUS, REALLY? IN THE MIDDLE OF ALL THIS?
SHUT UP, YOSHI.
WHAT'S GOING ON?
WE HAVE A DEAD BODY. SAMMI FOUND US. AND...uh... CHECK YOUR PHONES.
THE END OF THE WORLD JUST STARTED.
I NEED TO GET INSIDE.
DON'T YOU FUCKING LEAVE ME HERE. DIDN'T YOU HEAR HER?
YOU'RE GOING TO BE OKAY. I NEED TO MAKE SURE MY FRIENDS ARE, TOO.
KEEP YOUR EYE ON THE DOOR AND IF SHE WALKS OUT AGAIN, YOU SHOOT HER AND YOU KILL HER, OKAY?
WAIT.
IS IT REAL?
WHAT?
THE UNDERNET. IS IT REAL?
YEAH. IT'S REAL. I'M SORRY.
I HOPE YOUR LIFE HAS BEEN NICE UP TO NOW.
EVERYTHING IS ABOUT TO GET A LOT HARDER.

The change is starting. More and more have seen the light, and they are going to bring our new future to us.

THIS IS VERY IMPRESSIVE, SAMMI.

I REALLY THOUGHT I WOULD HAVE BEEN ABLE TO PUT MY PLAN IN MOTION BEFORE YOUR SIDE GOT THIS FAR WITH IT ALL.

You can't stop this. It'll only grow from here.

Hmm. LET'S SEE.

CLK

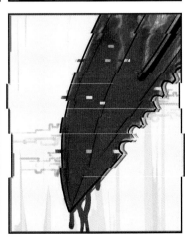

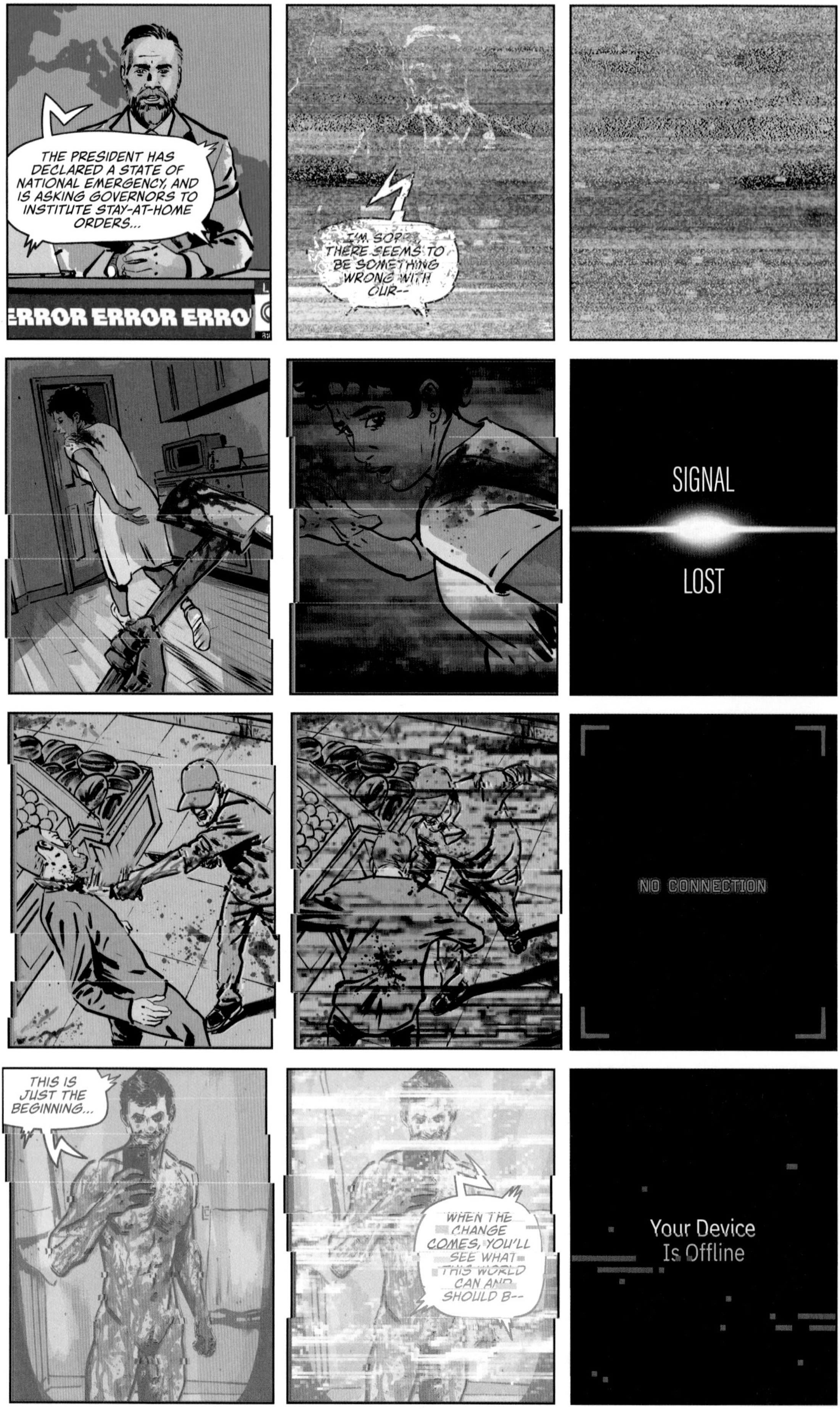
THE PRESIDENT HAS DECLARED A STATE OF NATIONAL EMERGENCY, AND IS ASKING GOVERNORS TO INSTITUTE STAY-AT-HOME ORDERS...
ERROR ERROR ERRO
I'M SOR-- THERE SEEMS TO BE SOMETHING WRONG WITH OUR--
SIGNAL
LOST
NO CONNECTION
THIS IS JUST THE BEGINNING...
WHEN THE CHANGE COMES, YOU'LL SEE WHAT THIS WORLD CAN AND SHOULD B--
Your Device
Is Offline

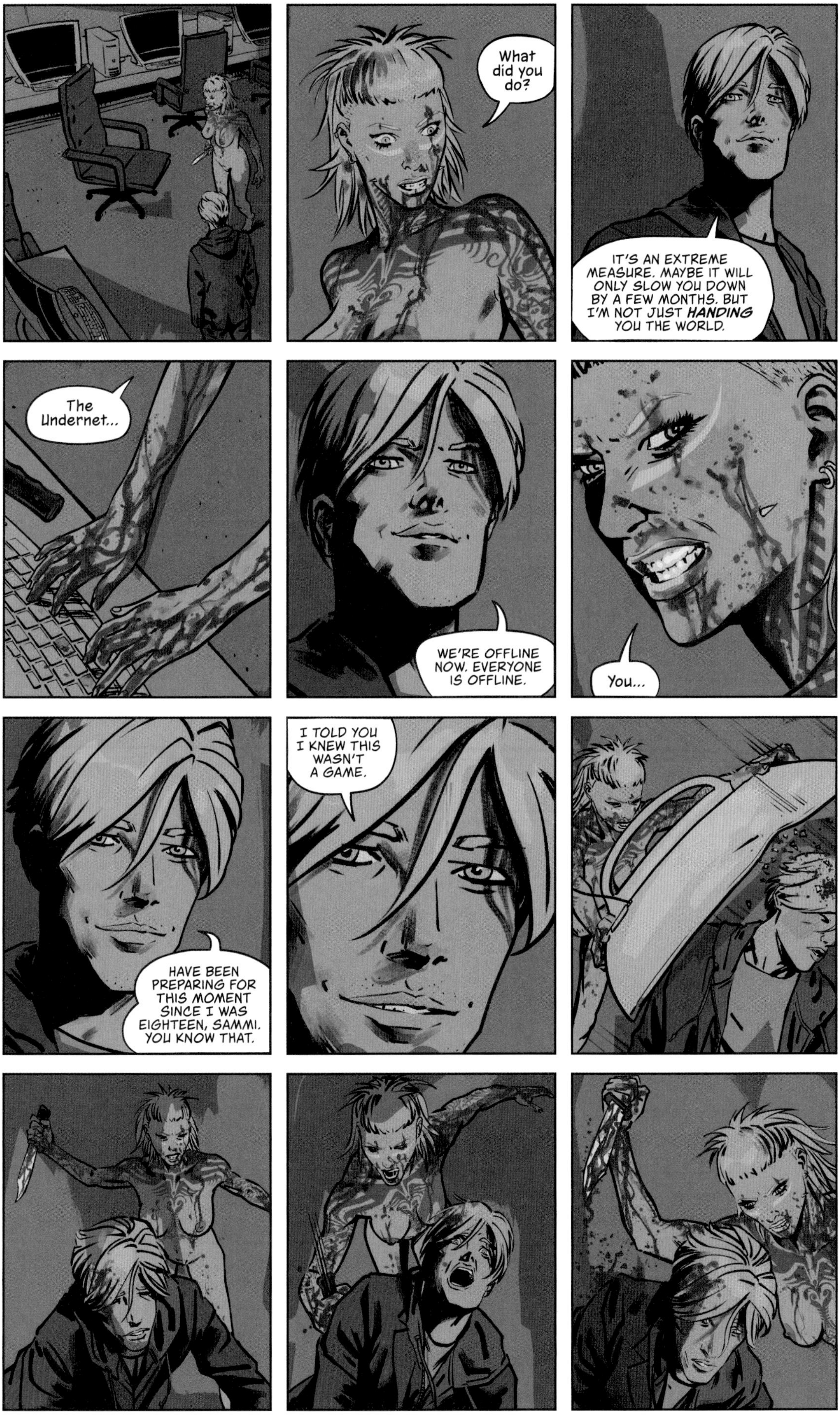

What did you do?
IT'S AN EXTREME MEASURE. MAYBE IT WILL ONLY SLOW YOU DOWN BY A FEW MONTHS. BUT I'M NOT JUST **HANDING** YOU THE WORLD.
The Undernet...
WE'RE OFFLINE NOW. EVERYONE IS OFFLINE.
You...
HAVE BEEN PREPARING FOR THIS MOMENT SINCE I WAS EIGHTEEN, SAMMI. YOU KNOW THAT.
I TOLD YOU I KNEW THIS WASN'T A GAME.

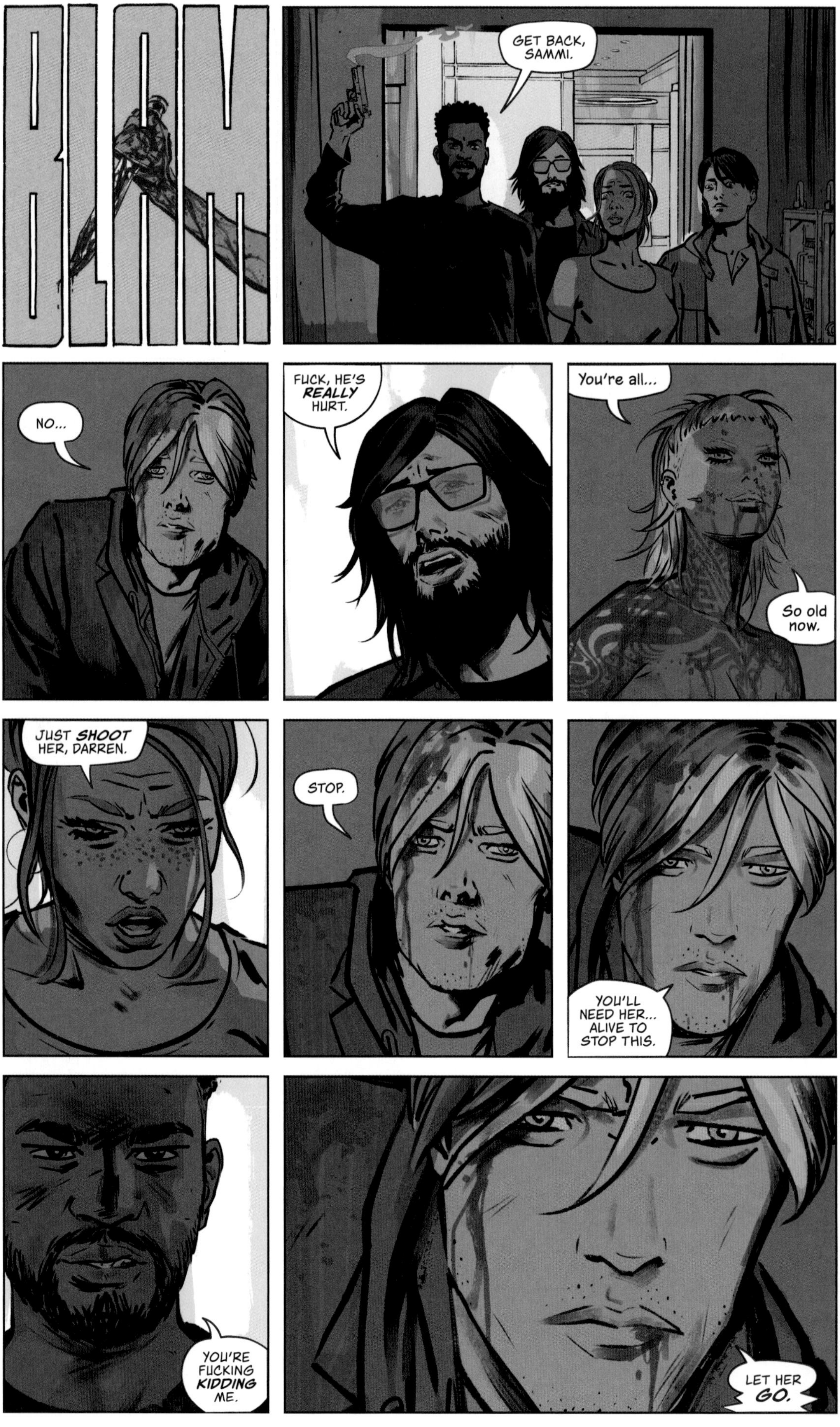
BLAM
GET BACK, SAMMI.
NO...
FUCK, HE'S REALLY HURT.
You're all...
So old now.
JUST SHOOT HER, DARREN.
STOP.
YOU'LL NEED HER... ALIVE TO STOP THIS.
YOU'RE FUCKING KIDDING ME.
LET HER GO.

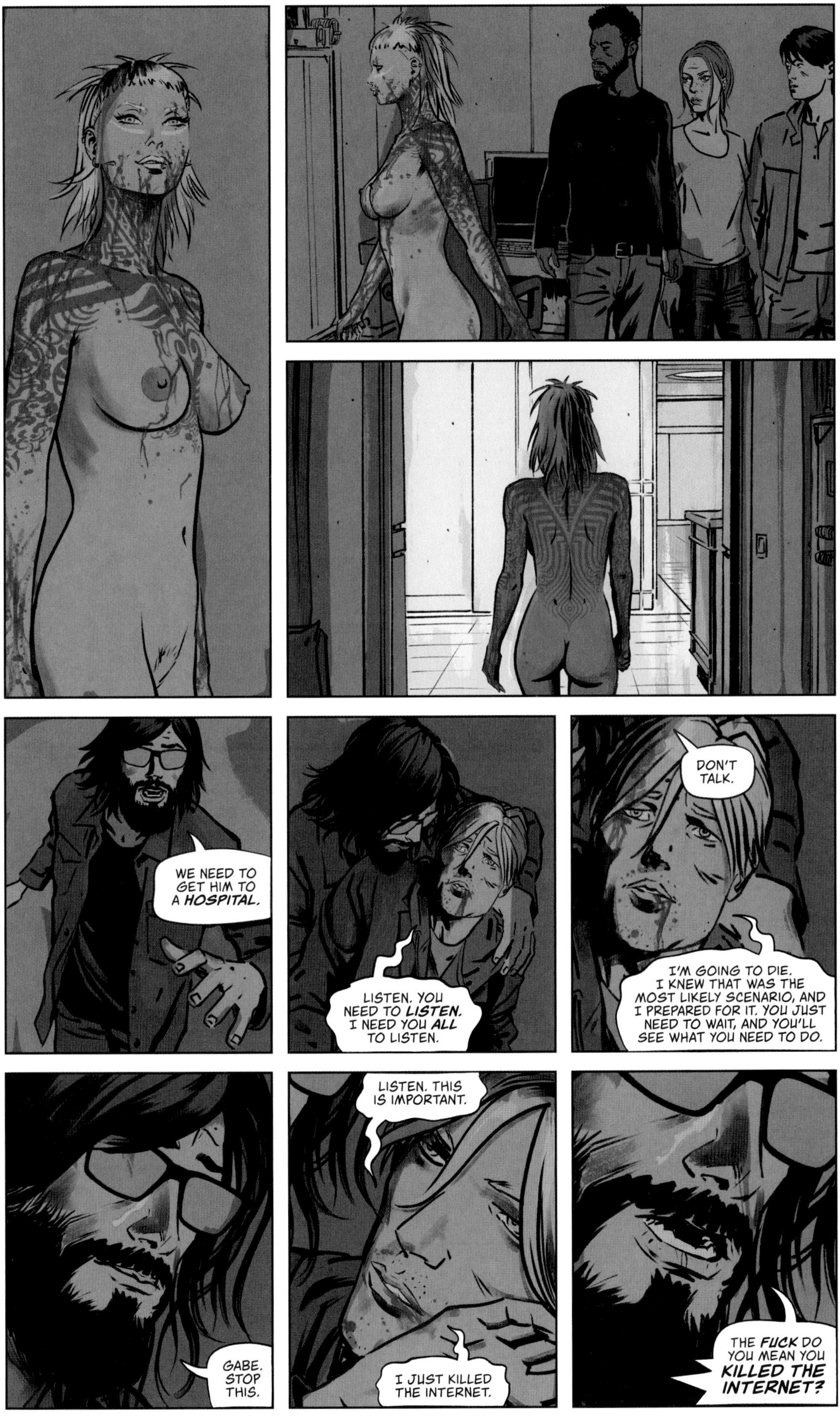
WE NEED TO GET HIM TO A HOSPITAL.
LISTEN. YOU NEED TO LISTEN. I NEED YOU ALL TO LISTEN.
DON'T TALK.
I'M GOING TO DIE. I KNEW THAT WAS THE MOST LIKELY SCENARIO, AND I PREPARED FOR IT. YOU JUST NEED TO WAIT, AND YOU'LL SEE WHAT YOU NEED TO DO.
GABE. STOP THIS.
LISTEN. THIS IS IMPORTANT.
I JUST KILLED THE INTERNET.
THE FUCK DO YOU MEAN YOU KILLED THE INTERNET?

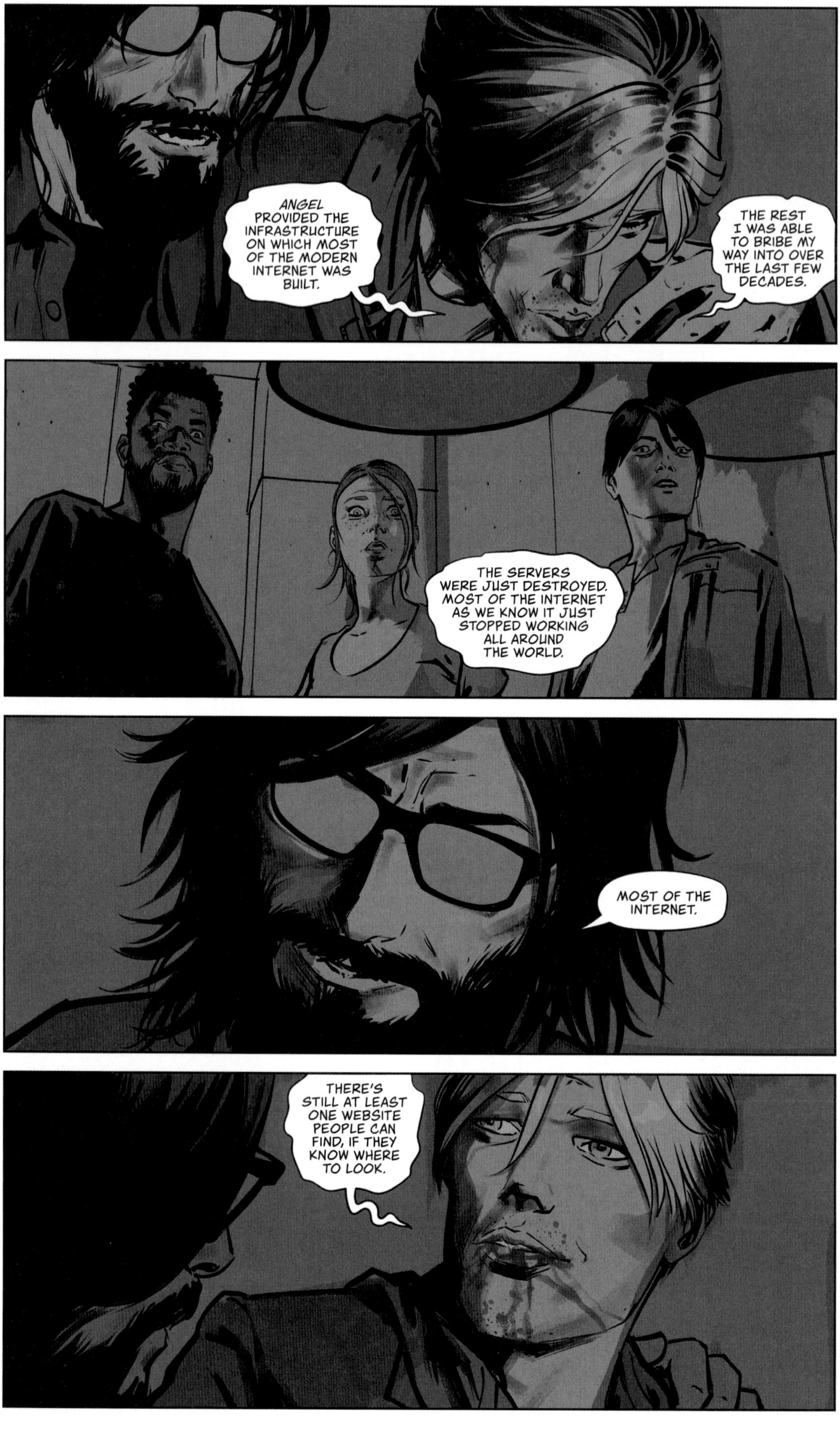
ANGEL PROVIDED THE INFRASTRUCTURE ON WHICH MOST OF THE MODERN INTERNET WAS BUILT.
THE REST I WAS ABLE TO BRIBE MY WAY INTO OVER THE LAST FEW DECADES.
THE SERVERS WERE JUST DESTROYED. MOST OF THE INTERNET AS WE KNOW IT JUST STOPPED WORKING ALL AROUND THE WORLD.
MOST OF THE INTERNET.
THERE'S STILL AT LEAST ONE WEBSITE PEOPLE CAN FIND, IF THEY KNOW WHERE TO LOOK.

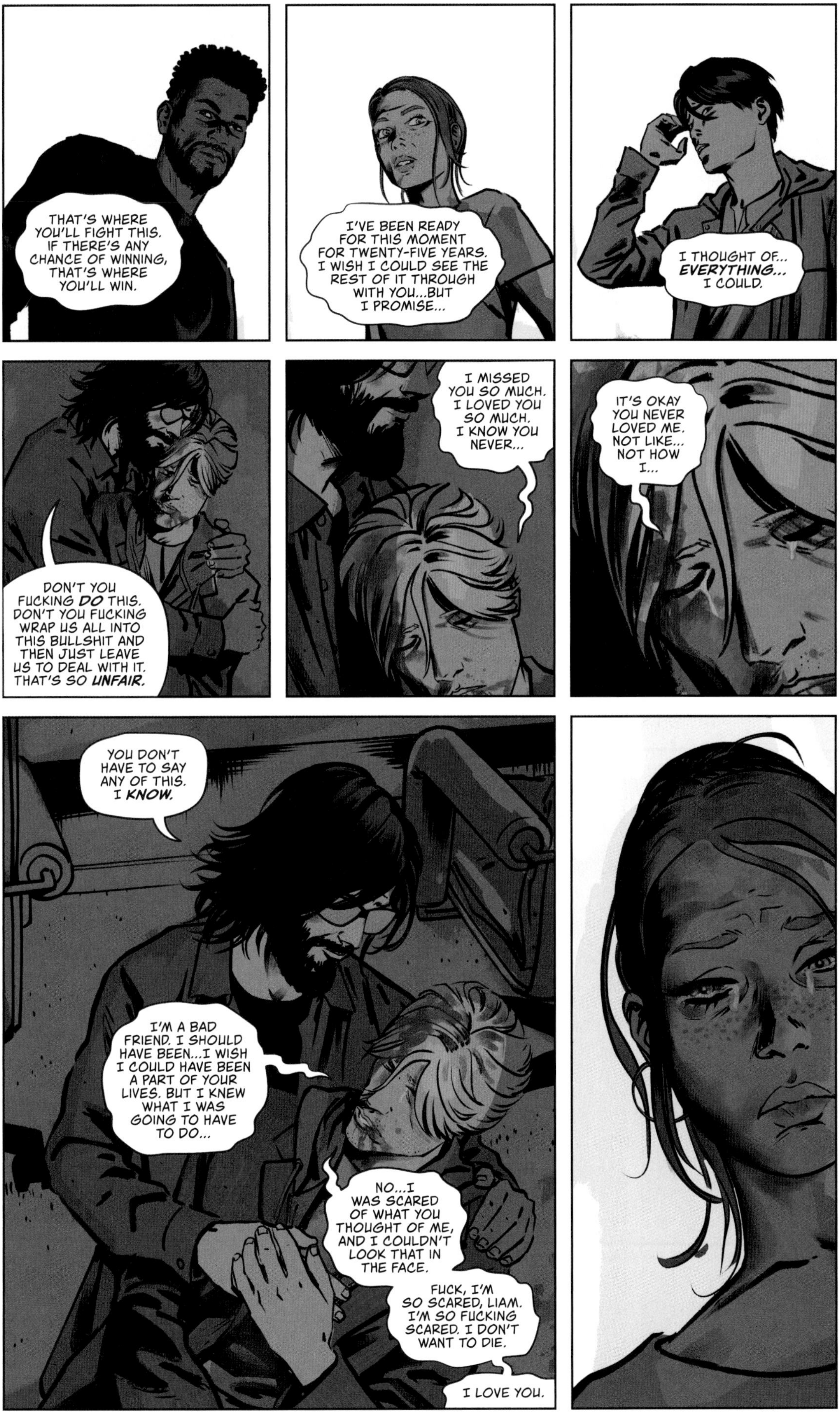
THAT'S WHERE YOU'LL FIGHT THIS. IF THERE'S ANY CHANCE OF WINNING, THAT'S WHERE YOU'LL WIN.
I'VE BEEN READY FOR THIS MOMENT FOR TWENTY-FIVE YEARS. I WISH I COULD SEE THE REST OF IT THROUGH WITH YOU...BUT I PROMISE...
I THOUGHT OF... **EVERYTHING...** I COULD.
DON'T YOU FUCKING **DO** THIS. DON'T YOU FUCKING WRAP US ALL INTO THIS BULLSHIT AND THEN JUST LEAVE US TO DEAL WITH IT. THAT'S SO **UNFAIR.**
I MISSED YOU SO MUCH. I LOVED YOU SO MUCH. I KNOW YOU NEVER...
IT'S OKAY YOU NEVER LOVED ME. NOT LIKE... NOT HOW I...
YOU DON'T HAVE TO SAY ANY OF THIS. I **KNOW.**
I'M A BAD FRIEND. I SHOULD HAVE BEEN...I WISH I COULD HAVE BEEN A PART OF YOUR LIVES. BUT I KNEW WHAT I WAS GOING TO HAVE TO DO...
NO...I WAS SCARED OF WHAT YOU THOUGHT OF ME, AND I COULDN'T LOOK THAT IN THE FACE.
FUCK, I'M SO SCARED, LIAM. I'M SO FUCKING SCARED. I DON'T WANT TO DIE.
I LOVE YOU.

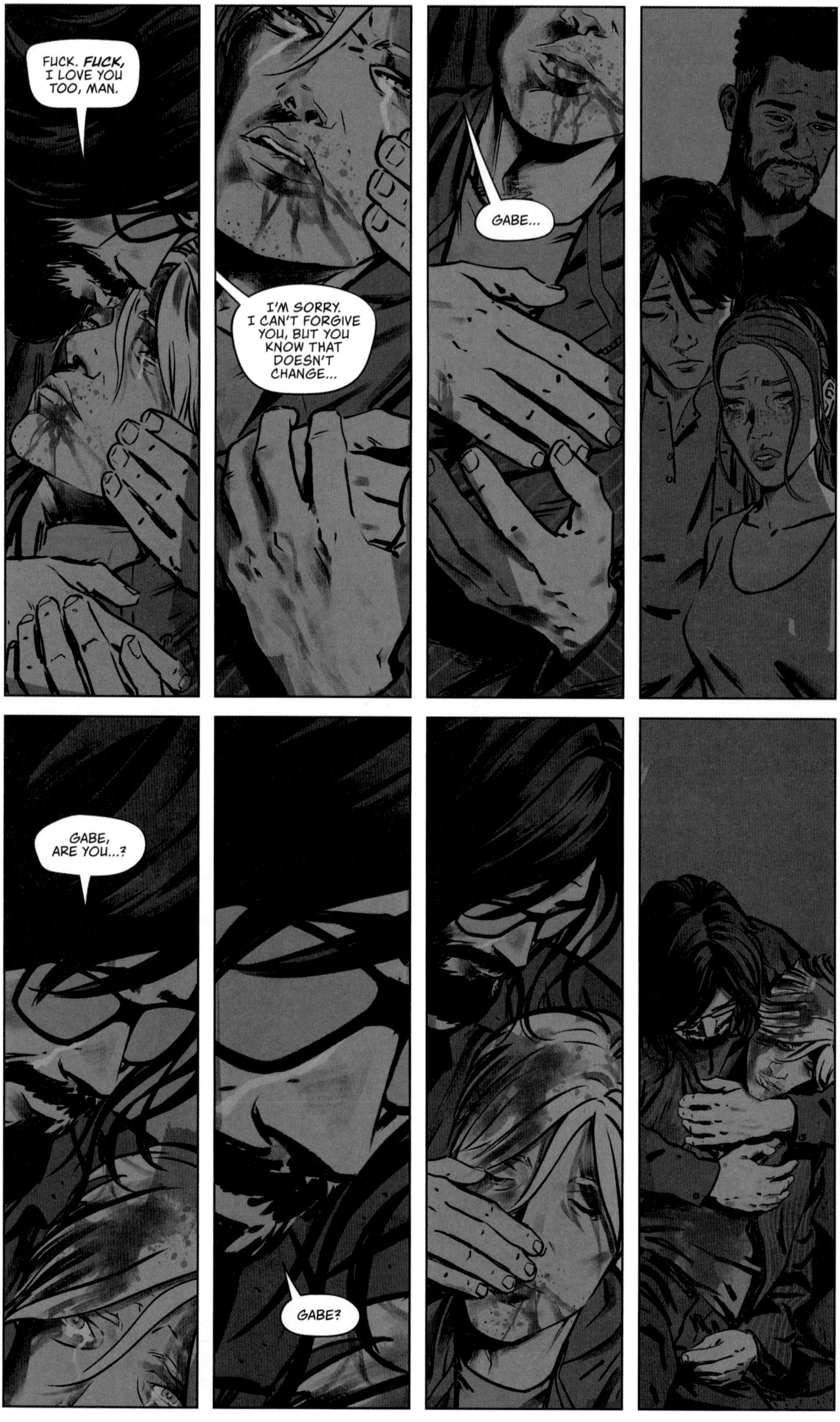
FUCK. **FUCK,** I LOVE YOU TOO, MAN.
I'M SORRY. I CAN'T FORGIVE YOU, BUT YOU KNOW THAT DOESN'T CHANGE...
GABE...
GABE, ARE YOU...?
GABE?

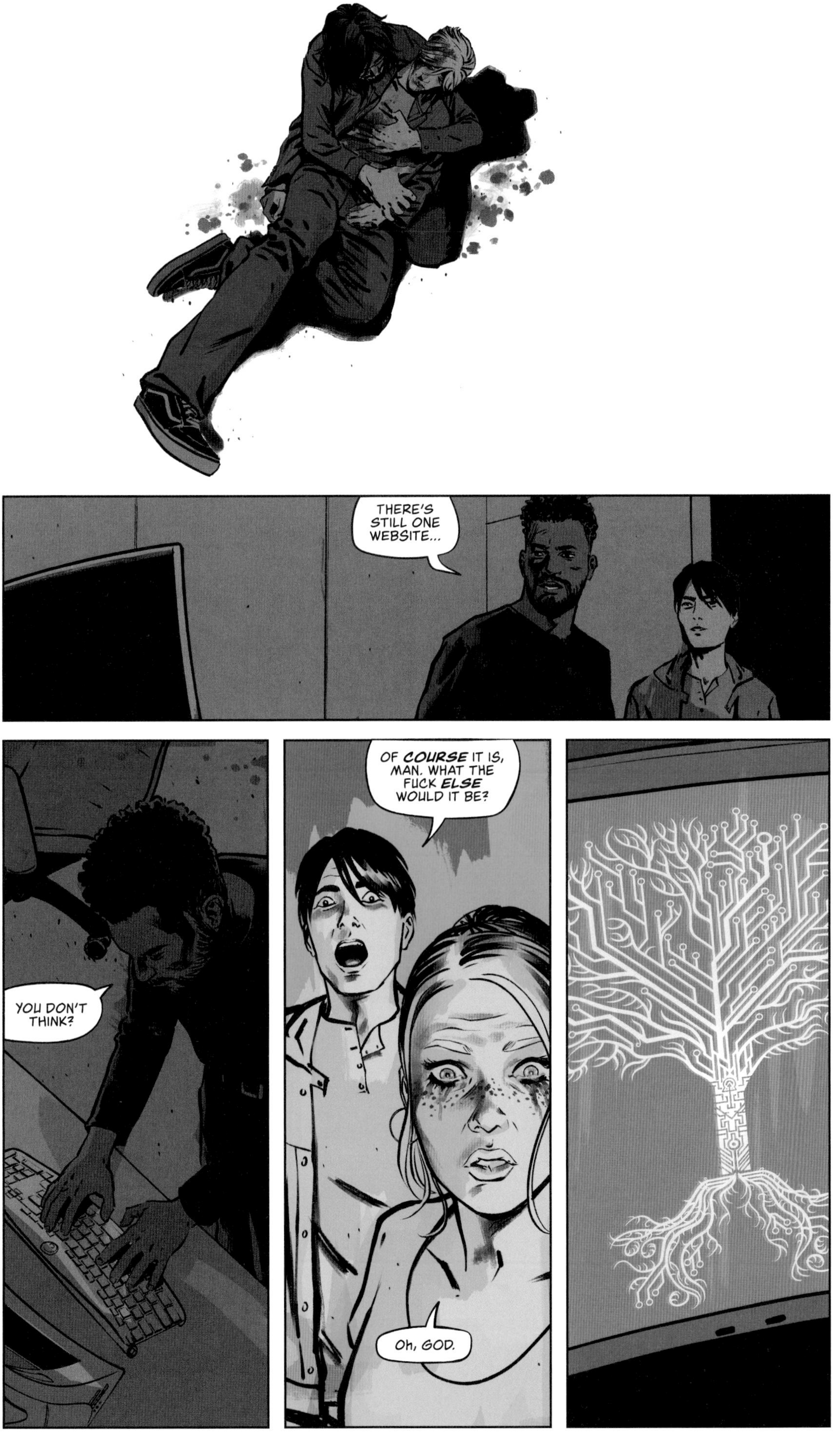
THERE'S STILL ONE WEBSITE...
YOU DON'T THINK?
OF COURSE IT IS, MAN. WHAT THE FUCK ELSE WOULD IT BE?
Oh, GOD.

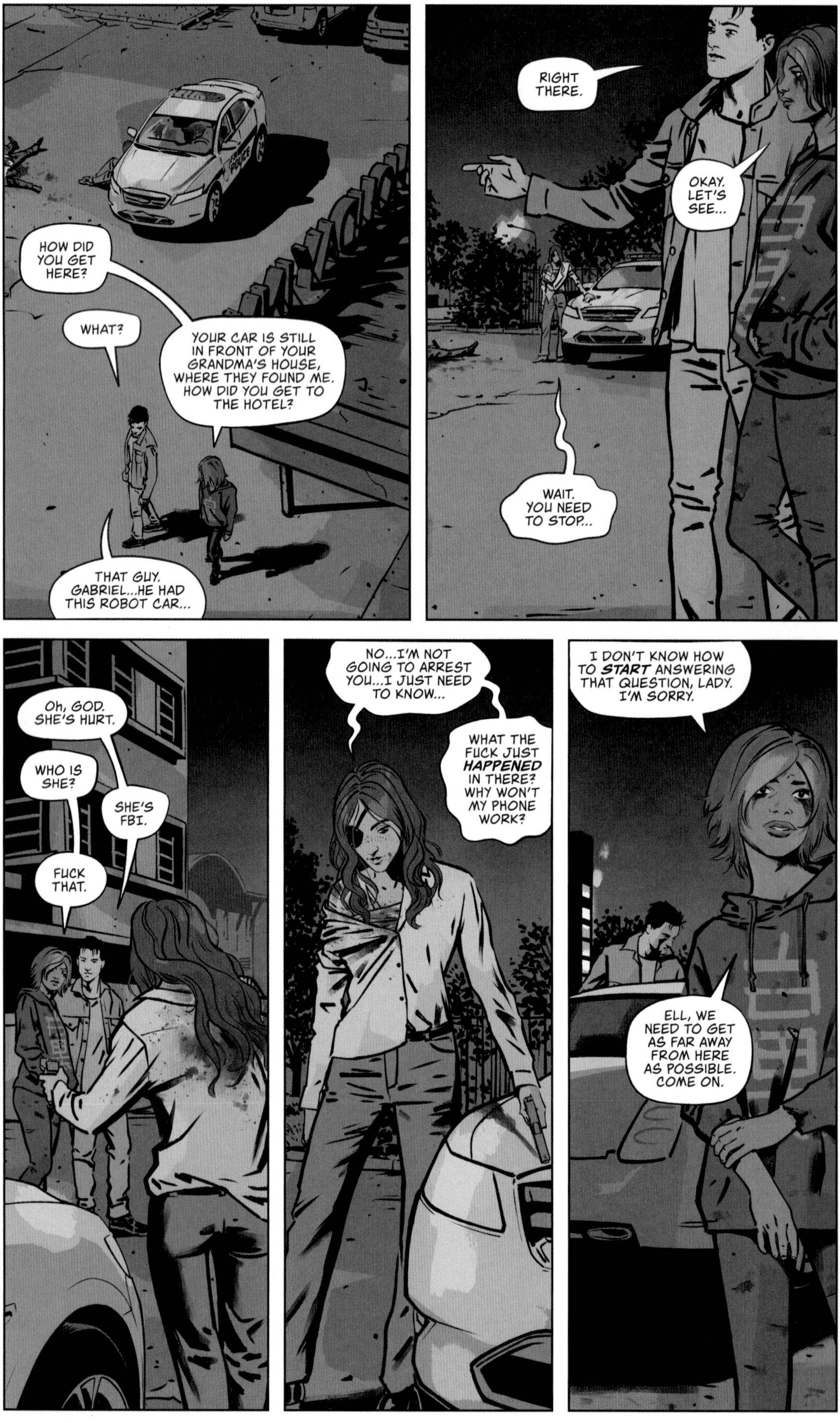
HOW DID YOU GET HERE?
WHAT?
YOUR CAR IS STILL IN FRONT OF YOUR GRANDMA'S HOUSE, WHERE THEY FOUND ME. HOW DID YOU GET TO THE HOTEL?
THAT GUY. GABRIEL...HE HAD THIS ROBOT CAR...
RIGHT THERE.
OKAY. LET'S SEE...
WAIT. YOU NEED TO STOP...
Oh, GOD. SHE'S HURT.
WHO IS SHE?
SHE'S FBI.
FUCK THAT.
NO...I'M NOT GOING TO ARREST YOU...I JUST NEED TO KNOW...
WHAT THE FUCK JUST HAPPENED IN THERE? WHY WON'T MY PHONE WORK?
I DON'T KNOW HOW TO START ANSWERING THAT QUESTION, LADY. I'M SORRY.
ELL, WE NEED TO GET AS FAR AWAY FROM HERE AS POSSIBLE. COME ON.

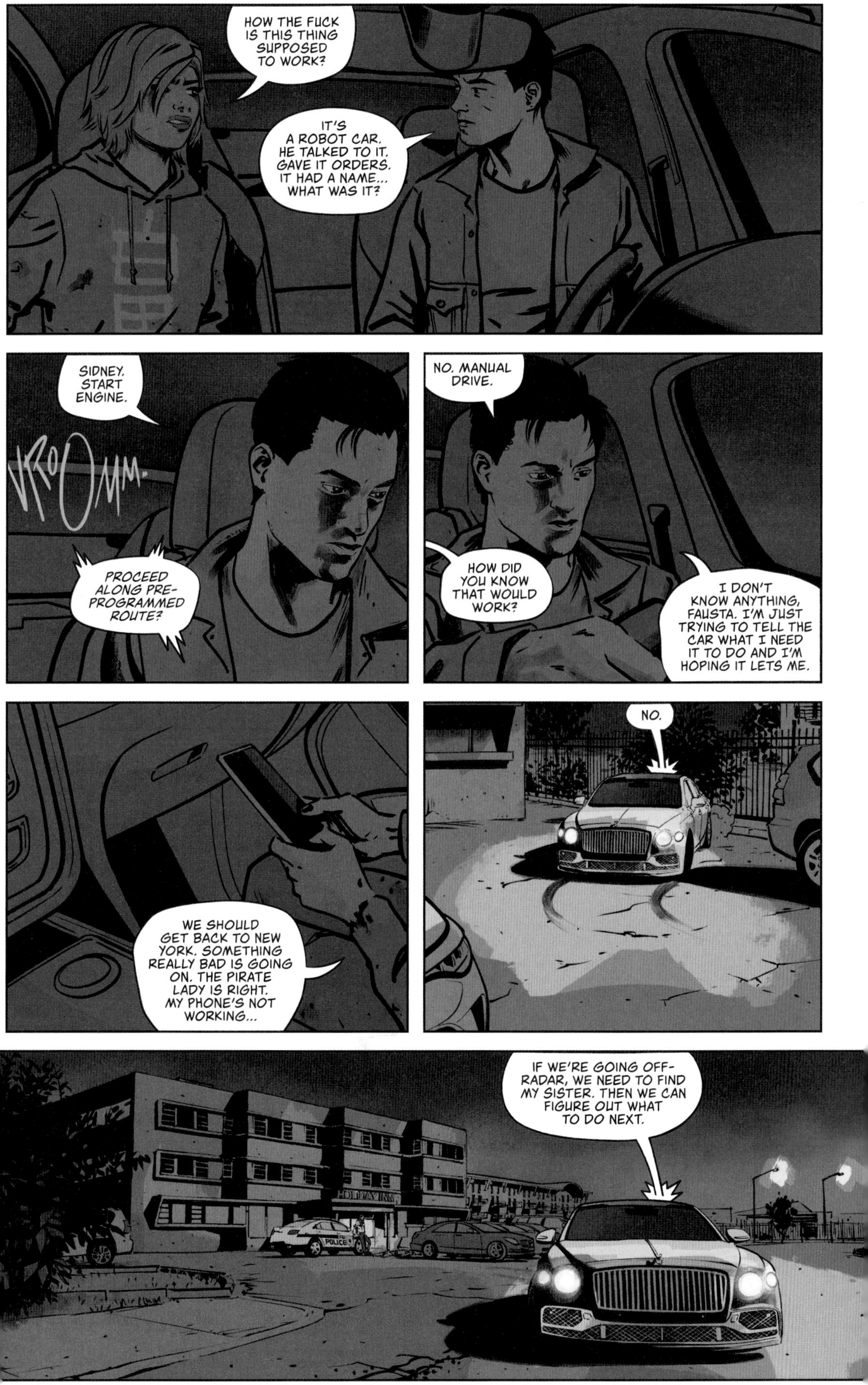
HOW THE FUCK IS THIS THING SUPPOSED TO WORK?
IT'S A ROBOT CAR. HE TALKED TO IT. GAVE IT ORDERS. IT HAD A NAME... WHAT WAS IT?
SIDNEY. START ENGINE.
VROOMM
PROCEED ALONG PRE-PROGRAMMED ROUTE?
NO. MANUAL DRIVE.
HOW DID YOU KNOW THAT WOULD WORK?
I DON'T KNOW ANYTHING, FAUSTA. I'M JUST TRYING TO TELL THE CAR WHAT I NEED IT TO DO AND I'M HOPING IT LETS ME.
WE SHOULD GET BACK TO NEW YORK. SOMETHING REALLY BAD IS GOING ON. THE PIRATE LADY IS RIGHT. MY PHONE'S NOT WORKING...
NO.
IF WE'RE GOING OFF-RADAR, WE NEED TO FIND MY SISTER. THEN WE CAN FIGURE OUT WHAT TO DO NEXT.
HOLIDAY INN
POLICE

2049

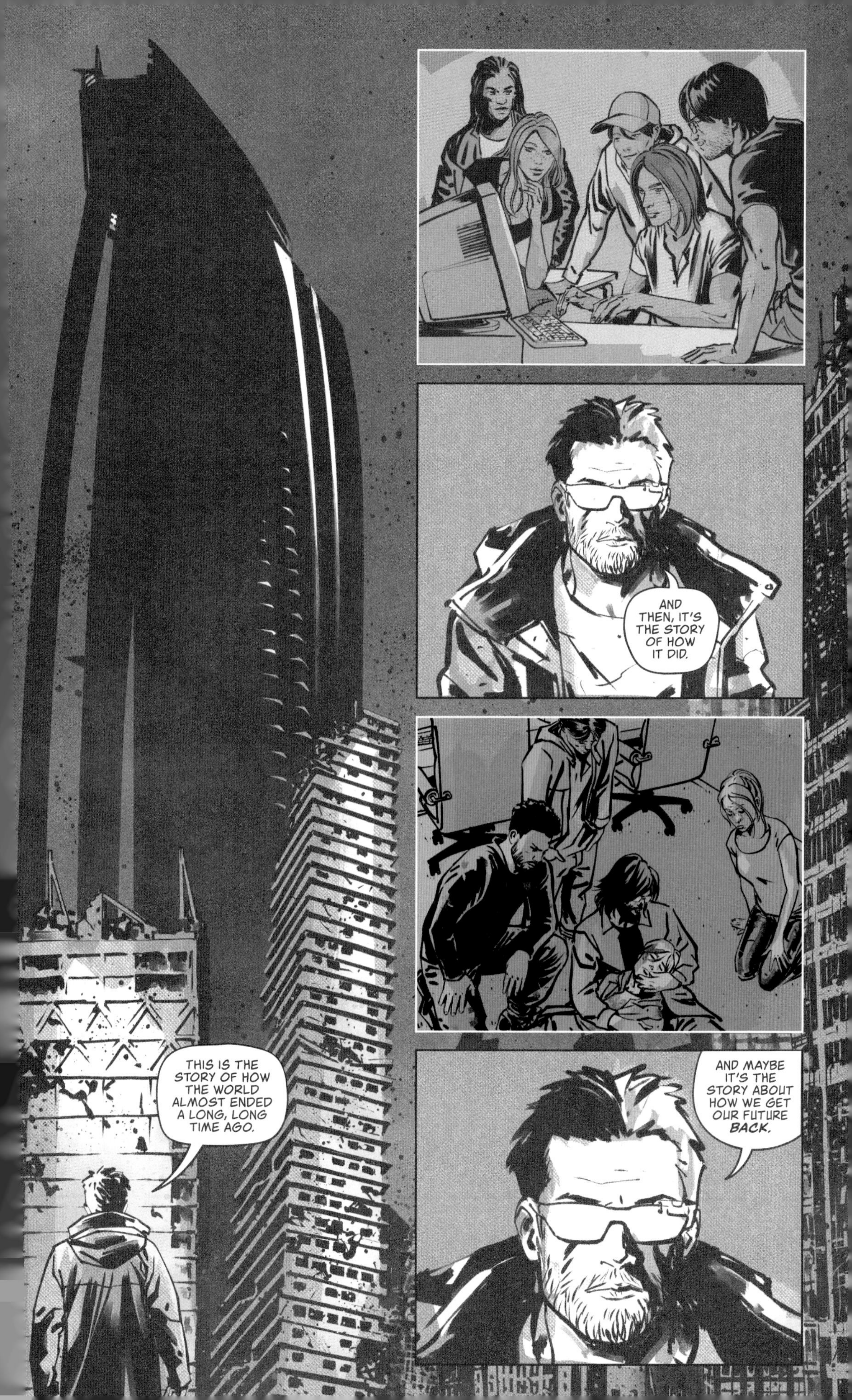
THIS IS THE STORY OF HOW THE WORLD ALMOST ENDED A LONG, LONG TIME AGO.
AND THEN, IT'S THE STORY OF HOW IT DID.
AND MAYBE IT'S THE STORY ABOUT HOW WE GET OUR FUTURE *BACK.*

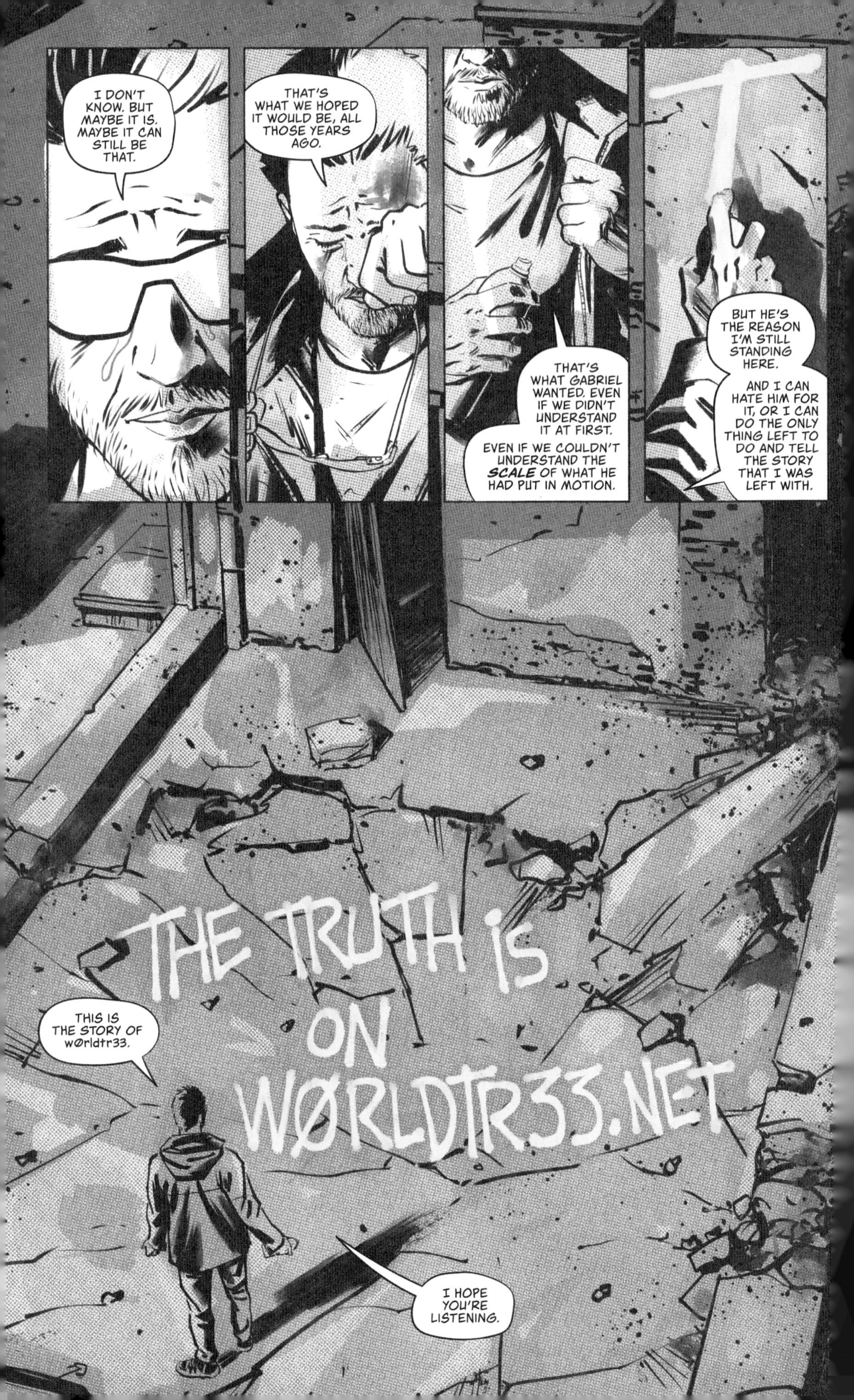
I DON'T KNOW. BUT MAYBE IT IS. MAYBE IT CAN STILL BE THAT.
THAT'S WHAT WE HOPED IT WOULD BE, ALL THOSE YEARS AGO.
THAT'S WHAT GABRIEL WANTED. EVEN IF WE DIDN'T UNDERSTAND IT AT FIRST.
EVEN IF WE COULDN'T UNDERSTAND THE SCALE OF WHAT HE HAD PUT IN MOTION.
BUT HE'S THE REASON I'M STILL STANDING HERE.
AND I CAN HATE HIM FOR IT, OR I CAN DO THE ONLY THING LEFT TO DO AND TELL THE STORY THAT I WAS LEFT WITH.
THE TRUTH IS ON WØRLDTR33.NET
THIS IS THE STORY OF wørldtr33.
I HOPE YOU'RE LISTENING.

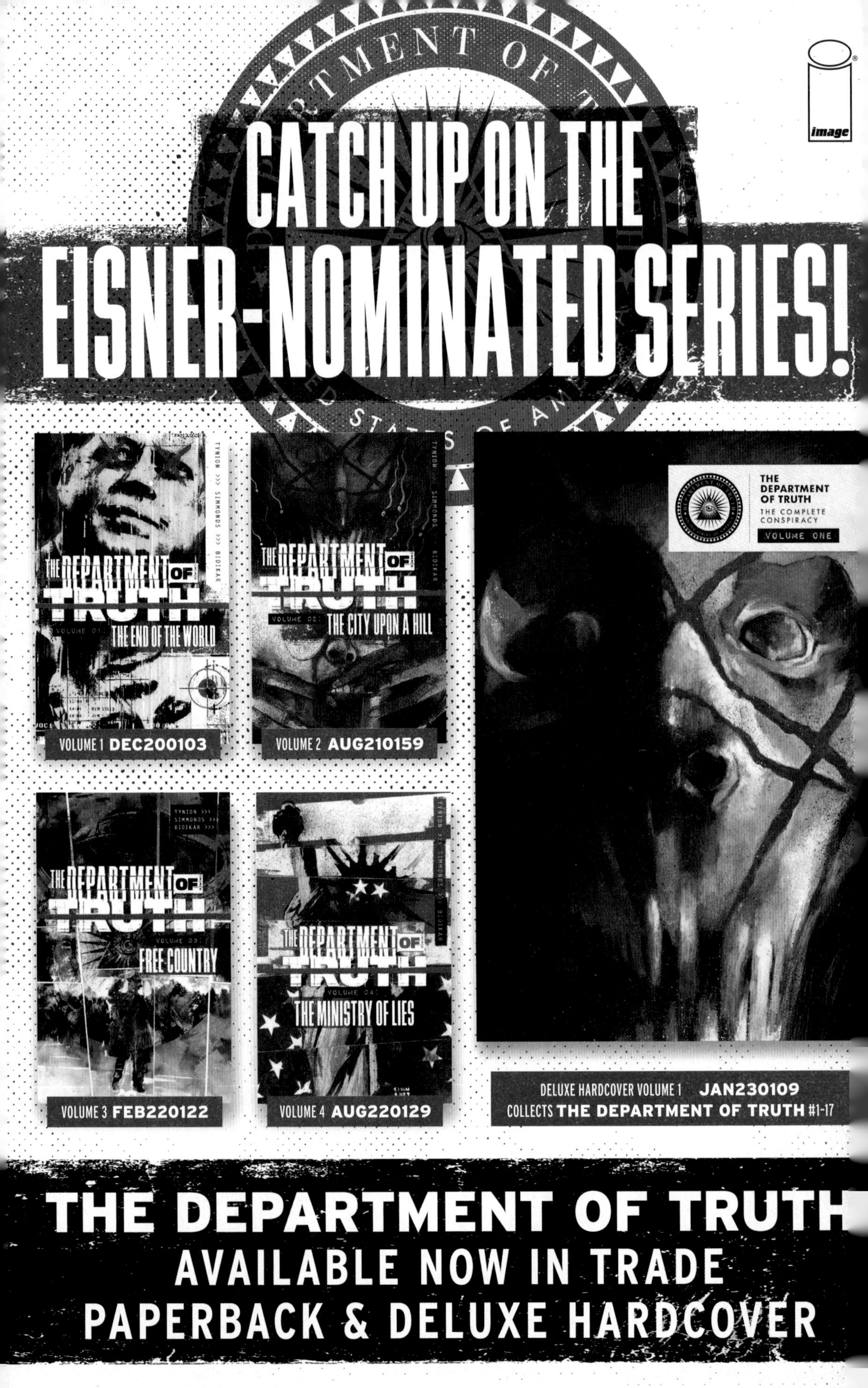
image
CATCH UP ON THE
EISNER-NOMINATED SERIES!
TYNION >>> SIMMONDS >>> BIDIKAR
THE DEPARTMENT OF TRUTH
VOLUME 01: THE END OF THE WORLD
VOLUME 1 DEC200103
THE DEPARTMENT OF TRUTH
VOLUME 02: THE CITY UPON A HILL
VOLUME 2 AUG210159
THE DEPARTMENT OF TRUTH
VOLUME 03: FREE COUNTRY
VOLUME 3 FEB220122
THE DEPARTMENT OF TRUTH
VOLUME 04: THE MINISTRY OF LIES
VOLUME 4 AUG220129
THE DEPARTMENT OF TRUTH
THE COMPLETE CONSPIRACY
VOLUME ONE
DELUXE HARDCOVER VOLUME 1 JAN230109
COLLECTS THE DEPARTMENT OF TRUTH #1-17
THE DEPARTMENT OF TRUTH
AVAILABLE NOW IN TRADE
PAPERBACK & DELUXE HARDCOVER

RAZORBLADES™

BOOK ONE

Over 350 pages of horror from some of the most cutting-edge names in the genre.

James Tynion IV

Steve Foxe

Ram V

Marguerite Bennett

Alex Paknadel

Ricardo Lopez Ortiz

Trevor Henderson

John J. Pearson

Tyler Boss

Jenna Cha

& Others

Available Now

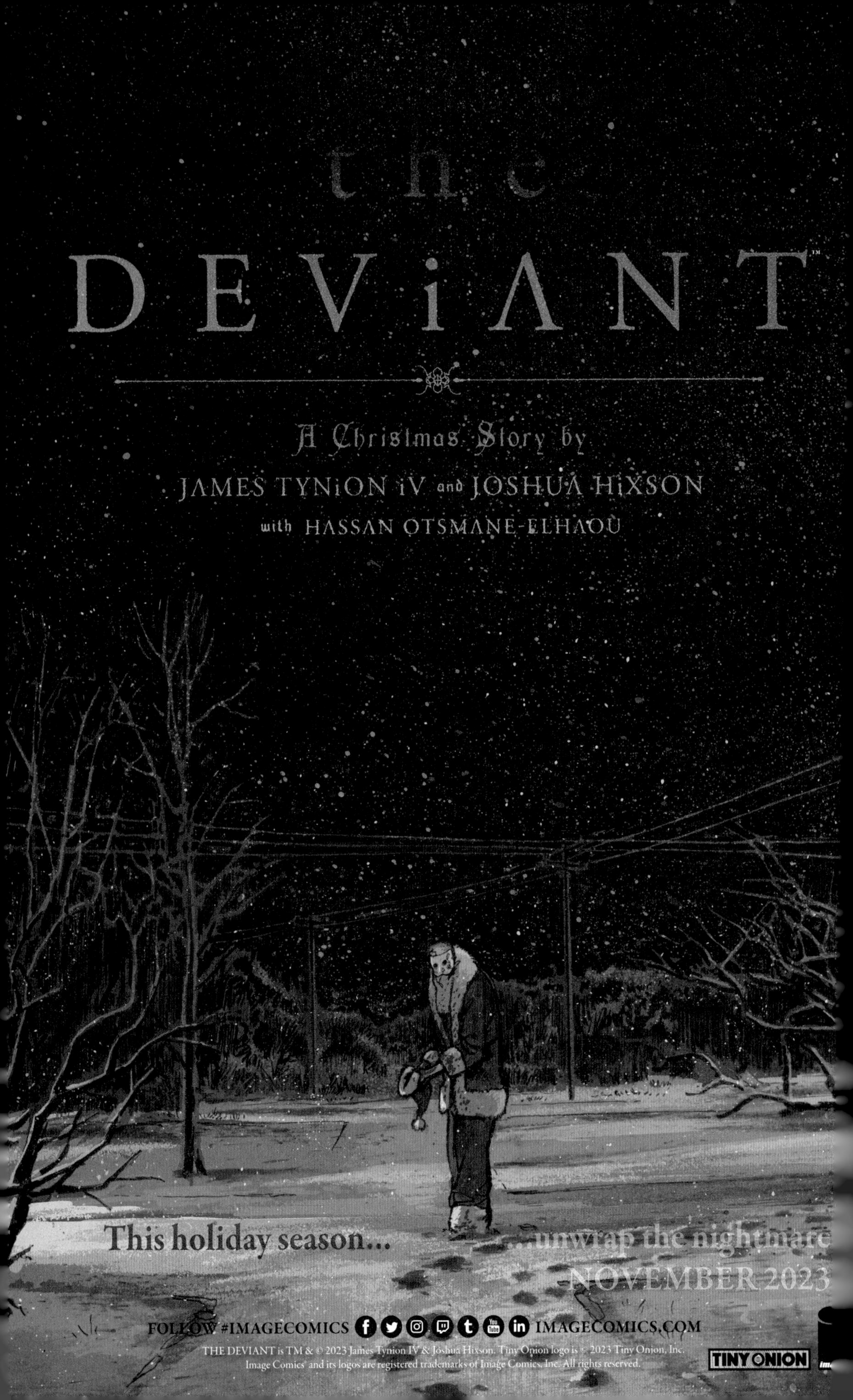

the
DEViANT™
A Christmas Story by
JAMES TYNiON iV and JOSHUA HiXSON
with HASSAN OTSMANE-ELHAOU
This holiday season...
...unwrap the nightmare
NOVEMBER 2023
FOLLOW #IMAGECOMICS IMAGECOMICS.COM
THE DEVIANT is TM & © 2023 James Tynion IV & Joshua Hixson. Tiny Onion logo is © 2023 Tiny Onion, Inc.
Image Comics® and its logos are registered trademarks of Image Comics, Inc. All rights reserved.
TINY ONION

That bump in the night just got a little louder...

From Eisner Award-winning writer James Tynion IV & fan-favorite artist Gavin Fullerton

AVAILABLE NOW!

THE CLOSET ™

TINYONION

SHOPTINYONION.COM

VARIANT COVERS **T-SHIRTS** **ENAMEL PINS**

EXCLUSIVE MERCHANDISE & MORE